HEAVENS ON EARTH

State v. Market

HEAVENS ON EARTH

HOW TO CREATE MASS PROSPERITY

J. P. FLORU

Biteback Publishing

First published in Great Britain in 2013 by
Biteback Publishing Ltd
Westminster Tower
3 Albert Embankment
London SE1 7SP
Copyright © J. P. Floru 2013

J. P. Floru has asserted his right under the Copyright, Designs and Patents Act 1988 to be identified as the author of this work.

ISBN 978-1-84954-519-8

10 9 8 7 6 5 4 3 2 1

A CIP catalogue record for this book is available from the British Library.

Set in Sabon

Printed and bound in Great Britain by
CPI Group (UK) Ltd, Croydon CR0 4YY

To Madsen Pirie and to Tom G. Palmer
who never tire to inspire
and
to leaders who don't redistribute what is,
but allow people to create what can be.

ABOUT THE AUTHOR

J. P. Floru is a Senior Research Fellow at the Adam Smith Institute. Attracted by its tradition of individual liberty and free market economics, Floru moved from his native Belgium to the United Kingdom in 1994. His witty and contrarian take on being a student, City lawyer, artist, entrepreneur and councillor in the City of Westminster is the subject of his first book, *What the Immigrant Saw*.

Floru is the founder of Freedom Week, an annual one-week seminar held at Cambridge where students are taught the philosophical and economic principles of a free society based on individual liberty and the free market. In 2009 he topped the poll of Conservative Party members in London for the European elections on the basis of a Eurosceptic and free market message. He then joined the Adam Smith Institute after a year working in Parliament for Steve Baker MP ('I learned how Parliament works – and how it doesn't').

A prolific writer, speaker and blogger, his articles appear in the *Daily Telegraph*, *City A.M.* and ConservativeHome.com.

CONTENTS

FOREWORD BY ALLISTER HEATH

It is high time for a proper debate about the relationship between the individual and the state. In a classically liberal society, people's incomes are seen as theirs, to be spent, invested or donated as they see fit, with taxation kept to the minimum necessary to provide certain services and help the poor (the size of these activities are, of course, subject to debate). The present, collectivist mood in the UK sees it differently: earnings are implicitly treated as public property, to be divided up according to how politicians see fit; tax cuts are even seen as a 'cost' to the Exchequer, as if it were automatically entitled to everybody's wealth.

There is a fundamental philosophical distinction between these two positions. This is not merely an abstract debate: shifting views on what we mean by 'justice' have economic consequences. The UK's relative prosperity – during its industrial heyday and then again during the 1980s and 1990s – was based on policies that assumed that individuals had a natural right to their earnings and property. By contrast, the post-war period, when envy and confiscatory taxation were rationalised on moral grounds, culminating with a 90+ per cent tax rate in the 1970s, was a disaster.

The situation is obviously nothing like as bad today. But Britain is now a very high tax, big government society by international standards, yet for some reason we wonder why the UK economy is stuck in the doldrums. The simple truth is that economic growth is never miraculous. In his latest book J. P. Floru investigates the sources of prosperity in countries which have achieved it. The evidence is there for all to see: capitalism and the market economy are the only way to drive sustainable economic progress, yet far too often our politicians choose to ignore or even deny it, preferring instead to fall back on yet another doomed scheme to reflate the economy by subsidising credit.

The story Floru tells is inspiring and one that Britain, one of the birthplaces of capitalist prosperity, needs to reacquaint itself with.

We have not yet come across limits to wealth creation: we have never run out of any raw material and we have never run out of people. The advances humanity has achieved in the last fifty years alone have lifted billions out of poverty. Wealth creation is the underpinning of civilisation itself. Redistribution by the state and wealth creation are communicating vessels: they can be combined, but the growth of the one will always reduce the other.

If there is one overriding lesson to draw from Floru's book, it is that Britain and other troubled Western economies need to rein back their bloated governments and find the courage to trust the individual, property rights, the rule of law and sound money. If we put the right conditions and institutions in place, and allow people the freedom to better themselves, the economy will take care of itself. We did it before – and now we must do it again.

Allister Heath is editor of City A.M.

ONE

THE UNITED STATES

I. A CASE STUDY IN WEALTH CREATION

930s and 1940s America saw the consecutive implementation of the two great ideologies the world has fought over since time began. The catastrophic economic crisis of 1929 brought Franklin Delano Roosevelt's 'Can-Do' government into power. Under the umbrella of the New Deal – a raft of programmes such as state employment schemes, welfare, public works and trade union rights – politicians attempted to end the economic crisis, poverty and uncertainty. This reached its apotheosis during the Second World War, when the state took control over the entire economy. Was FDR's interventionism successful in creating prosperity?

The electorate didn't think so: FDR's New Dealers steadily lost political ground until the Republican Party won a majority in both Houses in 1947. The Republicans' economic policy was the opposite of FDR's: people regained power over their lives and over their economic pursuits. The return of laissez-faire was short-lived, but the economic outcome was unequivocal.

The approaches of both economic systems are polar opposites – and so are their social and economic outcomes. Both want to create mass prosperity for all, but supporters of the first theory think it can best be achieved through government intervention, whereas supporters of the second believe it is best achieved by leaving people free. Each politician who wishes to create mass prosperity has to choose his camp. 1930s and 1940s America is a good case study to identify the characteristics and the economic outcomes of the two alternatives.

2. THE GREAT DEPRESSION

Who could have predicted that the policies resulting from an economic bubble which burst in 1929 would dominate the political discourse to this day? Crises like the 1929 one have happened since time immemorial. The economic boom of the 1920s had created a speculative bubble: in six years the stock market increased fivefold. When business activity started to decline, nervousness increased. On Black Thursday the bubble burst: the stock market lost 11 per cent, before rebounding to a 6.38 per cent loss. This was reported in the newspapers over the weekend, resulting in panic selling and a 13 per cent drop on Monday, followed by a 12 per cent drop on Tuesday. Between 1929 and 1932, the Dow Jones lost 90 per cent of its value. Many were ruined. Banks which had invested in shares made heavy losses. In the autumn of 1930 a number of banks in the Midwest and the South went bust. People tried to withdraw their savings, resulting in bank runs. As banks re-invest rather than keeping all cash ready in a vault, they invariably default if all their customers try to withdraw their savings at the same time. Three hundred and fifty-two banks failed in December 1930 alone.

How had such problems been solved before? During the crisis of 1907, the economy had recovered and bank runs had ended after the banks agreed between them only to pay out to deposit holders up to a limited amount, organising larger transactions on paper only. In 1930, though, the free market mechanism of banks agreeing measures between them without state intervention was not used, as the banks believed that the Federal Reserve System would solve the problem. Had it not been set up for precisely that purpose? In reality, the Federal Reserve Banks did little, though that was not widely known at the time. In 1932, under pressure from Congress, the Federal Reserve System finally shot into action. It started to purchase large amounts of government bonds in which the banks had invested. This gave additional liquidity to banks, to meet the demands from their depositors and customers. But when the favourable effect started, Congress adjourned and the Federal Reserve stopped its purchases. Between the election of FDR and his assumption of office at the beginning of 1933, there were more bank failures. Outgoing President Hoover refused to act without FDR's cooperation, and FDR refused to take responsibility until he took office. When FDR took office he declared a nationwide banking holiday and tried to tackle the crisis. Between 1929 and 1933, 10,000 out of 25,000 banks disappeared through failure, merger or liquidation. GDP halved. Unemployment rose to 25 per cent (13 million people). Suicide rates went up by one-third. The Great Depression quickly spread to the rest of the world. Countries introduced drastic restrictions on trade by way of tariffs and quotas. World trade halved.

Two political camps interpreted the crisis, and how it should be tackled, in two different ways. It determined their political faith. On the one hand were the free marketeers, who wanted to see this crisis solved as crises had been solved before: without government interference and by letting the markets take care of the correction. This view was mainly supported by Republicans. To the public, this sounded lame: it seemed as if the Republicans had no answers.

In the opposite camp were the interventionists. Their finger-pointing proved popular with the newly poor. They blamed

greedy bankers for reckless speculation and industrialists
for exploiting misery. They portrayed President Hoover's
Republican government as a 'Do-Nothing Administration'.
In fact, Hoover was an interference-happy big-government
Republican. He laid the foundation on which FDR built
the Depression: he ran greater deficits than FDR in peacetime; increased the federal budget by 50 per cent, expanded
public works, intervened in agriculture and pressurised businesses not to cut wages even when their sales fell. During
his administration the Smoot-Hawley Act came into being,
imposing record tariffs on imports; more than sixty countries took retaliatory protectionist measures against it. A
petition signed by 1,028 economists asked Hoover to veto
the legislation, to no avail. Most of Hoover's 'Do-Nothing'
politics were continued and expanded by FDR.

The interventionists saw government as the solution to
the country's woes. Government would hand out relief to the
poor, protect against the vicissitudes of life and regulate to
prevent a crisis from happening again. FDR's New Deal
for the Forgotten Man would turn government into a
protector instead of the Founding Fathers' independent
referee. In 1933 the Democrats swept into power with a
massive majority in both houses, and FDR became the
new President.

‡

The ideologies of the Depression
FDR's views on the economic crisis were deeply indebted to
the theories of John Maynard Keynes. These were fashionable with the intellectual and political elites at the time and
have become so again since the 2007 world economic crisis.
Keynes believed that the crisis resulted from a contraction
in demand for goods and services. When people save more in
times of economic uncertainty, their demand for goods and

services decreases, resulting in higher unemployment. Lower incomes reduce demand. Companies are reluctant to invest. This spiral can lead to a recession or even a depression.

Keynesians believe that the way out of such an economic crisis is for government to stimulate demand to achieve full employment. This can be done through tax cuts or through increased state spending. Keynesians find tax cuts less desirable because people will save some of the money rather than invest it; therefore direct state spending is more efficient. Keynesians don't mind governments going into the red ('deficit spending') in order to stimulate demand. The stimulus is financed by printing money and/or by borrowing. That the repayment of the loans mortgages future growth was not a concern for Keynes, who quipped that, 'In the long term, we are all dead.' Keynes's theories have been the main argument for massive increases in the size of the state in the West throughout most of the twentieth century.

Classical economists such as Adam Smith see things differently. For them, markets are the best method of achieving the subjective individual aims of the greatest number of people. Markets are also self-correcting: scarce resources are most efficiently allocated through the interaction between supply and demand, as signalled by prices. If demand for a product rises, it signals to producers that they should increase production. When they do, demand is satisfied. If prices rise, consumers reduce consumption and/or look for alternatives, resulting in demand reduction and a drop in prices. If people save more in times of uncertainty, interest rates go down as borrowers find it easy to attract capital. The low interest rates encourage people to invest again. Therefore, in a time of economic crisis, all that is needed is patience while those self-correcting adjustments take place. Government should not interfere in a way that might disrupt market mechanisms. For example, increased state borrowing to fund spending causes greater demand for money and consequent rises in interest rates. The private sector will then borrow and invest less. Government spending increases demand for labour and thus increases wages; this harms the profitability of the private sector. In other words, the public sector crowds the private sector out. The economy is stimulated in a sustainable way when productivity increases, not when government artificially stimulates the economy at the expense of productivity.

There are two alternatives to Keynes's explanation of what happened during the Great Depression. The first one, the Monetarist Theory, came too late as it was only developed from the mid-1950s onwards. The second, the Austrian Business Cycle Theory, was too unknown and too unpopular to have any effect in the 1930s. Both theories are averse to government interference (the Austrians in all fields, and the Monetarists in all fields except the money supply).

For Monetarist Theory, as developed by Nobel Prize Winner Milton Friedman, the money supply and central banking are central to macroeconomic policy. Monetary authorities must focus on maintaining price stability. Inflation is caused by an excess supply of money; a deflationary spiral, as during the Depression, is caused by an undersupply of money (a liquidity – or credit – crunch). People liquidate their risky investments and put the money under the mattress, or buy assets which they consider safe. The situation worsens when banks start to fail: people try to get their money back before they lose it, and bank runs result. Banks do not keep all money in cash. Most of it they invest, and if depositors all ask for it back at the same time, banks become insolvent. In the 1907 bank run, the crisis was ended through a free market remedy: the banks agreed between them that they would only pay out limited amounts in cash to their deposit holders; all other transactions were conducted on paper only. It worked, and the crisis was sharp but short-lived. The interventionists refused to leave crisis-solving to the uncertainties of the market and set up a new Federal Reserve System in 1907. The Republicans tried to keep the Fed's board independent, but the Democrats succeeded in having its members appointed by the President of the United States. From then on, whenever there was such a contraction, the Federal Reserve System was to pump money into the banks. Hence 'supply-side economics': the belief that crises can be ended by increasing the money supply. The money supply can be increased by the Federal Reserve Banks buying bonds on the open market or from banks. The Fed pays for it by creating ('printing') additional money. As increasing the money supply can cause inflation, it must be monitored in order not to oversupply. When there is a gold standard (as there was until FDR abolished it) the amount the Federal Reserve can inject in this way is limited by its gold reserves.

Milton Friedman proved that, contrary to what they had done in the decade before, between 1929 and 1933, the government-appointed Board of the Federal Reserve not only refused to increase the money supply, but actually reduced it, thereby exacerbating the crisis. A large number of other interventionist policies under FDR's New Deal Programme had further damaged the self-correcting free market system. In other words, Monetarists believed that the protracted nature of the crisis stemmed from the Fed refusing to act, and the government acting too much.

The Austrian Business Cycle Theory was developed by Nobel Prize-winner Friedrich Hayek in the 1930s. Similar theories were developed by Ludwig von Mises in 1911. Most of the exponents of this theory were born in Austria, hence the name 'Austrian School'. They reject the use of statistics and mathematics by mainstream economists: social phenomena, they claim, can only be explained by looking at the motivations of each individual. Government interference therefore typically fails, as it is not cognisant of all the information all individuals in society possess – this is called the

Knowledge Problem. Austrian School economists advocate laissez-faire: non-interference by government in the economy, so individuals who do have the information can act in the most efficient way. Admittedly, individuals' decisions fail too – but the consequences for society are less severe than if government fails. People learn which behaviours are most profitable for them through a process of trial and error.

The Austrian School sees economic crises as the inevitable result of economic bubbles. Pressurised by government, central banks keep the interest rate at which they lend money to banks artificially low to stimulate the economy. The low interest rates incentivise people to borrow, invest and speculate. Banks are able to lend ever-increasing amounts of money through the system of fractional reserve banking: banks only keep a fraction of the deposits in their vaults, and lend the rest – which in turn is deposited with the banks and lent out again. Together, these factors create a spiralling increase in the money supply and therefore in inflation. As the banks are flooded with ever more money to invest, they reduce the interest they pay to depositors further. Investors seek higher returns than the low interest rates (made worse by inflation) can offer, and flee into tangible property. This creates exceptional price rises or bubbles. The prices become irrational: for example, in 1929, share prices were completely divorced from the actual performances of the companies. The bubble is fuelled further by people seeing the spectacular price rises and wanting a piece of the action. This creates malinvestment: investment not based on reasonable or rational expectations of future returns, but on speculation (gambling, hence the term 'casino capitalism'). The bubble bursts when people start to blink: they sell their inflated assets, nobody wants to buy, and panic selling ensues. Panic selling started on Black Thursday 1929. When a price bubble bursts, it causes a sharp contraction of credit called 'recession' or 'credit crunch'. The market readjusts and allocates resources to more rational uses. Austrian School economists believe a recession is an inevitable readjustment of the market. Government interference in this market process is usually aimed at prolonging the bubble to give people a false sense of continued prosperity.

The Austrian School holds that Monetarists are misguided if they increase the money supply when there is a credit crunch. Central bankers simply do not have enough information to know when the money supply needs to be increased or decreased. In fact, for many Austrian School adherents, such as the eminent economist Detlev Schlichter, central banks and the state's monopoly on currency are themselves anathema to the free market. Instead of central planning and fiat currency (that is, currency whose value is not linked to any material good, such as gold), they prefer more open and diverse approaches to money and banking. Unlike Keynesians and Monetarists, they want a separation of the state from money. They want money to be treated like any other asset which can be produced, bought and sold in a free market and whose value and supply will therefore adapt more readily to market fluctuations.

‡

3. NEW DEAL OR RAW DEAL?

The New Deal was the Democratic Party's plan to tackle the 1932 economic crisis, to provide relief for the unemployed and the poor, and to reform the financial system to prevent a repeat depression. Instead of reviving the economy, the measures destroyed it further and prolonged the crisis into a ten-year depression. State jobs destroyed more private jobs, labour protection laws made companies less competitive, protectionism reduced trade, cartels were legalised and reduced competition, and welfare reduced incentives to work. The New Deal assembled all the main interventionist measures which became so popular in the second part of the twentieth century under one banner.

FDR was the inventor and driver of the New Deal. Born into an upper-class family, his compassion for the less favoured spurred him into paternalistic fervour. He believed that government intervention in the economy was both desirable and successful. Attracted by the additional tax revenue it would raise, he started his presidency by abolishing prohibition. 'Vote! Vote! We want beer!' chanted US Representatives from the Senate balcony to pressure their colleagues into voting for the Beer Act. FDR guided fifteen major New Deal laws through Congress in his first 100 days in office. The Democratic majority didn't bother scrutinising the proposals. Even crusty southern Democrats and many old-time Republicans voted promptly for bank closures, 100 per cent deposit insurance, a federal pension fund, a minimum wage and a cap on working hours; the Tennessee Valley Authority public power project (which would push many private providers out of the market); an interventionist agricultural policy including subsidies and competition-reducing measures; public works programmes and trade union rights. It all went so fast that opponents had no time to organise opposition.

The policies were not necessarily popular or effective, but FDR sold them well. After the election he immediately set about making regular 'fireside chats' on radio – the first President to do so. He used plenty of daily life analogies rather than statistics and he sounded like an elderly family member. The war turned him into a folk hero and relegated Congress to the back seat.

FDR's advisers became known as his Brain Trust. They were widely ridiculed in editorials and cartoons for being utopian dreamers. Many were Columbia and Harvard law professors who spent their lives self-assuredly advocating regulation to protect people from life's hardships. Harry Hopkins was a professional social worker who set up government employment programmes throughout his life. Frances Perkins, the first woman in a US Cabinet, can best be described as a welfare state activist who succeeded in turning her dreams into legislation; she introduced capped working hours, the minimum wage, overtime laws, state pensions and unemployment benefits. Rexford Tugwell was satisfied that state planning could solve just about any problem. His Resettlement Administration aimed at moving 650,000 struggling urban and rural families to state-planned cities. By the time this was judged unconstitutional, Tugwell was known as 'Rex the Red' and his plan labelled 'Communist'. A few years after the initial influx of New Dealers, Harvard law professor Felix Frankfurter's aides seemed to be everywhere, drafting laws and pushing them through Congress and the courts. When Frankfurter was appointed to the Supreme Court he became known for not applying the Constitution, that is, for not limiting the executive's actions as the Founding Fathers had intended. The inclusion of academics in FDR's circle illustrated the shift on campuses from a belief in the beneficence of a free market economy into a belief in the beneficence of an economy led by the state.

To achieve their aims, the New Dealers introduced an alphabet soup of programmes known by their acronyms. They can be subdivided into five categories: programmes to benefit specific groups such as farmers; employment programmes through public works; changes to labour laws; the introduction of social security; and economic measures such as the abandonment of the gold standard.

The important electoral constituency of farmers was struggling because increased efficiency had lowered food prices. The Agricultural Adjustment Act 1933 ('AAA') reduced the numbers of producers and introduced subsidies. Farmers were exempt from antitrust law: they could agree between them to reduce production to keep prices artificially high. The numbers of intermediaries were culled through licensing 'to eliminate unfair practices'. This again drove prices up. Farmers received subsidies to kill off livestock or to leave land uncultivated. The subsidies were paid for by a tax on companies processing farm products. The AAA also raised tariffs on imports, dictated farm acreage for specific crops and empowered the government to restrict farm production and purchase farm surpluses. Sharecropping and tenant farming disappeared. Traditionally landowners used tenant farmers and sharecroppers to work the land. The law now forced them to share the subsidies with their tenants. It incentivised landowners to get rid of their tenants and replace them with employees.

The farmers were pleased with the farm subsidies and the artificially high prices; the consumers' views were not heard. It was a classic example of concentrated benefits and dispersed costs: the Act directly benefited a well-organised special interest group, whereas the cost was dispersed over tens of millions of anonymous consumers who would not have blamed the government for the increase in the price of an apple. The anti-competitive measures continue to be the mainstays of a subsidy-dependent class of farmers in the United States today.

The Civilian Conservation Corps (CCC), the Federal Emergency Relief Administration (FERA) and the Works Progress Administration (WPA) were set up to reduce unemployment. The CCC provided work for unemployed unskilled manual labourers aged between seventeen and twenty-three from relief families, or veterans. The set-up was not unlike that of a professional army: the men could sign up voluntarily for between six months and two years. They received $30 per week as well as food, housing in camp barracks, a uniform and medical care. African-Americans and Native Americans were enrolled in segregated camps.

The CCC is mainly remembered for its nature conservation programmes. Its supporters state that it was responsible for planting 3 billion trees to help reforest America and for constructing more than 800 nature parks. Other outdoor tasks included the elimination of predatory animals; forest fire prevention; seed collection; mosquito control; building bridges, roads, and airport landing fields; irrigation and draining works. In nine years 2.5 million people participated.

One of the programmes set up by 'Do-Nothing' President Hoover, subsequently copied by FDR (who claimed credit for it), was the Federal Emergency Relief Administration. FDR appointed Harry Hopkins to head it, and told him to give immediate relief to the unemployed and to pay no attention to politicians and the public. FERA provided grants to create jobs in local and state government. Apart from doubtlessly worthy causes such as research into the vitamin C content of apples, FERA's work included arts projects, national park improvements and the repair and construction of public buildings. FERA's production-for-use projects came in for particular criticism. Bedding, towels, clothes and canned goods were produced and then distributed to the poor. Production-for-use as opposed to production-for-profit is a socialist concept. It is production of goods determined by human need rather than profit (though neo-classical economists see this as a false dichotomy, as businessmen can only make a profit if they sell products for which there is demand). Instead of businessmen, politicians decided what to produce. Businessmen strongly objected to production-for-use projects and they were terminated.

The Works Progress Administration 1935 was the largest New Deal project. It attempted to provide one paid job for every family which had suffered long-term unemployment. Public buildings and roads were built, slums cleared and large arts projects were set up. Elizabethton, Tennessee used the WPA to build a golf course; regional guidebooks were written, fences erected and painted. At its peak it gave jobs to 3 million unemployed men and women.

Supporters said that it was right for the state to spend more on the job schemes than on simply paying dole, as a job offered so much more: improved physical condition, increased self-esteem and employability. Critics retorted that the projects provided 'make-work' jobs: jobs that have fewer benefits than their cost ('digging a hole and then filling it'). Keynes would have approved of make-work jobs: he famously stated that income and capital wealth would increase if the Treasury buried bottles with money and let private enterprise dig them up after having paid for the right to do so. Many feared that the projects created lousy working habits which would make the recipients less employable in the private sector. They would then become a permanent drain on welfare. The most fundamental criticism was the opportunity cost. The state jobs were paid for by private sector taxes. The private sector could therefore invest less money and create fewer jobs. In other words, private sector jobs were replaced by state jobs. The amounts of taxpayers' money spent on the projects were eye-watering. In 1935, the Works Progress Administration alone spent 6.7 per cent of GDP.

Despite central orders, the uptake of projects in the states was slow. Many localities procrastinated or simply refused. In Oklahoma City, for example, officials were reluctant to introduce relief programmes. They campaigned to discourage people from moving to the City; local voters rejected a proposal to issue a bond to increase the relief funds; local papers failed to print the location of soup lines and the City Council refused to raise taxes to increase relief – and cut property taxes instead.

The third limb of the New Deal consisted of a number of labour laws such as the National Recovery Act 1933 (NRA) and the National Labour Relations Act 1935. The NRA aspired to economic recovery but achieved the opposite by increasing union protection and reducing free market competition. Trade unions were given protection and collective bargaining rights, leading to upheaval and strikes. Codes regulating industrial sectors could set minimum wages, maximum working hours and working conditions. Antitrust laws against cartels and monopolies were set aside. Labour laws like these harm the economy in a number of ways: (1) If cartels and monopolies enjoy legal protection, a few producers can set prices above that which would have ensued from normal supply-and-demand interaction in a free market. This is another example of concentrated benefits and dispersed costs: popular resistance against cartels will be limited, as the higher consumer prices are dispersed over many consumers, whereas the few privileged producers will have a direct financial incentive to defend their privileges. (2) When competition is restricted to existing companies by way of cartels or monopolies, their income security disincentivises them from trying to innovate or increase productivity. One ends up with antiquated production models. (3) Anti-competitive agreements typically block new competitors from entering the market, thereby excluding potentially innovative business models. (4) Caps on working hours and thresholds for wages increase production costs. This makes companies less competitive in the world market where such employee protection does not exist. The companies will reduce their workforce, or they may go bust. (5) The introduction of a minimum wage means that people with few skills find it more difficult to obtain a job. They may then end up on welfare.

The Act illustrates the traditional divide between the left and the right as to who should decide employment conditions. Those on the left believe that employers and employees are in an uneven bargaining position, with the former predominating. Thus, the government must be called upon to re-balance the equation by imposing statutory employment rights or strengthening trade unions. Those on the right do not accept that the bargaining position of the employees is necessarily worse than the employer's. If there is a labour shortage, or if the employee has desirable skills, his bargaining position will be better than the employer's, resulting in good contract conditions. If the economy struggles, the employer must be able to reduce his costs as fast as possible – or fire people – to survive the competition. The left generally does not accept that workers should see their employment terms worsen due to competitive pressures. Instead, they argue that company owners should be content with lower profits. And if the company goes belly-up, a generous taxpayer-funded welfare state must guarantee the living standards of the freshly unemployed.

Collective bargaining is possibly the most harmful of union activities. Protracted negotiations with unions may impede a businessman's ability to take decisive action in an environment of cut-throat competition. The union may force him to take the wrong economic decision. It might, for example, prevent him from replacing workers with machines even though competition demands it. The threat of strikes may increase wages above what is affordable. Job losses or the absence of new job creation may result. When FDR introduced the Act guaranteeing collective bargaining rights, unemployment stood at 20.1 per cent. The President's pro-union measures reduced competitiveness further; and this extended the economic crisis, with fewer jobs all around. But then, those who never found a job thanks to FDR's munificence to unions would probably not have linked cause and effect – they were told the misery had been brought upon them by greedy capitalists, rather than a President who needed the electoral support of unions and their members.

The fourth category of New Deal measures introduced social security. The Social Security Act 1935 introduced the first federal pensions, as well as benefits for the unemployed, dependent children, expectant mothers and the disabled. Most of these benefits are still in place today and have greatly expanded. The Federal Insurance Contributions Act invented the pay-as-you-earn system for welfare contributions. The employer withholds the contribution from the employee's pay, and sends it on to the government. The employee has to contribute as well, at the time of paying his income tax. This clever device allows the government to tax without the people ever seeing the money. Initially, the system was self-funding, as there were more contributors than beneficiaries. When the ratio reversed, contributors and taxes had to increase steadily to pay for the shortfall.

When the democratic welfare system grows, property rights and the rule of law eventually evaporate. Government employees, welfare recipients and their dependants may become a democratic majority. Numerically, this is not yet the case in the United States, but several European countries have majorities which are wholly or partly dependent upon the state. We end up in the realm of quasi-slavery: a majority of the population living off the labours of the minority.

	US Evolution of Social Security		
Year	Beneficiaries	Percentage of population	Dollars
1937	53,236	0.04 per cent	$1,278,000
1938	213,670	0.16 per cent	$10,478,000
1939	174,839	0.11 per cent	$13,896,000
1940	222,488	0.16 per cent	$35,000,000
1950	3,477,243	2.28 per cent	$961,000,000
1960	14,844,589	8.21 per cent	$11,245,000,000
2000	45,414,794	16.13 per cent	-
2008	50,898,244	16.87 per cent	-
Source: Historical Background and Development of Social Security, Social Security Administration website			

The fifth limb of the New Deal consisted in debasing the currency. The Classical Gold Standard, which existed in most Western countries from the 1870s onwards, brought about stable currencies. It made it impossible for governments just to print money to go on a spending spree as people were entitled to gold in return for banknotes. While the Classical Gold Standard existed, the West enjoyed unprecedented and unrepeated growth, free trade, and harmonious monetary relations, which were ended by the First World War. Germany was the first to leave the gold standard in 1914 to print money to finance the war (by 1923, inflation was 30,000 per cent per month). Keynes's favoured method of fighting an economic crisis was an increase in state spending, paid for by printing money. In 1924 Keynes announced that the gold standard had become a 'barbaric relic'. Britain abandoned the gold standard in 1931 in order to print money. On 15 June 1933, FDR nationalised all gold: gold coins, gold bullion, and gold certificates above $100 had to be turned in to the Federal Reserve in return for money at a fixed price. It became illegal for individuals to own gold. One year later, the government increased the price of gold, in effect devaluing the dollar by 41 per cent.

The New Deal umbrella soon proved to be leaky. The poor did not become less poor, unemployment stayed persistently high and there was no economic recovery. Both Hoover's and FDR's interventionist measures prolonged the economic crisis into a depression. If we discount the war years, the Depression lasted for FDR's entire term in office. But such was the enthusiasm and clout of the New Deal proponents, and so desperate were the millions who had voted for it, that the policies were continued and reinforced with great vigour.

Evolution of Unemployment During the Depression	
1929	3.2 per cent
1930	8.9 per cent
1931	16.3 per cent
1932	24.1 per cent
1933	24.9 per cent
1934	21.7 per cent
1935	20.1 per cent
1936	16.9 per cent
1937	14.3 per cent
1938	19.0 per cent
1939	17.2 per cent
Source: Historical Statistics of the United States: Millennial Edition, ed. Susan Carter, Scott Sigmund Gartner, Michael Haines, Alan Olmsted, Richard Sutch and Gavin Wright (Cambridge: Cambridge University Press, 2006), http://hsus. cambridge.org/, accessed 5 January 2009.	

There are two reasons why the New Deal failed to make the economy recover: (1) The aims of the New Dealers were much wider than mere economic recovery and poverty relief, and (2) the New Deal methods made economic recovery impossible. While its economic aims largely failed, its unspoken aims were extremely successful.

What were these unspoken aims? They were as diverse as their proponents. In his seminal book *Crisis and Leviathan*, Robert Higgs provides a highly amusing profile of the main New Dealers: a motley lot of semi-socialist national planners, semi-fascist members of a pro-business gang, consumerists, antitrust enthusiasts, avowed cartelisers, spending fanatics and budget balancers, agricultural reformers, every species of inflationist and monetary crank, and assorted proponents of panaceas that ranged from spreading the work to building garden cities. They used state coercion to advance their pet aims at the expense of all others. The Democratic politicians had one aim in common. State jobs, welfare, and labour protection laws were used to buy votes. Programmes were carefully targeted at constituencies which the Democrats needed to win or hold on to. New Deal politicians could quote the exact numbers of people they had given jobs to; whereas those who were never offered a job in the overtaxed private sector remained anonymous and unidentifiable. When New Deal workers were deployed to campaign for the Democratic Party, the outcry was such that the so-called Hatch Act was introduced to make it illegal for government employees to hold elected office or participate in political campaigns.

The methods used in the New Deal made economic recovery and reducing unemployment impossible. Keynesian stimulus for the economy needs to be paid for. It doesn't grow on trees. The profligate government trinity of printing money, raising taxes, and increasing borrowing was applied to pay for the schemes. The US top marginal income tax rose from 25 per cent to 63 per cent in 1932 and to 79 per cent in 1936. New Dealer Harry Hopkins came up with the quote 'We shall tax and tax, and spend and spend, and elect and elect.' In essence, printing money and borrowing are taxes, too. Printing money causes inflation, thereby reducing the value of people's savings; borrowing will have to be paid back by future generations, with interest paid in the meantime. The productive sector pays for the state's spending and can therefore invest less. The increased state spending merely shifts growth from the private sector to the public sector. Sadly, it is not even like for like: the state is less efficient and more wasteful than the private sector. There will be waste; an army of bureaucrats needs to be employed, and special interest groups will lobby government for state investment. State job creation will therefore always result in a net loss of jobs overall. Politicians love public job creation schemes as they can claim credit for specific improvements in employment figures, whereas the jobs killed off in the private sector to pay for these schemes are difficult to pinpoint.

4. TOTAL WAR

The policies of the wartime period can in many ways be seen as New Deal on Steroids: the apotheosis of an all-encompassing state. Although the war brought many New Deal programmes to an end or suspended them, the voter-specific targeting of defence spending and even policy – including the continued internment of Japanese-Americans in concentration camps until three days after FDR's re-election – wasn't ended.

Initially, the war effort was slow. New Deal interference in the economy had seriously harmed American production capacity. Robert A. Lovett, who toured aircraft factories, reported to the War Department that 'by European standards, the American aircraft industry is in the horse-and-buggy age ... alarmingly small, inadequately capitalized, and technologically backward'. When Communists, taking their cue from the Soviet Union's pact with Nazi Germany, tried to slow the war effort through strikes, FDR initially refused to interfere. He also protected resources for New Deal projects from being transferred to the war effort. Then came the attack on Pearl Harbour, spurring Congress into approving almost unlimited Presidential powers. The government took command of the entire economy. Government agencies and bureaucrats mushroomed. Commodities were rationed; all transport coordinated; price and wage controls introduced. All production and allocation of materials and fuel was centrally directed. Rent controls were introduced. Even the amount of cloth to be used for each garment was regulated.

In a free market economy, price signals indicate to buyers and sellers where there are shortages or surpluses. This allows them to take the right decisions to achieve maximum efficiency. When government regulations override these signals, it usually results in the misallocation of resources, abuse of position, and black markets. When price ceilings on fish were introduced, East Coast fishermen preferred to stay home rather than to lose money on their catch and a shortage ensued. When a wage ceiling was introduced for aircraft workers, they flocked to shipbuilding and the aircraft industry suffered a shortage of workers. In one more example of the regulatory failure spiral, the government responded to its failure by regulating more: 27 million workers were 'frozen' in their jobs; they were not allowed to move.

Rationing was ideally suited to abusing one's position. When gasoline was rationed, those with an A windscreen sticker obtained three to four gallons a week, B stickers (military workers, doctors etc.) obtained up to eight gallons, and X drivers (police, firemen, civil defence workers and religious ministers) obtained an unlimited supply. Within weeks it became clear that drivers had obtained X stickers without needing them ... including 219 Congressmen.

There were black markets in every American city where you could buy what your rationing coupons didn't offer. Producers withheld part of their output, and made fortunes. People with money could buy at exorbitant prices when others couldn't. According to surveys, one-third of business in certain products was done on the black market. This went hand-in-hand with organised crime, including counterfeiting coupons.

The war is routinely credited with ending the Depression. Keynesians claimed that the measures used in the Depression had been too timid. Now all the stops were pulled out, and it seemed as if Keynesianism was vindicated. Unemployment went down from 17.2 per cent in 1939 to 1.2 per cent in 1944. In the 1930s, state spending had been about 20 per cent of GDP; by 1945 it stood at 53 per cent. Economic growth was 50 per cent in 1944. It looked as if state command could indeed do better than the free market economy. Deficit spending went into overdrive: in the 1930s, the federal deficit had never been more than $3.5 billion per year. In 1943, the federal deficit stood at $55 billion. How was this paid for?

The usual state financing trinity of tax, borrowing and money printing was applied. Tax revenue (federal, state and local) rose from 19.1 per cent of GDP in 1933 to 30.2 per cent of GDP in 1945. In 1940, 4 million Americans paid tax; by 1942, 39 million did. In Congress, some politicians defended the principle of taking *all*. Senator Chandler said: 'The government can assert its right to have all the taxes it needs for any purpose, either now or at any time in the future.' Henry Ford observed: 'Did I invent the Model T, fine-tune the assembly line, innovate on the V-8 engine, and then retool my factories to make thousands of planes for the war only to have all my income for 1943 plus much more taken by the government?'

The bills were kicked into the long grass, left for the children to pay. In the 1920s, the federal debt had been about 20 per cent of GDP. In the 1930s, it rose to 40 per cent. By 1945, it was 116 per cent. In the next three decades it was paid back through taxes, thereby depressing private sector growth. One could of course argue that winning the war kept future generations free as well – but there were cheaper ways of winning.

The third means of paying for the war was the printing press. The Second War Powers Act of 1942 liberalised the authority of the Federal Reserve System to buy government securities 'without regard to maturities either in the open market *or directly from* the Treasury'. The printing press was used to help finance the government's gargantuan deficits. While money printing could be hidden from the public, rising prices couldn't – by 1941, prices rose at about 1 per cent per month. Regulatory spiral failure manifested itself in the introduction of price controls. These led to shortages, rationing, abuse and a huge black market.

Did the war truly reduce unemployment? As Robert Higgs states: 'Unemployment fell mainly as a result of the build-up of the armed forces. Between 1940 and 1945 the number of unemployed fell by 7 million, while the number of soldiers increased by more than 11 million. Any government that can conscript workers by the millions for free can eliminate unemployment.'

What would have happened if America had used private sector mechanics instead of a command economy to build up its wartime economy in order to wage war? It is difficult to say definitively, as it wasn't tried, but it's certainly true that free enterprise tends to outperform state enterprise. Why would it be different in a time of war? Given a different leader, the war might well have been won faster, and at a lower expense.

5. FDR'S WISH LIST

FDR knew what he was going to do after the war before it had even started. In his State of the Union address of 1941, which became known as his 'Four Freedoms Speech', he said:

> In the future days, which we seek to make secure, we look forward to a world founded upon four essential human freedoms.
>
> The first is freedom of speech and expression – everywhere in the world.
>
> The second is freedom of every person to worship God in his own way – everywhere in the world.
>
> The third is freedom from want – which, translated into world terms, means economic understandings which will secure to every nation a healthy peacetime life for its inhabitants – everywhere in the world.

The fourth is freedom from fear – which, translated into world terms, means a world-wide reduction of armaments to such a point and in such a thorough fashion that no nation will be in a position to commit an act of physical aggression against any neighbour – anywhere in the world.

That is no vision of a distant millennium. It is a definite basis for a kind of world attainable in our own time and generation.

In his State of the Union Address of 1944, FDR clarified what Freedom from Want meant: the right to a job; to adequate income to pay for food, clothes and recreation; to a decent return for farmers on their produce; to trade without unfair competition or monopolies; to a family home; to medical care; to education; and to adequate protection from economic fears of old age, sickness, accident and unemployment. FDR wanted to elevate New Deal-style entitlements into constitutional rights. He cleverly juxtaposed his new right of 'Freedom from Want' with freedoms of speech, expression and worship – traditional rights which were widely understood and valued. In due course, his widow Eleanor would ensure that the new Freedom from Want was enshrined into the Universal Declaration of Human Rights in 1948.

Traditional human rights, as reflected in the first ten Amendments to the US Constitution, protect liberty and property against excessive encroachment by the government. They are 'negative' rights, because they tell the government *not* to do certain things. For example, the right to private property means that the government is not allowed to take that private property away. FDR's rights were of an entirely different nature. It unleashed an avalanche of so-called 'positive' rights – that is, rights which require the government to act. It entitles every human to certain material goods. The problem with positive rights is that somebody needs to pay for the material good. In other words, your right to property is infringed. Positive rights were nothing new. The nineteenth-century philosopher Frédéric Bastiat observed correctly that 'the second half of the programme [positive rights] destroys the first half [negative rights].'

Sadly for the interventionists, FDR died before he could implement his plan. Besides, his adversaries had been planning the defeat of FDR's policies as far back as 1937. Shaken by the power of the unions, by FDR's 'socialist' policies, and by his attempt to pack the Supreme Court with New Deal judges, conservative Democrats, mainly from the South, had started to make common cause with conservative Republicans. They called for lower taxes on capital gains and profits, for cuts in government spending and for balanced budgets, for a restoration of the peace between labour and industry, and for reliance on free enterprise. The Conservative Coalition dominated Congress until 1963. Early on, they won a number of key votes. When the Republicans recovered electorally and reached near parity with the Democrats in 1942, Democrats became even more inclined to support conservative policies. FDR was able to bypass their obstruction of his policies through the wartime emergency legislation which had given him quasi-dictatorial powers. Nevertheless, a number of New Deal programmes were abolished by Congress, usually by withdrawing funding. Congress took particular pleasure in abolishing the National Resources Planning Board in 1943. Its members were enthusiastic Keynesians who wanted the state to provide just about everything after the war. Earlier in 1943 it had published a 640-page report urging the government to employ all the jobless, to introduce social security for all, to set up offices to inform people of their entitlements, and to pay for it all through taxes. The report was ignored – though its main tenets have now been implemented in most Western democracies.

Dominated by the Conservative Coalition, Congress then proceeded to defy the President when he asked for $10.5 billion in tax rises in the Revenue Act 1943. Congress believed the President was using the war to legitimise mass redistribution of income. FDR urged Congress to 'tax all unreasonable profits, both individual and corporate'. This was rather difficult, as the top income tax rate was already close to 100 per cent. Congress voted for its own Revenue Act, raising taxes only by $2 billion. FDR promptly vetoed it, stating that the bill provided 'relief not for the needy but for the greedy'. The Democratic Senate Majority Leader, Alben Barclay, who had faithfully carried FDR's banner for seven years, promptly resigned his post, under thunderous and almost unanimous applause from his colleagues. Congress overrode the President's veto by a large majority in both Houses.

As the war neared its end, the intellectual left started to agitate for a continuance of the command economy. They believed that the return of 12 million soldiers and 12 million citizens employed in soon-to-be-discontinued war industries would bring mass unemployment and a repeat of the Great Depression. They held the opposite view to the Conservative Coalition in Congress, but because the one held political sway while the other dominated the intellectual world, both were equally powerful. Who would come out on top?

6. BOOM

Vice-President Harry Truman was shown into the First Lady's sitting room. 'Harry,' she said, 'the President is dead.' Truman asked Eleanor Roosevelt whether there was anything he could do for her. Eleanor responded: 'Is there anything *we* can do for *you*? You are the one in trouble now.'

Despite his long-term ill health, FDR's death came

unexpectedly; he had just started his fourth term as President of the United States. His successor came woefully unprepared. He hadn't even been told about the Manhattan Project, America's development of an atomic bomb. Japan was still fighting in the Pacific. Invasions had been planned for 1945 and 1946, but America feared that Japan would fight to the death, as its soldiers had done in Iwo Jima and Okinawa. Four months after FDR's death, the atomic bombs were dropped and Japan capitulated.

The war had ended much earlier than expected. Nobody knew what the future would bring. Would the Great Depression return, together with the state intervention-ist measures of the New Deal? Or were people sick of the wartime garrison economy; would they want more freedom? It could go either way. FDR's early death, the early end of the war and Truman's inexperience tipped the balance. The Conservative Coalition was ready.

On 6 September 1945, Truman asked Congress for a Fair Deal: full employment through government schemes, an increase in the minimum wage and up to six months' entitlement to unemployment benefits. He pleaded for tax cuts (though only small ones), as his Fair Deal would devour money. Joseph Martin, the Republican Leader of the House, fumed that Truman was trying to out-New Deal the New Deal. Both Democrat-held houses thundered a resounding 'no'. In its Revenue Act 1945, Congress slashed taxes by $5.9 billion, or 13 per cent of total federal revenue. Income tax was reduced by about 10 per cent for all rates. The top marginal rate of 94 per cent was cut to 86.45 per cent. Corporation taxes were cut by between 2 and 4 per cent; the top marginal rate went down from 90 per cent to 38 per cent. Georgia Senator Walter George defended the Revenue Act of 1945 with thinking which today is called 'supply-side economics'. If the tax bill 'has the effect which it is hoped it will have,' George said, 'it will so stimulate the expansion of business as to bring in greater total revenue'. The tax cut was accompanied by a drastic reduction in state spending: from $93 billion in 1945 to $55 billion in 1946 and $34 billion in 1947. Government employees were laid off. Keynesians augured a gloomy future of mass unemployment and a return to the depression.

In the run-up to the 1946 Congressional elections, clear dividing lines were drawn between Truman and the Republicans. Truman still wanted to cut spending to reduce the debt and balance the budget. He suggested that taxes might have to go up. He also campaigned for a New Deal revival in which the state would guarantee rights to houses, healthcare, jobs and decent wages. Under the slogan 'Had enough?', the Republicans promised across-the-board tax cuts of 20 per cent and spending cuts of 50 per cent. The Democrats were wiped out. New Deal Democrats lost most of their seats. The Republicans obtained a comfortable majority in both Houses for the first time since 1933. Truman's daughter later quipped that: 'My father awoke aboard his special train, en route to Washington, and discovered that he had a bad cold and a Republican Congress.'

The Republicans quickly set about drafting a tax-cutting bill. They believed that revenue cuts were the only way to curtail the size of government. Republican Congressman Knutsen put it in colourful language: 'For years, we Republicans have been warning that short-haired women and long-haired men of alien minds in the administrative branch of government were trying to wreck the American way of life and install a hybrid oligarchy at Washington through confiscatory taxation.' Truman vetoed the bill three times, but eventually the veto was overruled with the help of Democrat votes. $6.5 billion of tax cuts took effect in 1948.

Apart from the large tax cuts, the 80th Congress also limited the presidency to two terms and introduced the Taft-Hartley Act, which reduced the privileged role labour unions had obtained under FDR. Labour laws were re-balanced, states became entitled to adopt 'right-to-work' rules and Communists were driven out of the labour movement.

The results of these policies were quite extraordinary. Economic growth reached the unheard-of peacetime level of 14.7 per cent in 1947. Notwithstanding the high numbers of soldiers returning from Europe and the transformation of the domestic wartime economy into a peacetime economy, unemployment rose by a mere 2 per cent immediately after the war and then remained stable at the low level of 3.9 per cent. In 1946 there was a fall in the total tax receipts but, as people started to work and invest again, total receipts went up until they reached near-parity with the 1945 levels in 1948. Americans were taxed much less, but the government raised just as much. Federal deficits were changed into surpluses, and the federal debt started to fall.

In addition, America saved Europe from post-war starvation. Unlike Britain, the US abandoned most rationing and price controls quickly from 1945 onwards, to allow the free market to balance supply and demand. The spike in production was especially significant after market regulation was abandoned. When farmers no longer held back food from 'official' production to sell on the black market, production increased by almost 18 per cent. When the alarming reports of hunger in Europe reached America, the interventionists called for the return of rationing, to send the surpluses to Europe. Truman refused, opting for growth instead. Agricultural subsidies were increased, and the US government bought food on the market, which it sent to Europe. While subsidies are certainly not a recommendable practice, they worked in the emergency period. Sadly, the subsidies – like many New Deal programmes – continued to exist well beyond the emergency. Unlike emergencies in daily life, emergencies which occasion public policy and public spending supposedly never abate.

	Real GDP	Tax Revenue ($ billion)	Unemployment	Fed Deficit/ Surplus ($ billion)	Debt ($ billion)
1945	+2.5 per cent	67.4	1.9 per cent (soldiers returning)	−47.4	256
1946 (tax cuts)	+7 per cent	61.5	3.9 per cent	−15.9	269
1947* (tax cuts)	+14.7 per cent	62.1	3.9 per cent	+4	258
1948* (tax cuts)	+9.5 per cent	67	3.8 per cent	+11.8	252
1949	+3.1 per cent	65.6	5.9 per cent	+0.6	253
1950	−1.4 per cent	66.7	5.3 per cent	−3.1	257

The Republican spring was short-lived. In the 1948 Presidential election campaign they promised even more cuts. But because Democrats had lent their crucial votes to overrule Truman's veto, the electorate did not clearly identify the Republicans as the tax-cutting party. In addition, with the Cold War starting, polls showed voters were happy to pay their taxes if it went to the right spending streams, such as defence. In this atmosphere, Truman's labelling of the 80th Congress as the 'Do-Nothing Congress' was a vote winner. He revived the old New Deal coalition of blacks (by promising overdue civil rights), farmers (by promising state support) and trade unionists (by promising to repeal the Taft-Hartley Act). He defeated the Republican Presidential candidate and the Democrats won back both Houses.

Around the time of the disappearance of free market thinking in America in 1948, one erstwhile enemy introduced it. In Germany the effect was so pronounced that it was called a miracle: the *Wirtschaftswunder*.

TWO

GERMANY

I. WHEN GERMANY STARVED

The Level V ration card allowed for so few foodstuffs that it was known as the Death Card. Non-productive adults, such as housewives, the sick, the elderly, the disabled, the unemployed and former Nazis were entitled to it. Other categories of people received food in proportion to the work they carried out: a manual labourer might be entitled to 600 grams of bread a day; an office worker to 400 grams. Sometimes the goodies had all been handed out by the time the queuer came to the head of the line. People would queue for hours; families took turns. In the summer of 1946, rations were halved in the British occupation zone. The daily fat allowance now stood at 7 grams a day, about one-quarter of the minimum recommended to remain healthy.

Many topped up their rations with food they had stored away. There was also the black market, which, although illegal, operated quite openly. But how to pay for it? The German currency had lost its value; cigarettes and coffee were used instead. The wealthy bartered antiques or jewellery. Some Germans worked for the occupying army, for example, as translators. Few ordinary businesses remained. In the Soviet zone, industrial structures were dismantled and shipped to the Soviet Union in lieu of reparations. Those who had nothing else to trade sold themselves: they were called *Ruinenmäuschen* (mice of the ruins). Many Germans scavenged. Not just in the ruins, but also the countryside – called 'hamstering'. If they were lucky, they found or bought food. If not, they returned empty-handed, and took shelter in what remained of their homes. Sometimes they were arrested on the way back into town, accused of being black marketeers.

There is no shortage of figures showing the catastrophic situation Germany was in. In the zones occupied by France, America and Britain, 40 per cent of the housing stock had been destroyed. The population of Cologne had dropped from 750,000 to 32,000. Most German cities were mounds of rubble. Traditionally, this was where industry had been located, in order to be near the workers. Before the war, Germany had been the most industrialised country in Europe. In 1946, the German economy was 28 per cent of the size it had been in 1936.

Raping and plundering is the preserve of every war; but the Germans feared the Soviet army far more than the armies from democratic countries. The Soviet propaganda encouraged atrocities and the Nazi propaganda exaggerated them to encourage the Germans to fight harder. The Nazis had behaved with extreme brutality on the Eastern front, and the Russians were certainly not going to show any mercy now. In addition, the Russians were poorer than the Western Allies: when they entered the Reich 'proper', they often couldn't believe the luxuries they found. After twenty-eight years of Communism their living standards were far lower than those of the Germans.

Ten million Germans fled ahead of the Soviet army. At the Potsdam Conference (1945), America, Britain and the Soviet Union had redrawn the European borders: Germany ceded about 30 per cent of its territory. Poland moved westwards and the Soviet Union obtained part of East Prussia. Together, they expelled about 7 million Germans; Czechoslovakia, about 3 million. Between 5 and 7 million Germans and ethnic Germans were expelled from other European states. Before the Wall was built, another 3.5 million East Germans fled to the free world. In the five years after the Second World War, 15 million Eastern Europeans fled to the West.

At the Potsdam Conference it had been agreed that Germany would be divided into four zones which would be occupied by France, Britain, the Soviet Union and the United States. Each zone was to support its own population, and pay war reparations. In view of their own massive losses, the Soviets were also allowed to confiscate property in the western zones; in return the western zones would receive food from the Soviet zone. The agreement quickly fell through, and eastern Germany, which had always been the agricultural supplier of the rest of Germany, was now firmly out of bounds.

It wasn't just Germany which endured food shortages after the war; many western European countries suffered. Britain tightened rationing in 1946 – including bread, which had never been rationed during the war. The Allies wondered how to keep the Germans alive. It wasn't popular with the home electorate: in opinion polls, the American and British showed willingness to forgo food to remedy the starvation of Europe, but when they were asked whether they were happy to forgo food for Germans, the results were less enthusiastic.

The Nazis had behaved appallingly during the war, and people were not about to forget it. Germany had introduced rationing in 1939, but as Hitler regarded rationing as one of the reasons morale had dropped during the First World War, even by 1944 German rations were still well above 2,000 calories (Jews and Poles in the occupied territories obtained starvation rations). By VE Day this had halved, and it dropped further after that. The estimated required calorie intake for a healthy person today is something between 2,000 and 3,400 calories a day, depending on activity. During the war, Germany plundered its food from the occupied territories. The Reich never managed to feed itself. Not for want of trying though: the interventionists attempted it through two pieces of legislation and a large bureaucracy. The Hereditary Farm Law of 1933 declared all farms under 308 acres to be hereditary estates which were protected through the old laws of entailment against division, foreclosure and mortgaging. Those who could trace their Aryan pedigree back to 1800 could become *Bauer* (Farmer); their entire estate would be inherited by their eldest or youngest sons. The flipside of the coin was that he was bound to the soil, just like a serf in medieval days. Agricultural labourers were forbidden from leaving their employ, too (though allegedly this rule was largely ignored). The Reich Food Estate 1933 abolished free market farming. All aspects of farming were put under central command, with an overall aim to protect farmers and to achieve food self-sufficiency. The interventionists achieved neither. Even official prices were increased by 20 per cent; and the profit to farmers evaporated in higher prices for machinery and fertiliser.

2. THE NAZI ECONOMY

The destruction of the economy was not just the result of Allied bombs during the war; it started on the day the Nazis took office (and some say well before). The economically illiterate Hitler appointed an assortment of interventionists to achieve his aim of reviving the economy, in order that he might win the allegiance of his people and pay for the expansionist war which was to follow soon after.

What economic model did the National Socialists adhere to? Officially, they rejected both socialism and capitalism, and promised a 'third way'. The main influence came from the *völkische* (people's) wing of the Historical School. In *The Jews and Modern Capitalism*, the economist Werner Sombart, initially a Marxist, claimed that the Jews had invented capitalism because they had been excluded from the medieval guilds. In *Händler und Helden*, Sombart showed his contempt for the commercial views of the English people, who had lost their warlike instincts. He dismissed the striving for the happiness of the individual, and welcomed the German War which would end commercialism and individualism and replace them with a German state which was based not on individuals but on the *Volksgemeinschaft* (People's Community). In *German Socialism*, he welcomed the demise of capitalism and proletarian socialism and their replacement by German Socialism (National Socialism). All life was to be regulated by a planned economy in which individuals would have no rights but only duties. German Socialism would be guided by the *Volksgeist* (National Spirit), which was not racial but metaphysical. The antithesis was the Jewish Spirit, which was metaphysical as well: it did not mean being born Jewish or believing in Judaism; the Jewish Spirit meant a belief in the capitalistic spirit. The English people had the Jewish spirit and National Socialism was to destroy it.

Keynesianism was also very influential. Dr Hjalmar Schacht, who became Minister of Economics in 1934, admired Keynes, and his policies bore some resemblance to FDR's New Deal. The difference was the extreme brutality by which the National Socialists applied it. In the German edition of his *General Theory*, Keynes included this gem:

[T]he theory of output as a whole, which is what the following book purports to provide, is much more easily adapted to the conditions of a totalitarian state, than is the theory of production and distribution of a given output produced under the conditions of free competition and a large measure of laissez-faire.

One of the chief socialist deceits is to portray Nazi Germany as a capitalist society. One could be fooled into believing that Nazi Germany was capitalist, as outwardly it continued to allow for private property. In reality, while you were allowed to own property, the government decided what you could do with it. Production, prices, labour and trade were all heavily regulated. The free market economy was replaced by central planning. It became even worse when Göring was put in charge of the Four Year Plan in 1936. He was to prepare Germany for total war: 'guns instead of butter', as he called it. Germany was to become self-sufficient. Even though he was barely more economically literate than Hitler, Göring had total power over the economy. Albert Speer wrote in his memoirs that, upon becoming a Minister, he had decided to ignore Göring's observation that he could do anything as long as it didn't interfere with the Four Year Plan. As the Plan embraced the whole economy, it would have meant doing absolutely nothing at all. By the end of the 1930s, the entire economy had become wholly subservient to the state. Fritz von Thyssen, an industrialist who helped Hitler to power, observed that 'soon Germany will not be any different from Bolshevik Russia; the heads of enterprises who do not fulfil the conditions which the "Plan" prescribes will be accused of treason against the German people, and shot.'

Even today the myth that Hitler revived the German economy is alive and well. Economic catastrophe had brought the Nazis to power. When the United States terminated its loans to Germany to support its economy at the start of the Great Depression, severe unemployment resulted; by 1932 it was over 30 per cent. This fed the Nazis' electoral successes. The Nazi government immediately set about stimulating the economy by increasing state spending on employment programmes, public works (waterways, railroads and highways), and – far outweighing the former – the army. To the uninitiated it looked as if Nazi Germany was one big beehive of activity. Unemployment fell from 6 million in 1932 to less than 1 million in 1936. GDP rose by 102 per cent between 1932 and 1937. Nazi Germany's 'economic miracle', as it was called at the time, was a classic case of smoke and mirrors: displacement of the private sector by the public sector, and deficit spending paid for by inflation. By 1939, a debt of 38 billion Reichsmark had been built up. State rearmament spending was destabilising the economy and price controls failed to control inflation. In the weeks before his dismissal from his last post as President of the Reichsbank, Schacht warned that Germany was heading towards a foreign exchange crisis. The economy stood at the brink of the abyss and only the war deflected from that.

Let us look in some detail at the methods the National Socialists used to bring the entire economy under their control. Under Nazism, the free market economy was comprehensively destroyed. Some businessmen were initially quite positive about the National Socialists coming to power, as the trade unions were outlawed, strikes forbidden and collective bargaining abolished. Workers became akin to medieval serfs when assorted decrees restricted a worker's freedom to move from one job to another. In 1938 labour conscription was introduced: henceforward workers could not resign and could not be fired without approval from the state. They had to take the jobs the state assigned to them. The Four Year Plan quickly erased the smiles from the businessmen's faces. In an attempt to become self-sufficient, imports were slashed and state companies set up. Wage and price increases were forbidden, under penalty of being sent to a concentration camp. The result was that the shops were soon empty, as nobody wished to sell at the compulsory low prices. In 1939, rationing was introduced. During the war disobedience to the price controls became punishable by death.

One of the chief instruments used to give the state complete control over the economy was the introduction of compulsory state cartels. Through cartels, businessmen agree to restrict competition and keep prices artificially high. The victim is the consumer, who has to pay more than he would have under free competition. Free market economies often have rules to prevent cartels. Some say that such rules are unnecessary: cartels are inherently unstable, as it will be financially enticing for a member to break the agreement or for outsiders to compete with the cartel. Cartels are stable, however, when the state enforces them, and that is what the Nazis did. In their new 'classless society', the employers' federations were declared obsolete and new cartels were set up by the government. They were used to execute decrees. Membership was compulsory. Monopolistic price fixing became the rule in most industries. The cartels initially pleased the big coal, steel and shipbuilding businesses, but it was just a prelude to the state taking control completely. Free agreements between businessmen were not quite what the statists had in mind. In 1937 the Reichsbank took control of all exports, thereby reducing the power of cartels, and the formation of new cartels was restricted. By the end of 1943, 90 per cent of the cartels were dissolved: henceforward the state took all economic decisions.

The amount of red tape one had to weed through during the Nazi period was mind-boggling. Businessmen spent an inordinate amount of money on greasing the palms of officials, on bypassing regulations, and on plain simple advice on how to interpret the government's diktats. It started at the top: Hermann Göring, the totalitarian master of industry, became extremely wealthy through corruption and bribes. So far from making production more efficient to wage war, the Nazis slowed production down and made rearmament more expensive.

How was the National Socialists' apparent stimulus of the economy paid for? The usual holy trinity of profligate government was applied: money printing, taxing and borrowing.

Initially the rearmament had to be kept secret from the Allies – so the Nazis resorted to printing money. They were able to do this as the gold standard had been abolished to finance the First World War. In a clear-cut example of regulatory failure spiral, within two years the resulting inflation had to be hidden through price controls. In 1934, the highest marginal income tax rate was raised to 50 per cent. (Taxes on the poor were kept very low.) From 1937 the business tax rate was raised to 30 per cent; later, corporate profits above 100,000 Reichsmark became subject to an additional tax of 40 per cent. Large corporations were largely exempt from taxes on profits but were private in name only. Many readers may recall the film *Schindler's List*, which illustrates quite well the dependence of corporations on the Nazi commands. State borrowing on the money markets had the disadvantages that interest needed to be paid and that it was visible to other European countries. Therefore, Nazi Germany borrowed in the form of 'Mefo-bills': armaments were paid for with IOUs created by the Reichsbank and guaranteed by the State. The total amount was kept secret. Insurance companies, banks and others were forced to buy government bonds. Dividends above 6 per cent had to be invested in government bonds. By 1939 there were 12 billion Reichsmarks' worth of Mefo Bills and 19 billion of normal government bonds. A fourth source of revenue was added to the state financing trinity: outright theft – the confiscation of property belonging to 'enemies of the state' (Jews).

3. THE ALLIED POLICIES IN POST-WAR GERMANY

The outrage of the world against Nazi Germany became even stronger after the liberation of the concentration camps. The Allies were divided into two factions: those who blamed the Nazis, and those who blamed the entire German people. Of a collectivist mindset at the best of times, FDR belonged in the second category. FDR's Secretary of the Treasury, Henry Morgenthau Jr., came up with a plan which bears some resemblance to the destruction of Carthage by the victorious Roman armies in 146 BC. The Germans were to be reduced to subsistence farming, and some were to carry out forced labour outside Germany. The country was to be split up and its industry to be dismantled and carried off by the Allies. FDR enthusiastically endorsed Morgenthau's plan. He wrote to his Secretary of State that rather than be lenient, it would be a better policy to have the Germans 'fed three times a day with soup from Army soup kitchens', so 'they will remember that experience the rest of their lives'. FDR then tried to convince Churchill. At first, the British Prime Minister refused violently, but later he caved in and agreed to sign a reduced version of the plan. Why did Churchill change his mind? It has been suggested that his policy adviser, Lord Cherwell (who was firmly in the collective responsibility camp), convinced Churchill that taking out competitor Germany would save Britain from bankruptcy. The US also promised another $6 billion Lend Lease Agreement for Britain. The plan was leaked to the press, and FDR denied the reports. Nazi propaganda chief Goebbels used the Allies' plan to stiffen the resolve of the Germans to keep fighting.

The spirit of the Morgenthau Plan permeated the schemes devised by the Allies at the Potsdam Conference. The German standard of living was to be lowered; 1,500 manufacturing plants were to be closed; steel production was to be drastically lowered; car production would only be allowed at 10 per cent of pre-war levels etc. In the American occupation zone the Morgenthau Plan was implemented through Joint Chiefs of Staff Directive 1067 (JCS 1067). The American occupying army in Germany was to take no steps towards reviving the economy. It was merely ordered to keep starvation, civil unrest and disease below levels at which

they would pose a danger to the occupying troops. When
FDR was asked whether he wanted the German people to
starve, he replied: 'Why not?' Charitable relief organisations were prohibited from distributing food in Germany
until mid-1946. What the Germans in the British zone
could expect was typified by a board put up by the military
commander of Essen. It basically said: 'You started the war.
We now have to help those who suffered from your actions.'
And the final sentence, which the reader Ernst Schmitt never
forgot for the rest of his life: 'The best advice that I can offer
you is to tighten your belt and keep your chin up.' This is not
the place to debate whether the occupation policy was right
or wrong. But it must be pointed out that the belief in collective guilt is based on a collectivist ideology which denies that
responsibility is individual. Perhaps it was not so surprising
that FDR supported the Morgenthau Plan. Churchill was
of a different mindset. At the second Quebec Conference he
attacked the original Morgenthau Plan, concluding: 'You
cannot indict a whole nation.'

In the Soviet zone, the National Socialist command economy was transformed into a Communist command economy.
Moscow-trained German Communists headed by Walter
Ulbricht were flown in during April 1945. When it became
clear that there were too few native Communists, and that
they certainly couldn't win an election, the Soviet Military
Administration forced the Social Democrats of the SPD into
a union with the Communists' Socialist Unity Party in April
1946. By 1948, the SED was a strict Stalinist Communist
party. Estates over 100 hectares and all Nazi-owned land
was expropriated and redistributed to small peasants, agrarian workers, the state and refugees from the east (this was
not revoked when Germany reunified in 1990). Mining
concerns, banks, and industries were nationalised. Small
companies were squeezed out of the market. Large industries
were dismantled and taken to the Soviet Union. Some were

left in place but were put under Soviet ownership. Of hunger, the Communists saw little. At Communist headquarters in Berlin there was an entirely different rationing system for Communists, according to rank. While the general population was nearly starving, Party Secretaries received meals of several courses with wine. The different economic outcomes of the Communist Germany and the free market Germany soon became visible to all.

It is unclear precisely when the Morgenthau Plan was buried. General Clay, Commander of the American zone, stated that Germany was not to be starved. He urged for a united, democratic and self-governing Germany. In September 1946, US Secretary of State James F. Byrnes descended from Hitler's train (in whose bed he had slept) and stated that Germans had the right to work hard and to enjoy the fruits of their labour. In March 1947, former President Herbert Hoover said: 'There is the illusion that the new Germany left after the annexations can be reduced to a "pastoral state". It cannot be done unless we exterminate or move 25 million people out of it.' In July 1947, President Truman finally revoked JCS 1067 and replaced it with a directive which stated that 'an orderly, prosperous Europe requires the economic contributions of a stable and productive Germany'. There were many reasons to change the policy: public opinion, the realisation that reducing Germans to the begging bowl meant that the Allies would have to fill it, and the fear that Nazism would revive, or Communism take hold. It was at this time that Ludwig Erhard came to the fore.

4. LUDWIG ERHARD

There have been few instances in history where individuals who were fundamentally opposed to state intervention in the economy were put in charge of it. Ludwig Erhard's belief in free markets was probably instinctive at first. He was raised by a farmer's son who had moved to the city to set up as a draper. Ludwig's father was active in the Freisinnige Volkspartei, a small classical liberal party. Even though Ludwig had been rather lazy at school and did not obtain the grades necessary to enter university, he subsequently obtained a degree in economics. His intended career in academia was thwarted because the University of Nuremberg wouldn't accept his second dissertation. By this time the university was a Nazi stronghold, and Erhard had refused to join the Nazi Party and the Nazi professors' organisation. In the dissertation, he had attributed the depression in Germany to cartels and monopolies. As these groups dictated prices, prices could not signal demand, resulting in overproduction. Erhard advised breaking up the cartels and allowing prices to float freely to steer supply and demand.

He went to work at the Vershofen Institute, a think tank. Its founder, Wilhelm Vershofen, believed cartels worked for the common good. Ludwig was an amenable man and, in a move which may sound familiar to many free market-oriented academics and politicians, he often watered down his free market beliefs so as not to annoy his employers. In 1939, Erhard published an article which was a veiled attack on the Nazis' economic interventionism. He pointed out that state interference had made prices irrelevant as they no longer reflected supply and demand. As, without prices, it is impossible to know consumers' demands, the state planning replacing it would fail and result in rationing (it did).

In 1942 Erhard set up his own think tank, the Institute for Industrial Research. In January 1942, Hitler made speculation about post-war Germany illegal. Erhard was nevertheless asked to write a study on how to transform the war industry to a peace industry after the war by the Reichsgruppe Industrie. At this time, Speer was eliminating the last remnants of the free market economy to wage total war. Money and prices had become irrelevant. Erhard did not expect Germany to win the war. He argued for a gradual reduction of regulations and the reintroduction of competition. The war was being paid for by the state forcing banks and companies to buy state bonds, and by printing money. Instead, Erhard proposed to reduce the money supply. The free market would be supervised by the government; he expressly stated that the role of the government should never again be restricted to the role of night watchman. A free market with real competition remained the overall goal. His industrial supporters did not like the urge for free market competition much. The paper nevertheless drew the attention of a few high-ranking Nazis. For a few years Erhard acted as an economic adviser to Gauleiter Bürckel. Erhard continued to refuse to join the Nazi Party and later said that he had taken the job 'to make the best out of a bad situation'. His work for Bürckel was probably the reason why Erhard was not condemned when Count von Stauffenberg attempted to kill Hitler on 20 July 1944. He had reason to be scared: as part of the Stauffenberg plot, co-conspirator Carl Goerdeler had asked Erhard to write a paper on post-Hitler economics. Erhard duly wrote it and sent it to Goerdeler by ordinary post. When the coup failed and its instigators were arrested, Erhard destroyed his correspondence with Goerdeler and prepared to go into hiding. In the event he was not arrested, though 4,980 people were executed by the Nazis as a direct consequence of the attempted coup.

As Erhard often stated that he neither believed in totalitarianism, nor in unbridled free market capitalism, commentators have claimed that he tried to find a 'third way'. The self-effacing Erhard would have been horrified by such a conceit, but he did not help himself by calling his beliefs *Soziale Marktwirtschaft* (Social Market Economy). Far from wanting to stifle the free market, Erhard wanted to build a legal framework to strengthen it. Without a legal framework, it was not competition, but the most powerful bullies – such as special interest groups and cartels – that would reign supreme. Erhard's legal framework would prevent this from happening.

For career reasons, Erhard had to compromise throughout his life. When he became actively involved with politics, he again had to be careful not to annoy his more statist party colleagues. Joining the centre party CDU instead of the classical liberal Free Democrat Party was a compromise, too: he joined the strongest party to have as much political support as possible. In public he called for the cautious, gradual implementation of his free market reforms (while barging full speed ahead), and left certain aspects of the welfare state untouched even though he did not agree with it.

When the eminent philosopher Friedrich von Hayek asked why he embellished 'free market' with 'social', Erhard replied: 'I hope you don't misunderstand me when I speak of a social market economy. I mean that the market as such is social, not that it needs to be made social.' Erhard's market was social because it benefited consumers: that is, everyone. In the wake of the interventionists' appropriation of the phrase, 'consumer protection' suggests state intervention. That was not how Erhard used the word 'consumer': for him, consumers were simply individuals operating in the marketplace. Consumers, rather than the state or cartels, were to steer production, by what they desired and, thus, bought, as evidenced by the price mechanism. The capitalism which Erhard did not like is called 'crony capitalism' today: capitalists conspiring to increase their profits at the expense of the individual through government action. Erhard's state would prevent this form of banditry.

According to Erhard, democracy and a free economy logically belong together, like dictatorship and a state economy. The Weimar Republic had not been a free economy, as state and cartels had constantly connived against consumer wants. Erhard's state would create and maintain the market system, keep an eye on the social effects of the economy and promote growth and free trade. It would set the ground rules for competition, and supervise. It would never participate in, or attempt to steer the market. He wanted to deregulate the economy to free individuals from petty bureaucrats. Erhard refused insuring businessmen against risk: they had to bear the burden of risk and failure. Only the consumer was to decide the businessmen's faith. In a limited number of fields, Erhard compromised: the state could create infrastructure such as schools and utilities. During the crisis atmosphere around the establishment of the new independent West Germany, he did not believe that the market could satisfactorily shape agriculture, fuel markets, housing and utilities – though he hoped that it could be left to the free market in the future.

Erhard saw economic growth as the solution for social problems: to increase the pie so there is more for everyone, rather than to redistribute the existing pie and create winners and losers. The market is social because it increases people's standards of living. Or, as he said: 'The freer the economy, the more social it is.' Foreign aid should come in the form of setting up schools where people from underdeveloped countries could learn how to build an economy which creates prosperity through growth. Erhard rejected redistributive justice as he believed it was a society in which 'everyone had his hand in the pocket of everyone else'. Redistribution would discourage people from being responsible for their own actions. He never proposed to dismantle progressive income tax or welfare programmes – this can be seen as another example of his political awareness. To give people a stake in society, Erhard wanted to increase property and share ownership. This would encourage them to become responsible citizens, and independent of demagogues. Property ownership was to be obtained by saving, not as a present from the state.

He strongly opposed cartels and was in favour of legislation to curtail them. Cartels reduce competition: they lower output and artificially inflate prices; inefficient producers remain in existence; production is determined by what the producers decide to produce instead of by what consumers demand; barriers to entry are instated to prevent new competitors from establishing themselves. He did not object to large companies: if a company did well, it was to be allowed to profit from its success. Erhard rejected special interest groups. He believed people should not express their interests in groups. Asking for special favours for groups is at the expense of the whole of society (all individuals together). People asking for group favours become dependent upon the government's gifts.

He believed in freely convertible currencies, unrestrained by government interference. He wanted stable prices and monetary values. There is no free market without free prices. Only if the free market sets prices without government or conniving businesses interfering will supply and demand harmonise. He believed in balanced budgets: the state should only start spending after having received the income. He rejected Keynesian deficit spending. International relations are to be determined by free trade. Erhard therefore opposed the establishment of large international bureaucracies, including the plans for European unity. He believed those bodies would keep themselves busy with planning – and that always fails.

Erhard's beliefs were a ringing endorsement of the theories of Adam Smith, John Locke, Ludwig von Mises, Friedrich von Hayek and Karl Popper. In 1950, Erhard joined the Mont Pelerin Society, the worldwide organisation of classical liberals. It was a mutually satisfying link-up: Erhard was able to discuss his plans with them, and they saw their ideas being tried out in real life. But how did Erhard bring his beliefs into practice – and did they work?

After his house had been bombed by the Allies, Erhard was living with friends in his native city, Fürth. On 19 April 1945, the day after the Americans occupied the city, he walked into the American military authorities' headquarters and offered his services. They told him to restore Fürth's economic activity. By the end of May he had written a report to the US Authorities recommending reviving the German economy with a currency reform and a gradual return to the free market economy. He was quickly promoted to economic adviser to the military authorities for Central Franconia, northern Bavaria. He preached the virtues of the free market wherever he went. He often seemed completely alone, and was opposed by interventionists from all sides.

If anyone had stated in 1945 that Ludwig Erhard would do away with centuries of German state intervention in the economy, he would have been shown the way to the lunatic asylum. Everything pointed to a statist future for liberated Germany. There was a long tradition for this: prices and markets had been regulated by the state for centuries. Under the philosophy of the *Gemeinwirtschaft* (social economy), the state corrected the market economy. Although there was private property, the state decided what could be done with it 'in the interest of the community'. The eminent philosopher Ludwig von Mises's book *Gemeinwirtschaft* was published in English under the title *Socialism*; he believed the words were synonyms.

Many still remembered the Depression and blamed capitalism for having caused it. The left believed that big business and the Nazis had mutually supported each other. The socialists of the SPD wanted nationalisations and an economy planned by the state. The Christian socialists thought capitalism morally repugnant. Some Christian democrats of the CDU wanted an end to bourgeois society and the socialisation of key industries and natural resources – though they rejected violent class struggle. Konrad Adenauer, the CDU leader in the British zone, wrote a programme in 1947 advocating the nationalisation of heavy industries, codetermination for workers, and central planning. He dreamed of a return to a pre-capitalist society in which people would be represented as members of social orders and receive care and protection from a benevolent government acting on Christian principles. At times it seemed as if all saw capitalism, rather than statism, as the fount of all evil. As the eminent philosopher Ludwig von Mises said so poignantly:

> The interventionist policies as practised for many decades by all governments of the capitalistic West have brought about ... wars and civil wars, ruthless oppression of the masses by clusters of self-appointed dictators, economic depressions, mass unemployment, capital consumption, famines ... The interventionist doctrinaires and their followers explain all these undesired consequences as the unavoidable features of capitalism. As they see it, it is precisely these disasters that clearly demonstrate the necessity of intensifying interventionism. The failures of the interventionist policies do not in the least impair the popularity of the implied doctrine. They are so interpreted as to strengthen, not to lessen, the prestige of these teachings. As a vicious economic theory cannot be simply refuted by historical experience, the interventionist propagandists have been able to go on in spite of all the havoc they have spread.

The occupying forces were not helpful, either. The Russians quickly established a totalitarian government in their zone. The French had no intention of Germany ever again becoming economically significant. The British zone was influenced by British domestic politics. The socialist Prime Minister Clement Attlee was busy nationalising industries, increasing ever more progressive taxes, nationalising healthcare and the Bank of England, socialising the law and introducing and expanding the welfare state. The British Labour government now tried to implement the same in the British zone in Germany: their attempts to collectivise the industries in the Ruhr disrupted production and brought people on the brink of starvation. And the Americans? That was hit and miss, too. FDR was dead. The neo-New Dealer Harry Truman was

President, but was unable to do much as the Republicans were quickly gaining political terrain. The policy in the American zone was determined by JCS 1067, which aimed at reducing Germany to a nation of farmers. No attempts were to be made to rebuild its industry. This meant that the US became responsible for the hand-outs to keep the Germans alive. Fortunately for Erhard and his free market ideas, the Commander of the American zone, General Lucius D. Clay, believed in the free market, too.

The wartime destruction, the movement of millions of displaced people and the catastrophic controls over all aspects of the economy meant that Germany was slowly perishing. The Allies simply continued the Nazis' rationing, wage and price controls. Soon the black market accounted for about half of the country's economy. People saw that the controls didn't work. This was Erhard's moment. Thankfully he had tried his luck with the Americans, rather than with the British or the French. He was appointed by the Americans to Economics Minister in the newly formed Bavarian government. They wanted him as a counterweight to the socialist Prime Minister Wilhelm Hoegner. Erhard built up useful political contacts and continued to advocate the virtues of the free market economy. It was around this time that he was approached by the pro-free market Free Democratic Party (FDP) for the first time – but Erhard refused to join any party. When the electorate gave the Hoegner government the boot in 1947, Erhard lost his job. On the basis of evidence gathered by a Communist civil servant, the socialist SPD now asked for an investigation into Erhard's time in office. It cleared him of all wrongdoing. At the instigation of the Americans and the FDP, Erhard was appointed to the Special Office for Money and Credit in 1947. This was an advisory body to the Economic Council (effectively the Parliament for the Bizone, the merged American and British zones). Erhard was made chairman. He was in a constant battle with the interventionists. While

Erhard pleaded to abolish rationing, others wanted minimum allocations of goods for each person. Some argued that the rich should be taxed to enable the government to invest the receipts; Erhard replied that the wealthy would reinvest it much better. When it was stated that freeing the prices would create inflation and allow profiteering by capitalists, Erhard pointed to the failure of price-setting as evidenced by the huge black market. Erhard often stood completely alone and his free market views were met with incredulity. In early 1948 he urged General Clay of the American zone and General Robertson of the British zone to implement currency reform urgently and not to let them be delayed by Soviet recalcitrance. They assured him they wouldn't.

In the beginning of 1948, the position of Director of the Administration for Economics (in effect the Economics Minister) became vacant. The incumbent pro-free market Johannes Zemler was fired by Robertson and Clay after Zemler had called the Allies' food aid 'chicken feed'. Erhard obtained the support of the FDP and of pro-free market CDU-ers, but the powerful head of the CDU in the British zone, Adenauer, preferred another candidate who did not believe in free market competition. Death intervened: Adenauer could not be present at the discussions between CDU and FDP to decide whom they would support for the post as he was with his dying wife in Bonn. Notwithstanding the strong opposition by the socialist SPD, the CDU and the FDP elected Erhard to become the new Director of the Administration for Economics. On 2 April 1948, the free marketeer Ludwig Erhard became the most powerful man for Germany's economic future.

Erhard was aided by an Advisory Council, of which several members were free marketeers like him. He also managed to turn a few unlikely members into supporters. Wherever Erhard spoke, he reiterated his determination to liberate Germans from the command economy. The elected representatives in the Economic Council, weaned on state paternalism, were sceptical, but the Allies were sympathetic: the Bipartite Control Office agreed that the currency reform would have to be accompanied by a reduction of economic controls.

On the afternoon of 15 June 1948 Clay and Robertson informed Erhard that the new Deutsche Mark currency would be announced on 18 June and that it would be distributed on 20 June. Every German would immediately receive 40 DM; money owned by Germans would be proportionally reduced and 5 per cent would be put into new savings accounts for use immediately, with a further 5 per cent to be freed within ninety days. Ninety per cent of the money supply would disappear. Erhard was thrilled.

He now moved very quickly – a bill allowing him to abolish price controls was rushed through the Economic Council and approved in the early hours of 18 June 1948. Erhard didn't bother trying to obtain approval of the Bill from the Allies, as he knew they would not have concurred, and quickly announced that prices would be freed on 20 June. He also used his existing powers to announce the abolition of rationing for household goods at the same time. Rationing would be maintained for goods of which there was a shortage such as coal, gas, electricity, oil and rental housing.

The Allies were not pleased that he had not sought their approval. Robertson particularly objected – Britain was still under rationing. Erhard was called into Clay's headquarters and it looked as if he would be fired and the economic liberalisation would be killed off. He was given a bollocking by Clay's advisers. Clay then saw Erhard face-to-face in his office and told him that in abolishing price controls without the Allies' approval he had acted beyond his power. With regards to the other issue of abolishing rationing, Clay admitted that that was within Erhard's power. When Clay said that all his advisers were opposed to the liberalisation, Erhard replied that his advisers were opposed to it, too. Clay realised that if the proper

procedure had been followed, the British would have vetoed
Erhard's proposals. He himself was in favour of free markets.
Clay then took the risk and approved Erhard's actions.

On 25 June, prices were freed in the Bizone. On 30
June, the British and the Americans approved Erhard's bill
to abolish price controls, and a substantial part of rationing was abolished. Rationing ended, except on food, raw
materials, shoes, clothes, textiles and soap. Prices were freed,
except for staple foods, raw materials and rents. Monopolies
were abolished where possible, and an anti-cartel and anti-
monopoly law would soon be prepared. Wages were freed.

Immediately after the market liberalisation, the Allies
and the Economic Council implemented dramatic tax cuts.
Lower incomes saw their taxes cut in half; middle and upper
incomes by 25 per cent. The high punitive marginal tax rates
were reduced, too. Although the highest rate remained 95
per cent, the threshold was increased from 6,000 DM to
250,000 DM. Corporation tax, which had varied from 35
per cent to 65 per cent, was reduced to a flat rate of 50 per
cent. When Erhard asked for more, the Allies introduced tax
exemptions for saved and invested income. Rapid deprecia-
tion allowances encouraged investment.

5. BOOM

The results were spectacular. Within weeks the shops were
full. Hoarding stopped; the black market disappeared.
Instead of keeping themselves busy black marketeering,
people found it lucrative to go to work again: absenteeism
dropped from an average of 9.5 hours per week to 4.2 hours
per week. Between June and December 1948, the industrial
production in the Bizone rose by 50 per cent.

As Erhard had predicted, though, all was not well: it
took the market almost a year to adjust and to find the new

appropriate market price levels. With the new hard currency, employers could no longer afford to keep on useless employees – so they fired them and unemployment rose. Prices rose and inflation went up. Erhard took transitional measures to soften the shock.

During the growing pains of the new free market economy, Erhard continued to be attacked from all directions – especially by the socialists, who were demanding fresh price controls, state planning and Erhard's removal. Although the American military authorities were generally in favour of free markets, they were also prisoners of their risk-averse planned barrack mentality. American New Dealers had not died out either. The British urged the socialism they were introducing at home.

Erhard doggedly persisted. He continued in his usual style: refusing to be bogged down in administrative detail and preferring the long-term overall picture instead. He refused to attend lengthy bureaucratic meetings and refused to read memoranda. He refused to compromise on his free market beliefs, something he was attacked for by his more political and career-oriented colleagues. He sought and found support though: when the new Federal Republic of Germany came into being in 1949, he joined the Christian Democrat CDU (although he never actually filled in his membership form). His heart was with the classical liberal FDP: his father had been a supporter, they shared his ideological beliefs and they had been the first ones to support his candidacy to become the de facto Economics Minister. But they were small, and Erhard realised he needed more powerful allies. For many years he clashed with the most powerful person in the CDU, Konrad Adenauer. Adenauer was in favour of private property, but not of free markets. He wanted to avoid collectivism and saw the future in a communitarian paternalistic society instead. By 1958, industrial production per capita was three times as high as before the reforms.

	1947	1948	1949	1950	1951
UK & US Aid in Mill US $	1,020	955	481	428	114
GDP in billion DM	37.5*	83.8	89.7	113.6	126

*Second half of 1948 only

Source: *Germany and the Political Economy of the Marshall Plan* by Helge Berger and Albrecht Ritschl, 1994.

The CDU government (later joined by the FDP) was so successful in its free market approach that the socialist SPD had to drop its Marxism and hostility to capitalism and adopt the much more moderate Godesberg Programme in 1959 in order to appeal to the electorate. It shows the strength of the approach Erhard advocated: his political opponents had to change course to regain power under Willy Brandt.

‡

Erhard, Kennedy and the Laffer Curve
Others later copied West Germany's example. When the young John F. Kennedy visited West Germany in 1961, Erhard impressed upon him that cutting high marginal tax rates would pay off even more for the masses than for the classes. Erhard told him to avoid the British high tax model, to cut America's wartime tax rates and to stop punishing wealth creation. Kennedy overruled his left-wing advisers and cut corporation tax in 1962. He then cut the top rate of taxation from 91 per cent in 1963, and three months after his death it was cut again to 70 per cent. It brought the longest economic expansion in America's history: between 1961 and 1968, the inflation-adjusted economy expanded by more than 42 per cent, a yearly average of more than 5 per cent. During the same period, tax revenue grew by a solid 62 per

cent. Even Walter Heller, the Keynesian economist who was Chairman of Kennedy's Council of Economic Advisers and who had tried to stop the President, had to admit that the tax cuts had paid for themselves by way of increased revenue.

Many left-wingers criticised the Kennedy tax cuts as 'tax cuts for the rich'. According to Leon Keyserling, who had been an economic adviser to Harry Truman, the richest 12 per cent of Americans obtained 45 per cent of the benefits. Cutting the highest tax rates inevitably benefits the highest earners more in a system of progressive taxation. The reason to do away with high tax rates is that the higher the rate is, the less incentivised people are to work (and the more incentivised they are to pay for expensive tax experts or to avoid tax in legal and illegal ways). Therefore, if you want to encourage people to work hard, it is the highest tax rates that you should cut first. This almost always leads to higher total tax receipts. This theory was made famous by the American economist Arthur Laffer. He famously explained the phenomenon to senior politicians in the Nixon–Ford administration by drawing what became known as the 'Laffer Curve' on the back of an envelope.

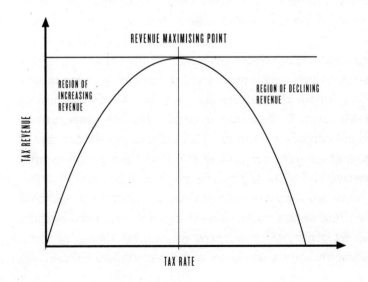

REVENUE MAXIMISING POINT

REGION OF INCREASING REVENUE

REGION OF DECLINING REVENUE

TAX REVENUE

TAX RATE

When taxes are 0 per cent, there is no tax revenue for the state. When taxes are 100 per cent, the economy comes to a standstill, so there is no revenue either. The maximum tax-take is somewhere in between the two extremes, and usually at a level which is much lower than average Western taxation. Governments are therefore advised to cut taxes to receive more.

‡

Keynesians would later claim that Germany's recovery was due to the stimulus created by the Marshall Plan (America's programme of aid to Europe), and not Erhard's liberation of the economy. In fact, nothing could be further from the truth. As Professor David R. Henderson states:

> [The] Marshall Plan aid to West Germany was not that large. Cumulative aid from the Marshall Plan and other aid programs totalled only $2 billion through October 1954. Even in 1948 and 1949, when aid was at its peak, Marshall Plan aid was less than 5 per cent of German national income. Other countries that received substantial Marshall Plan aid exhibited lower growth than Germany.

Moreover, while West Germany was receiving aid, it was also making reparations and restitution payments and paying for the costs of occupying Germany, well in excess of the foreign aid received. Economist Tyler Cowen notes that other European countries which placed greater reliance on free markets recovered faster as well. Belgium, for example, recovered long before the Marshall Plan.

Ludwig Erhard clashed repeatedly with the Americans over the Marshall Plan. Erhard did not object to receiving help from the American taxpayers, but he did object to the statism and interventionism that came with it. Erhard was, for example, required to draft an economic plan to receive the support. He dragged his feet for as long as he could.

Germany had a number of advantages which other European countries did not have. The massive immigration from the east of people who wanted to build a better future for themselves helped to stimulate the economy: it brought in cheap labour and specialised workers, tradesmen and professionals, who increased competition and productivity. Germany's special interest groups were largely destroyed, if not by the Nazis (e.g. the trade unions), then by the Nazis' collapse and loss of the war (big industry).

Ludwig Erhard was Economics Minister under Adenauer for fourteen years. He succeeded Adenauer, but disliked power and only served as Chancellor for three years. All along, he kept his free market zeal. He unilaterally liberalised foreign trade – an act which was followed by other European countries. Throughout the 1950s he reduced Germany's tariffs unilaterally to the low rates current in the Benelux countries. Erhard campaigned vigorously against the setting up of a European customs union with strong common institutions, as he feared it would end up being a trading block with high protective external tariffs. A customs union would mean making foreign trade policy subject to European group decisions. Erhard favoured a European free trade zone, with tariffs with third countries to be decided by the individual countries. He was much more willing to be subject to the pro-free trade OECD and GATT rules than to European majority rule. He lost that battle, and Europe did become a customs union.

To this day, post-war Germany's rising from the ashes is called the *Wirtschaftswunder*, the economic miracle. Other economic booms have been called miraculous – the most recent ones being the Asian economic miracle, the Chinese economic miracle, and the Brazilian economic miracle. The earliest example of the use of the word 'miracle' to describe phenomenal economic growth took place in eighteenth-century Britain. Almost 250 years before the American and German post-war revival, another country boomed – by applying similar methods.

THREE

BRITAIN

I. A MIRACLE?

'**M**ove your eye which side you will: you behold nothing but great riches and yet greater resources,' wrote Arthur Young in the second half of the eighteenth century. Others described Britain's rapid economic development as 'almost miraculous', and 'unparalleled in the annals of the world'. One wrote: 'A traveller who visits Birmingham once in six months supposes himself well acquainted with her, but he may chance to find a street of houses in the autumn, where he last saw his horse at grass in the spring.'

It was no accident that words like 'miracle' and other biblical imagery were used. Those who lived it were short of words to describe what they saw. There were no apparent earthly planners who could credibly claim to be the architects. It certainly wasn't the King's doing: ever since the overthrow of King James II in the Glorious Revolution, the Bill of Rights had severely limited his powers. Parliament was divided and power dispersed. Some who believed that the social order was laid down by God wondered whether the economic bounty came down from heaven as well.

One writer believed it was all geography and geology:

Consecrated in the purposes of Providence to the beneficent

task of expounding to the world the laws of trade, the land we inhabit was so arranged as to afford to every species of industrial enterprise the most favourable sphere of development. Although denied the warm temperature and luxuriant vegetation of tropical climes, it would be impossible to find a spot on which greater natural advantages have been bestowed. Every facility seems at hand for starting us on a manufacturing career. Those metals which are of greatest utility in the useful arts, and the coal which is requisite in working them, are distributed conveniently, and in inexhaustible abundance, throughout the land. With our insulated position we have a greater line of sea coast, and a greater number of capacious harbours, as compared with the extent of land surface, than any other nation in the world.

If God, Providence, geography or geology created such great wealth in the eighteenth century, why had they not done so before? In 1723 in the Scottish port of Kirkcaldy, across the Firth of Forth from Edinburgh, a boy grew up alongside sailors, fish merchants, nail-makers, customs officials and smugglers. Kirkcaldy was a busy trading port which exported coal from local mines and brought back scrap iron for the iron-working industry. He witnessed the growing prosperity around him and identified the reasons why it was happening. His name was Adam Smith.

2. CHANGING WORLD

Thanks to the intellectual atmosphere of the Enlightenment – the belief that one could improve one's circumstances through reason – there was a great deal of interest in experimentation and inventions. The number of books on medicine, science and technology increased by almost 300 per cent in the eighteenth century. It encouraged individuals to use technology to produce prosperity, instead of trying to use the government to increase their wealth (rent seeking).

British inventions were changing the world. In 1709, Abraham Darby invented a new method to increase production of cast iron at a reduced cost. Cheap iron was used in most industries and became the master material of the industrial revolution. Steam power carried coal and iron to all parts of the country and beyond. As the scientific writer Dionysius Lardner put it: 'Nor are [steam power's] effects confined to England alone; they extend over the whole civilised world; and the savage tribes of America, Asia and Africa, must ere long feel the benefits, remote or intermediate, of this all-powerful agent.' From 1775 onwards James Watt and Matthew Boulton produced more efficient steam engines to generate motive power. These gradually replaced the traditional methods of water wheels, windmills and horses. 'The people in London, Manchester and Birmingham are steam mill mad,' Boulton wrote to Watts. The machines would eventually be used for coal, steel, spinning factories, flour mills, breweries, and mills for crushing sugar cane. Manchester was nicknamed 'cottonpolis'. Raw cotton fibres had been imported from as far back as the thirteenth century, but cotton had always lagged far behind wool and silk, Britain's traditional textiles. In the eighteenth century, improved spinning and weaving methods increased productivity and cotton became Britain's main export product: the export value increased 300-fold. Silk and wool were unable to compete. Since medieval times, their guilds had restricted competition to keep prices high. The industries were comfortable in their protected position and hostile to change. They were easily out-competed by the modern cotton industry.

The astonishing fact about the eighteenth-century inventions was that they were accepted at all, without being choked off and limited by controls intended to preserve social stability. The inventors were spurred on by profit, despite the hostility from the protected crafts and the constant risk of litigation. Many businessmen were Jews and religious dissenters such as Quakers, who were not allowed to obtain academic degrees (Jews were also excluded from several mercantile organisations). The plants were usually small; the businessman did everything. The workforce had to be 'tamed': having only known the irregular agricultural hours, they now needed to keep to specific hours and organisation. Most businesses financed themselves by thriftily reinvesting their profits.

The transportation costs for bulky goods such as coal reduced when private companies dug canals. These paid dazzling dividends to their investors – the Oxford Canal paid on average 30 per cent for more than thirty years. Roads – often mere dirt tracks – became better maintained when they were privatised. An Act of Parliament made it legal to 'turnpike' an existing road. Local luminaries became trustees with a duty to maintain the road. They recovered their initial investment through the levying of toll. Profit making was the main aim; the legal vehicle of a charitable trust was merely used because in the wake of the South Sea Company collapse, the government, 'to protect the public', had made it difficult to set up joint stock companies. Between the 1750s and 1760s, over 300 turnpike trusts were created totalling 10,000 miles. By 1770 all the major roads into London had been turnpiked.

The financing of the industrial revolution occurred without state planning, too. A large number of individuals acted as intermediaries or providers of capital. Traders and industrialists provided local means of payment; lawyers received money in trust and gave investment advice. In 1784 there were more than 100 country banks in England; in the next ten years their number trebled. None of this was regulated by Acts of Parliament; instead they were subject to common law (e.g. liability for negligence) like everyone else, without distinction.

Stock exchanges flourished as private self-regulating institutions without government meddling. Initially, stock brokers traded at the Royal Exchange, in between grocers and clothiers. When the government tried to regulate the stockbrokers in 1696, they voted with their feet and left the Royal Exchange. They started to trade their shares in private places such as coffee houses. The exchanges thrived because they self-regulated. If a broker failed to live up to his promises, he was labelled a 'lame duck': he was banned from the coffee house, and his name was written on a blackboard. As this meant losing one's income, brokers had an interest in acting honourably. Having to mingle with the hoi polloi in a coffee house eventually became too much for some, and in 1762, 150 brokers transformed Jonathan's Coffee House into a private members' club. They admitted only reputable brokers and expelled the unruly or dishonest ones. Jonathan's became a highly respected and successful private stock exchange.

Ever more capital was needed to build ever larger factories. Joint stock companies were the obvious device to achieve this. In 1844, the onerous requirement of a Royal Charter or a private Act of Parliament was abolished, and joint stock companies could now be registered by paying £10. The number of joint stock companies increased from fifteen to 150 in six years.

Industrial towns mushroomed. Unincorporated Birmingham doubled its population between 1760 and 1800. The industrial towns were growing so fast that visitors were shocked by the congestion, smoke and squalor. Newly wealthy individuals often paid for or organised improvements. Private charitable institutions were set up to care for the aged, the sick, prisoners, orphans. Some complained that philanthropists and public authorities were over-indulgent with the idle and the lazy. Joseph Townsend, a vicar who wrote a book about the Poor Laws, stated categorically in 1783 that 'no human efforts' could improve the state of the poor and that only hunger could induce 'sobriety, diligence and fidelity'.

Self-help was far more popular than charity. The eighteenth and nineteenth centuries saw the rapid growth of friendly societies for labourers. The illness or death of the breadwinner often meant penury. People took pride in being self-sufficient and many refused to accept charity. Groups of friends put a little bit of money in a pot at the end of each week. If any of them fell upon hard times, he would receive some money. Some friendly societies were very informal, others had strict rules. They functioned well because the members knew each other. Because most arrangements were informal, they remained largely undocumented – hence early social reformers in the statist mindset portraying people who fell on hard times in the eighteenth century as 'left to charity'. Mutual societies helped themselves, not outsiders – they were emphatically not charitable. Later they accumulated reserves and federated with other friendly societies. In 1801 there were 7,200 societies with 648,000 adult male members (population 9 million). When compulsory social insurance for 12 million people was introduced in 1911, at least 9 million were already covered by voluntary insurance associations.

Policing was entirely private, until George II began paying some London and Middlesex watchmen with taxpayers' money. Crime victims gave rewards to private thief-takers to catch the criminals. The criminals were then compelled to return stolen property and pay restitution. Private watchmen were paid by private individuals and organisations. In 1828 there were private police units in forty-five parishes within a ten-mile radius of London.

Living standards rose, and not just for the rich. There

have been long debates between those who say that people were worse off with the onset of the industrial revolution and those who say they were better off. The critics blamed the industrial revolution for forcing artisans from a bucolic existence into wage slaves subject to the factory bell. The reality was quite different. In the pre-industrial era, people who produced piecework at home (the 'domestic system') had a low quality of life. The first factories increased productivity and offered a better pay. Many voluntarily abandoned the domestic system and flocked to the factories. As is shown by the rapidly increasing population, their living conditions improved. In 1700, England had a population of 5.5 million; by 1750, it was 6.5 million. Critics claimed that the poor bore more children so they could send them as additional earners into the factories from age six. In fact, the birth rate did not go up much. People simply lived longer than before. The increased income factory work gave them kept people alive when previously they would have died.

For the first time ever, labourers were able to purchase cheap goods for themselves. The first factories focused on mass production of cheap goods for the poor. Shoes, for example, were produced for the proletariat – the rich bought made-to-measure shoes. This was different from France, where the government's mercantilist product standards, designed to uphold quality, ensured that nothing was produced for the poor at all. In France, mercantilism continued to be state policy for much longer than in England. This is the reason why industrialisation took fifty more years to arrive on France's shores.

People did not just 'stay alive': many did exceedingly well. Friedrich Hayek showed that the industrial revolution created mass prosperity, and that the outrage over poverty increased as poverty became more exceptional and therefore more striking. The poverty awareness industry which sprang up at the end of the eighteenth century is often used as evidence of increasing squalor. The philosopher Schumpeter observed that the industrial revolution allowed for the financial maintenance of a class of intellectuals who had nothing better to do than to interfere in other people's lives – usually by attacking the very capitalist society which had brought intellectuals into existence.

The industrial revolution occurred when the state intervention guided by mercantilism waned. To understand why the industrial revolution happened, we have to look at what it replaced.

3. MERCANTILISM AND ITS DEMISE

In the centuries before the industrial revolution, economic development was stifled by mercantilism. Many mercantilist practices had existed in the Middle Ages (notably through the guilds), but between the late fifteenth and eighteenth centuries it was the West's dominant economic policy. Kings and princes intervened in the economy to preserve societal stability, to protect infant industries and to maintain a positive balance of trade to increase the amount of gold in the country. Merchants could not be left to their own devices; they had to be guided to serve the national interest. The mercantilist aims were pursued through a raft of regulations which Schumpeter called 'pre-analytic': its protagonists were pamphleteers full of assertions, opinions and axes to grind, rather than analysts. Mercantilism failed for three reasons: (1) the basic tenets of what constituted the wealth of a nation, and the finite nature of wealth, were erroneous, (2) special interest groups captured the government's interventionist zeal for their own profit, and (3) the interventionist measures and their side-effects destroyed wealth and potential wealth rather than increasing it.

There are two diverging views as to what people's lives

were like on the eve of the industrial revolution. The philosopher Ludwig von Mises describes one side:

> The authors begin by sketching an idyllic image of conditions as they prevailed ... At that time, they tell us, things were, by and large, satisfactory. The peasants were happy. So also were the industrial workers under the domestic system. They worked in their own cottages and enjoyed a certain economic independence since they owned a garden plot and their tools. But then the Industrial Revolution fell like a war or a plague on these people. The factory system reduced the free worker to virtual slavery; it lowered his standard of living to the level of bare subsistence – in cramming women and children into the mills, it destroyed family life and sapped the very foundations of society, morality and public health. A small minority of ruthless exploiters had cleverly succeeded in imposing their yoke upon the immense majority.

Adam Smith saw things quite differently. Before industrialisation, under the domestic system, many artisans who manufactured piecework at home had a terrible quality of life. The hours of labour were long. 'A shepherd', observed Smith, 'has a great deal of leisure, a husbandman ... some, a [domestic] manufacturer has none at all.' A seventeenth-century writer states that 'many a poor weaver sits at his loom from four in the morning till eight, nine, and ten at night'. In frosty weather the yarn spoiled in the drying – weaving came to a standstill and this meant no income at all. The work was tedious and repetitious. Tailors worked twelve to fifteen hours, shipbuilders and nail makers twelve. Child labour was universal in the domestic system before the industrial revolution. Some say that the domestic system at least allowed a family to stay together, and to take off time when desirable. In reality it offered the opportunity to starve *en famille*.

Becoming unemployed was an unmitigated disaster, as an assortment of rules made it near impossible to find alternative employment. You could work your garden plot if you were so lucky to have one, or help with the harvest – but a weaver could not suddenly become a shipbuilder. From the earliest times, the guilds managed to keep their income high by regulating their professions (village communities regulated agriculture). They regulated prices, working conditions and wages. Jews were excluded. Apprenticeships were strictly limited. They lasted up to fourteen (!) years; far in excess of the time needed to acquire the skills. Once you jumped through these hoops, you became a legal craftsman, as opposed to an illegal one. The state assisted in the enforcement: under the intervention-mad Tudor and Stuart kings, the guilds' restrictive practices became state law. The Statute of Artificers (1558) restricted the free movement and the wages of workers and limited the quantity of people entering the profession. Special interest groups always claim to act in the common interest. Apprenticeships, for example, were claimed to uphold quality. This in turn would help to obtain a positive balance of trade with foreign competitors. Guilds also pointed at the hardship the professional organisations' members would suffer if competition were allowed. Monopolies granted by government made it difficult to start new companies and to compete. One of the pieces of legislation which reduced the poor's options most was the Poor Relief Act of 1662 (known as the Act of Settlement). This Act made it impossible for the poor to seek a better life elsewhere. If a person moved to another parish and there was a complaint against him that he was a pauper and risked becoming a burden upon the parish, he could be removed. All of this meant that the poor were stuck in poverty. Many were forced into the navy, or lived from the meagre crumbs provided by seasonal work. Others were saved from starvation through private charity and the poor laws.

A large part of the population lived in abject poverty. Those who survived expected their children to live in equally abject poverty. The enclosure movement privatised previously collectively owned land. As private owners took greater care of their land, agricultural productivity increased a great deal (similar to the situation in the Soviet Union in the 1980s, where private land was more than ten times more productive than collective land). But by losing the use of the common land, some became destitute. The proletariat roamed the country, often as beggars, thieves and prostitutes.

Apart from the guilds, the government also gave privileges and monopolies to other special interest groups, which made wealth-creating free markets impossible. And just like today, this mercantilist state interventionism led to a regulatory failure spiral: government tried to tackle the unwanted side-effects by more failing regulations. Good examples are the price controls which governments tried to introduce after they had granted a monopoly on coal transport. In the seventeenth and eighteenth centuries, nothing excited the citizenry more than the price of coal. The dearth of wood had made coal indispensable. The agitation to regulate the prices, the actual regulation, the failure of the regulation resulting in its abandonment, followed by new demands to regulate prices, lasted for several centuries and is nothing short of farcical. All the problems started when, at the beginning of the twelfth century, King Henry I had the bright idea of decreeing that all coal from the banks of the River Tyne (the richest deposits in England) had to be shipped from the Newcastle quayside. Before the roads were privatised and improved, road transport was much more expensive than shipping. The coals were shipped to the rest of England, to Scotland, France and Flanders. The Hostmen, who owned the ships by which coal could legally be shipped from Newcastle, effectively policed the monopoly for half a millennium. Several kings confirmed the monopoly and received a cut in return.

The excessive prices charged by the Hostmen were often complained about, usually by Londoners. This resulted in court cases, which the Hostmen usually won. Repeatedly, government tried to impose a maximum price on coal. The suppliers always refused to sell at that low price, resulting in shortages and the eventual return to free pricing. Complainants displayed an astonishing incomprehension of the interaction between supply and demand, and only ever blamed conniving middlemen or greedy merchants for high prices. For centuries the House of Commons held inquiries into the price of coal. For most of the 500 years that people paid too much for coal because of a legal monopoly granted by the state, taxes exceeded the prime cost.

Under mercantilism, international trade was a matter of state: it was to ensure a positive balance of trade; it showed the power of the nation (and its ruler!); it brought in tax revenue; self-reliance was to be maintained for security reasons. It was feared that Britain could be brought to its knees if trade were cut off, and an assortment of foreign foes from Spain to Napoleon tried to do just that. In 1568 the Spanish ambassador told his king that 'if your majesty and the French King choose to stop English commerce, without even drawing the sword, they will be obliged to adopt the Catholic religion'. As the philosopher Thomas Hobbes had popularised the view that global wealth was finite, becoming richer could only be achieved by making another poorer (zero-sum thinking – still popular today). Through a myriad of regulations the rulers tried to maintain a positive balance of trade, that is, to ensure that more gold and silver came into the country than left it. This encumbered trade. When, for example, the East India Company wanted to take gold out of England to pay for Indian goods, the issue was hotly debated by politicians and limited accordingly. Exports were encouraged with export subsidies and privileges for trading companies, and imports hindered through import duties and other barriers. In medieval times this even applied at local level: local governments levied tolls on goods entering and leaving their patch.

'In the interest of order and government' the king and, later, Parliament granted monopolies to a handful of trading companies, using the navy to keep the trade routes open and to protect the trading companies' activities. This caused a never-ending stream of military conflicts. In return for the monopoly, the trading companies claimed to provide a number of 'public benefits': well-organised and well-regulated trade; high prices for British producers; protection of quality; navigation skills including fighting pirates; prevention of customs fraud; enforcement of government decisions; and acts of piety and charity such as building chapels and providing for distressed mariners and soldiers. And last but not least: 'lending' money to the Crown. Elizabeth I, for example, 'borrowed' £30,000 from the Merchant Adventurers shortly after her accession. The trading companies were powerful, and with their privileges they constituted a state within the state – and beyond.

The chief monopolistic trading companies were the Merchant Adventurers, the Eastland Company, the Levant Company, the Muscovy (or Russia) Company, the East India Company; the African Company and the Hudson's Bay Company. Regulated companies were governed by their members, who traded with their own capital on their own account; others were joint stock companies which operated as single entities with their own capital and loans.

The Merchant Adventurers firmly restricted its membership as it perpetually claimed to be overcrowded. One could become a member through parentage, by an apprenticeship of at least eight years, or by purchase. The members bought goods in Britain for their own account. As important buyers, they had a strong bargaining position. The company's ships brought the goods to their foreign destination. As the foreign

rulers or cities were eager to have their goods taken back
to England, they enticed the merchants with privileges such
as lodgings, preferential duties, their own jurisdiction and
protection. The trading company placed its members under
strict discipline: apprentices had a curfew and were obliged
to marry before the end of their apprenticeship. Merchants
who switched away from the established religion were sent
home, and he who had the temerity to marry a local woman
lost his membership. The trading companies claimed that
they forced their suppliers to provide high quality and were
held responsible by their buyers for slippage.

Above all, the trading companies ensured that their
members maintained a high income. They reduced competition by restricting membership, restricted the number
of apprentices and restricted the quantities of goods each
member could trade. Sometimes the members agreed prices
between them. They did not allow their members to sell
beyond the trading cities or directly to consumers. Assisted
by the British government and the host cities, the trading
companies waged an unrelenting war against competition
from free traders and rival foreign trading companies such
as the Hanseatic League.

Joint stock companies were different in that everybody
could buy or sell the shares (whereas merchants in regulated
companies had the monopoly of profit). This allowed them to
raise more capital, which was needed for riskier ventures and
longer voyages. Companies such as the East India Company
were constantly under attack from competitors, especially the
Dutch, and had to maintain forts and safe depots for their
trade. Sometimes a joint stock company was set up for just one
voyage to India. But their monopoly on trade restricted competition even more, as they operated as one company, whereas
traders in regulated companies still competed with each other.
The EIC did allow some individual merchants to trade in India
(and later Persia and China), provided they paid for it.

How did these trading companies maintain their monopolies for so long? It was a classic case of concentrated profits and dispersed costs, those profiting being the Crown, the merchants who were part of the trading company, and/or the shareholders; those losing out being the anonymous mass of consumers who had fewer job opportunities (competing in the trade was prohibited), low incomes (trading companies forced producers to sell cheaply), and had to pay high prices for imported goods.

Apart from intervening in trade by granting monopolies to trading companies, the government also tried to prevent foreign ships from being used for trade between England and its colonies through a succession of Navigation Acts. Ironically, the trade restrictions were imposed to fight the positive consequences of trade liberation elsewhere. After the Eighty Years War, the Dutch Republic and the Spanish Empire agreed to trade freely between themselves. The ensuing economic boom in those countries made English goods uncompetitive. Instead of liberating trade as well, Britain banned foreign imports to English and Scottish markets, and allowed its colonies to trade only with the mother country. This was one of the causes of the American Revolution. There is clear direct evidence of the harm these restrictive trading Acts did. When Cromwell introduced the first Navigation Act in 1651, the Levantine suppliers of raw cotton, no longer suffering competition from Holland and France, immediately raised their prices. Twenty thousand poor in Lancashire who were employed in making fustian threatened that unless they obtained dispensation from the Act, they would take their manufacture to Hamburg. No exception was obtained – presumably part of the Lancashire poor became even poorer when their jobs disappeared.

Although its influence waned significantly during the industrial revolution, mercantilist policies are still very much alive today. Governments are still obsessed with their balance of trade. Other countries' trade surpluses are portrayed as a national calamity. Most countries still try to hinder certain imports 'in the national interest'. It is widely accepted that government ministers, Presidents or royals intervene in or lobby for international commercial contracts, even though they are neither directors nor shareholders of the companies involved. When countries enter into trade agreements, complex calculations ensure that on balance not one penny more goes to one than the other, for fear of endangering the balance of trade. As one writer put it:

> There is nothing extraordinary about mercantilism, as the use of subsidies, tax rebates, tariffs, and quotas to attempt to protect and encourage American industries at the expense of the rest of the world is standard modern practice. If every member of [the American] Congress and every president had the economic background and viewpoints of Adam Smith and David Ricardo, we would not pursue such policies. But they do not, and we do pursue them, *as do all other governments in the world today and as they did throughout the seventeenth and eighteenth centuries.*

Adam Smith saw through the mistake of mercantilism and rejected it lock, stock, and barrel. Virtually the whole of his seminal book *The Wealth of Nations* is devoted to its dissection and rejection.

‡

Colbertism: the apotheosis of mercantilism
Internationally, mercantilism's most famous protagonist was Louis XIV's humourless Minister of Finance, Jean-Baptiste Colbert. His 'Colbertism' gold-plated mercantilism with eye-watering levels of government interference for the greater glory of the French state and its Sun King. He was a boundless

sycophant: on the occasion of a military victory, he once wrote to the king: 'One must, Sire, remain in silent wonder, and thank God every day for having caused us to be born in the reign of a king like Your Majesty.' The king's favour brought Colbert and his family great riches. Those who opposed him were labelled narrow-minded, short-sighted and selfish; he repeatedly called merchants 'little men with only little private interests'.

Colbert was reputed to have rescued France's finances, but his mercantilist interventionism actually impoverished the country. The excessive public spending incurred on his watch (including the expansion of Versailles and the maintenance of the court's lavish lifestyle) was paid for by borrowing, by tax increases (e.g. the '*taille*', from which the nobility was excluded) and by the granting of monopolies. He once said that 'the art of taxation consists in plucking the goose so as to obtain the largest number of feathers with the least possible amount of hissing.'

He managed to obtain a positive balance of trade through the combination of export subsidies and extreme tariffs and qualitative restrictions on foreign imports. His trade monopolies restricted competition, thereby stifling innovation and jacking up prices.

Like other mercantilists he believed that the total number of ships and the total production of manufacturing was fixed. Trade was therefore synonymous with war and conflict, as one country's fortune could only come about at the expense of another. Colbert rejoiced in France's wars irrespective of the misery they inflicted on others. In 1669 he wrote to King Louis XIV: 'This state is flourishing not only in itself, but also by the want which it has inflicted upon all the neighbouring states.'

No action could be left to the individuals involved. Colbert imposed a raft of product regulation which stifled innovation and choice. If you sold a product below state standard three times, you were whipped in public. The poor were not given the option of buying a product of a lesser standard for less money.

Intellectual and artistic life was brought under strict state control so as to be orderly and always in the service of the king. The arts were grouped into strictly regulated academies which enjoyed legal monopolies. The composer Lully had, for example, bought the monopoly over all musical performances with more than two instruments after his predecessor managed to go bankrupt. One theatre had the monopoly over all theatrical performances in Paris. The Académie Française was nationalised and put in charge of the French language. Artists and intellectuals also enjoyed a raft of pensions, no-show appointments and exemptions from taxes and protection against creditors. This did away with any semblance of artistic or intellectual independence.

Colbert micromanaged the guilds: entry into the professions was hindered through the imposition of apprenticeships of three or four years. One master could have only one or two apprentices, to prevent his company from growing too big. French workmen were prohibited from emigrating, as 'losing their crafts' was seen as a loss to the state. Industries were fixed in the hands of specific bourgeois; professions were inherited. Social mobility became virtually impossible for the lower classes. Colbert forced 'the idle' to work for the state: vagabonds were to be driven out of the country or put to forced labour as galley slaves. Holidays were reduced so people would work harder.

An impressive bureaucracy enforced the regulations. Civil servants known as intendants used inspections and spies to detect violations of the plethora of cartel restrictions and regulations. The spies also spied on each other, including the intendants themselves.

Colbert was one of the most notorious statists of all time. When he died there was rejoicing in the street. His successors expanded his interventionism further.

Interestingly, it was a meeting between Colbert and a group of French businessmen which occasioned the birth of the most famous free market dictum. The statist Colbert eagerly asked them what the state could do to help to promote commerce. He must have been deeply disappointed when the answer was '*laissez-nous faire*' ('leave us be', or 'leave us alone'). 'Laissez-faire' has been the purest explanation of free market economics ever since. Sadly, interventionists have scared many into believing that laissez-faire is a call for wicked lawless anarchy – while most free marketeers agree that a legal framework must protect individual liberty, including private property.

‡

4. ADAM SMITH

The world's greatest book on economics was written out of boredom. Adam Smith was accompanying the young Duke of Buccleuch on the Grand Tour in his capacity as tutor, and found the duty so tedious that he started idling the hours away by jottering about economics. *An Inquiry into the Nature and Causes of the Wealth of Nations* became an instant bestseller. It explained how wealth in society could be increased. It also investigated what stopped it from happening: government's misfiring interference.

Contrary to his detractors' caricature, Adam Smith did not want to leave people to their own devices altogether. He saw a role for government in protecting property rights, national defence, setting up a framework to guarantee the rule of law, and for a number of other issues. He wanted to limit the state's powers to intervene. He also proved that keeping individuals and markets free to pursue their self-interest is in the interest of society as a whole – especially for its poorest members.

Adam Smith rejected mercantilism in its entirety. One country's increase in wealth does not need to be at the expense of another's. The wealth of a nation can be increased by production and commerce. One must not confuse gold with wealth: gold in a vault does not increase wealth. Gold is merely a conduit to facilitate trade.

An increase in productivity can be achieved through specialisation. Smith illustrated this with the now quaint-sounding example of a pin factory. At least eighteen different operations were needed to produce one pin. On his own, one person was able to produce twenty pins a day. But through specialisation, that is, separate individuals doing one operation each, ten men could produce 48,000 pins a day. The surpluses could be traded.

Trade increases wealth, too. When two parties agree to trade something, they both obtain more than what they had before – otherwise, they would not engage in the trade in the first place. There are no losers: both have gained. The more trade, the wealthier people become. This contrasts sharply with the belief of development economists today that trade is a conspiracy by one person to enrich himself at the expense of another.

Self-interest, and not a concern for the other person's welfare, is what drives this wealth creation. As Smith famously put it: 'It is not for the benevolence of the butcher, the brewer, or the baker, that we expect our dinner, but from their regard to their own interest.' By self-interest, Smith did not mean greed or selfishness, but an eighteenth-century concern to look after our own welfare.

Goods have no intrinsic value. What they fetch on the market depends on what another is willing to pay and on how many goods are brought to the market. If demand outstrips supply, prices will rise. The higher prices will encourage others to bring similar products to the market or to produce alternatives, and prices will decrease again.

In a normal free market, equilibrium of supply and demand is reached at a market price. It is no different for the scarce resource of labour. If industry and trade are increasing, more workers will be needed, and their salaries will rise. Therefore successful trade and industry is in the best interest of workers, as they will earn more.

Special interest groups try to co-opt government power to twist the normal market system for their own financial advantage. Producers will try to convince the government to limit the number of fellow producers to achieve higher prices. Medieval guilds reduced the number of entrants into the profession. As Smith said: 'People of the same trade seldom meet together, even for merriment and diversion, but the conversation ends in a conspiracy against the public, or in some contrivance to raise prices.'

The rich always try to convince governments to overrule the market process for their own benefit. They will typically try to restrict competition. The poor have not enough clout to influence government, and they have therefore the most to gain from free markets.

Smith drew a distinction between the productive and the unproductive sectors – what today is called the manufacturing and the services sector. To produce goods or services, we consume production factors (labour, raw materials). In the productive sector, the production exceeds the production costs. The surpluses (e.g. the pins) can be sold to re-invest in machinery to increase productivity further: it is a virtuous circle. Capital accumulation is vital to increase growth. In the unproductive sector, we create no surpluses which can be sold to reinvest. We 'eat' our capital which could have been used to reinvest (e.g. by paying civil servants, doctors, artists). The more we consume now, the more future growth we must forgo.

People will usually save for later, whereas governments are usually only interested in spending for the here and now. Most government revenue is spent on the unproductive sector: 'It is the highest impertinence and presumption ... in kings and ministers, to pretend to watch over the economy of private people ... They are themselves always the greatest spend-thrifts in the society.' Big government may force taxpayers to part with so much capital that all the frugality of indi-viduals won't compensate for the resulting waste. Smith is an optimist though: 'The uniform, constant, and uninterrupted effort of every man to better his condition ... is frequently powerful enough to maintain the natural progress of things toward improvement, in spite of both the extravagance of government, and of the greatest errors of administration.'

Adam Smith believes that some taxation is necessary. However, as 'there is no art which one government sooner learns of another than that of draining money from the pock-ets of the people', government's power to tax needs to be restrained. Taxes should be in proportion to people's income, which they enjoy under the security of state protection. The rich should pay a slightly higher proportion of tax than the poor. Taxes should be certain and not arbitrary at the behest of officials, and taxes should be simple. Taxes should not create side-effects: not be so onerous as to create evasion, and not hinder industry. Taxes on companies are unwise because capi-tal can be moved quickly and easily to another country.

Adam Smith's concern for the less well-off permeates *The Wealth of Nations*. He tirelessly explains how the market improves their welfare. When production increases, wages rise and prices fall. One person becoming much richer does not mean that another person is becoming poorer: in *The Theory of Moral Sentiments*, Smith describes what interventionists have denigratingly called 'the trickle-down effect'. The 'unfeeling landlord' won't be able to eat his whole harvest. He will distribute the rest to those who prepare what he consumes; to those who fit out his palace, and to those who provide and maintain 'the baubles and

trinkets' which show his greatness. He will not give those
benefits out of humanity, but in return for what he needs.

> The rich ... are led by an invisible hand to make nearly the
> same distribution of the necessaries of life, which would have
> been made, had the earth been divided into equal portions
> among all its inhabitants, and thus without intending it,
> without knowing it, advance the interest of the society...

(Think wealthy footballers.)

The Wealth of Nations has been described as 'a clumsy,
sprawling, elephantine book'. I have met few people who
have ever read all of it – it takes some stamina to plough
through fifty-odd pages on the price of silver. Adam Smith
was neither a great orator nor a forceful personality able to
impose his views on the great and the good. He is described as
of middle height, shy, absent-minded (he once brewed bread
and butter instead of tea), muttering to himself while walk-
ing the streets, constantly digressing and always losing his
train of thought. He attacked extremely powerful interests,
in particular, governments which subsidised and protected
their merchants, farmers and manufacturers against 'unfair'
competition. He exposed those who were profiting from
unfree markets, collusive prices, tariffs and subsidies, and
outdated production methods. Yet as a teacher, his repute was
such that students from as far away as Russia came to see
him. Why did *The Wealth of Nations* become so influential?

5. ADAM SMITH AFTER ADAM SMITH

It is usually thought that the industrial revolution ran from
1750 to 1850. In fact, the economy had started to expand
well before that. The mercantilist privileges which had held
back the economy for centuries were firmly rejected from

the Glorious Revolution of 1688 onwards. In *The Wealth of Nations*, Smith described the factors which caused the unparalleled advance of his age, and interpreted them in a coherent and novel manner. After it was published in 1776, the book inspired demands for a greater future, and as such it accelerated the industrial revolution it was describing.

No single factor can be identified as the root cause of the industrial revolution, although the way the English Constitution evolved was of significant importance. After they deposed the Stuart king, Parliament invited the Dutch Stadtholder William III of Orange to become King of England on condition that he accepted the Bill of Rights. The Bill of Rights of 1689 ended moves towards absolute monarchy by restricting the monarch's powers: the king could no longer suspend laws, make royal appointments, impose taxes or keep a standing army at peacetime without Parliament's consent. William and Mary's reign marked the beginning of the transformation from the absolutist Stuarts to the parliamentarian Hanoverian dynasty.

The Hanoverian kings were ineffectual and therefore benign: the first didn't speak English, the second one wasn't interested and the third one was part-time mad. The new English Constitution became finely tuned and balanced in the eighteenth century. Power became dispersed away from the king and towards Parliament and public opinion. This made buying privileges a pricey business. Instead of bribing the king, special interest groups now also had to bribe majorities in both Houses of Parliament – at a time when Parliament was reluctant to part with any of its new-won powers.

The more trade developed, the more the monopolistic trading companies became subject to competition from rival foreign companies and interlopers. For centuries, kings had granted them privileges in return for 'loans' which allowed the king to live above his station and wage war all over the place. After the Glorious Revolution, Parliament became distinctly hostile to monopolies and friendly to free trade, and one by one they lost their privileges. The Merchant Adventurers' privileges came to an end when an Act of Parliament allowed all persons to export cloth to any part of the world. Producers could sell their wares to any merchant, any merchant or ship could transport the goods, and prices depended upon supply and demand instead of the price fixing by the trading companies. The Eastland Company had already seen its privileges reduced in 1673 with the announcement of free trade with Sweden, Norway and Denmark. The Muscovy Company lost its monopoly on English–Russian trade in 1698. Also in 1698, the African trade was freed: all goods exported and imported from Africa became subject to a 10 per cent duty which was paid to the African Company to maintain its forts. The company had to provide the same protection to all traders, irrespective of membership. The Levant Company's membership was thrown wide open in 1754 – one no longer had to be a merchant and a freeman of London – and the admission fine was fixed at £20. The East India Company maintained its privileges about 100 years longer than the Merchant Adventurers: trade with India was eventually freed in 1813, and with China in 1833.

All but the old monopolists profited from the freeing of trade. Competitors tried to sell more British goods abroad. They competed with each other, and took smaller profits. The British producers obtained better prices and the workers better wages than before. The most efficient and innovative traders flourished at the expense of the less efficient. International trade boomed. When the African Company tried to regain its exclusive privileges a decade later, the angry response from merchants shows the prosperity the freeing of trade had brought. They declared that the trade to Africa had greatly expanded; the shipbuilders said that many more ships had been built and fitted out, the wool manufacturers had sold more cloth and the gun-makers, cutlers and other metal manufacturers affirmed that they had exported more metal goods than ever before.

It was profit which incentivised the inventors of the industrial revolution. Traditionally, inventions were protected by 'letters patent' granted by the king. Gradually the system had been subverted into bought privileges. Elizabeth I, for example, sold patents granting monopolies not just for inventions but also for common commodities such as salt and starch. The privileges ended up with courtiers, office holders and speculators rather than real inventors. With the Statute of Monopolies of 1624, Parliament repealed all past and future patents and monopolies, except those created in the future for new inventions. Henceforward, a monopoly would be granted to new inventors for a period of twelve years – the guaranteed recovery of the development costs and the potential of great riches spurred them on. The English system was less bureaucratic than the Dutch and the French systems: in England a patent was granted upon simple registration, without an investigation and examination beforehand. Between 1720 and 1799, an average of twenty-five patents were registered annually, but in the final decade that rose to sixty-five patents a year.

The socioeconomic climate changed, away from privilege sanctioned by state diktat towards a marketplace based on merit. New inventors and traders could now compete with the older, heavily regulated and restricted trades and professions. The new industrialists became richer than the old privilege-holders and advocated economic freedom. For the first time since cultivation started, land and agriculture were no longer the main sources of wealth: trade and industry became far more lucrative. The landed aristocracy became relatively less wealthy and lost influence. Ever since the twelfth century, Enclosure Acts had been passed sporadically. Lands previously held in collective ownership were privatised. They became 'enclosed': fences were put up and old rights for local people to cultivate the land, cutting hay or using it for grazing, were abolished. The new private owners increased the productivity of the land. Between 1761 and 1800, 4,939 Acts of Parliament privatised land. Where mercantilist labour restrictions had turned people who lost the use of common lands into paupers, they could now go and work in factories. Everybody was driven by self-interest: people realised that they could better themselves through their own efforts. Prosperity became an aspiration and real possibility for the many, rather than the automatic outcome of the professional and state privileges granted to a few.

Most of the eighteenth century enjoyed benign – some would say ineffectual – government. When George I was called over from Hanover, he realised all would be well as long as he didn't rock the boat. In order not to appear too greedy for the English throne, his mother never taught him English, which, according to the historian Lord Acton, was 'a circumstance of the utmost value to England'. The ladies in his company didn't interfere in politics, either; they merely 'offended one part of the public by their morals and the remainder by their ugliness'. George I and his son, the later George II, spent so much time fighting each other that they interfered little with government.

George I left government to his Prime Minister. Power was effectively transferred to elected politicians who were grouped into a majority party and an opposition party. Robert Walpole, who was Prime Minister for twenty-one years, is said to have been 'more zealous to retain his power than to make heroic use of it, and was a good administrator but an indifferent legislator'. Lord Acton saw Walpole's following of public opinion as his greatest contribution to British freedom. Sadly, in order to keep power he constantly compromised with special interest groups. Although he believed in free trade, he impoverished Ireland for the benefit of English landlords. For that reason, Acton called him 'a false Whig'.

George III had eight Prime Ministers in twenty-one years. The Prime Ministers tried to refill the state's coffers after the mercantilist Seven Years War had nearly bankrupted the country. Taxes on the American colonies were mixed up with mercantilist attempts to reduce foreign competition for goods which England exported to America. Goods imported from outside the British Isles were taxed heavily. The Revenue Act of 1767 levied import duties on paper, paint, lead, glass and tea, which the colonies were only allowed to buy in England. The Indemnity Act and the Tea Act exempted the East India Company from paying duties, allowing it to dump their tea cheaply onto the American market; even undercutting smuggled Dutch tea. The tax cut in England was offset by a tax on all tea in the colonies. The British said that it was only fair that the colonies should contribute to the motherland's coffers – taxes in Britain were much higher. The Americans were not entitled to send Members of Parliament to Westminster, and rebelled because, according to the British Constitution, British subjects could not be taxed without the consent of Parliament ('no taxation without representation').

The loss of the American colonies was a defeat for tyrannical taxation and for mercantilist interventionism. It was of tremendous significance for British freedom and prosperity. It led to a fast boom in trade between Britain and America. It also led to William Pitt the Younger becoming Prime Minister in 1783. Pitt was a follower of Adam Smith and believed in free trade. His opponent Charles Fox readily admitted that he hadn't read Smith's *Wealth of Nations* as the subjects were beyond his comprehension. Even though he was not expected to last beyond Christmas, Pitt thankfully stayed in office for twenty years.

Pitt was always more interested in economics than in foreign policy. His introduction of a system of open bidding reduced the king's power of exerting influence through government contracts. While the king was out of action due to mental illness Pitt took over. As a disciple of Adam Smith, Pitt feared the effect of 'some mistaken policy' on the wellbeing of the country. From about 1750 onwards, governments started to free trade and innovation from their mercantilist constraints. This increased after Pitt came to power. Pitt's time in office saw capital accumulation, rising exports and rising business prosperity. When he compared the state's financial situation of 1783 with that of 1791, he observed that it had improved by £4 million, and that three-quarters came from increases in the national income and from the increased tax-take after he made smuggling unprofitable by reducing import duties from 119 per cent to 12.5 per cent.

In 1786 he concluded a free trade agreement with France. The Eden Treaty, named after its English negotiator, reduced a number of import duties in both countries. Britain reduced duties on French oil, vinegar, wines and spirits, and France reduced duties on British leather goods, hardware, cutlery, cottons, porcelain, glass and wool. Previously, 4 million gallons of brandy were smuggled into Britain annually; duty was only paid on 600,000 gallons. There was an immediate and massive increase in the import of French wines, replacing the previously imported port, which had enjoyed lower taxes. (Pitt had a special interest in this: he peaked at a daily intake of around six bottles of port, two bottles of Madeira and one and a half bottles of claret, and drank himself to death at the age of forty-six.) While old industrialists such as silk manufacturers, paper makers and leather producers who had benefited from the previous protectionism complained, Manchester businessmen were toasting the prosperity of free trade and wise government. In Birmingham, metal finishers were singing 'And whilst mutual friendship and harmony reign, our buttons we'll barter for pipes of Champagne'.

It was said at the time that the Eden Treaty was far more favourable to Britain than to France. Britain, with its population of 8 million, was eagerly eyeing the French market with its 20 million potential customers. The duties which were lifted on French imports were negligible as compared to the duties lifted by the French. Observe that carefully measuring each party's trade advantage was a peculiarly mercantilist way of seeing things. With the outbreak of the war between Britain and revolutionary France, the Treaty effectively ended. A mercantilist like most of his compatriots, Napoleon claimed that it had bankrupted France and that it was the cause of the French revolution. The economist David Ricardo would later prove that even freeing trade unilaterally is advantageous. British historians have largely ignored the Treaty as it ended so quickly. In fact, its influence went far beyond its seven years' course. It was a major blow to mercantilist protectionism, and the first victory of free trade. It inspired generations of British free traders.

Pitt was permanently busy with putting the government's finances into order. By repaying the national debt he hoped to stem the tide of endlessly accumulating taxes. He achieved balanced and surplus budgets. Economic prosperity, partly based on booming trade with the former American colonies, started to rise rapidly. Sadly this all evaporated when the war with revolutionary France commenced.

Britain won the almost continuous war with France between 1793 and 1815 because of its free market economy. Britain could afford a Royal Navy to keep the sea routes open thanks to its sound finances, which stemmed from its economic boom. It was so effective that marine insurance actually *fell* during the war. The British economy continued to prosper: the cotton and wool industry blossomed (Bonaparte's soldiers were wearing British greatcoats when they fought the Russians in 1807), and the iron industry boomed with war orders. In contrast, French trade languished and Napoleon's attempts to hinder British trade through his protectionist 'Continental System' largely misfired. Napoleon was unable to stop the smuggling of British goods into France.

‡

Napoleon's disastrous Continental System

After losing the Battle of Trafalgar in 1805, Napoleon lost all hope of either invading Britain or defeating its Royal Navy. The industrial revolution was turning Britain into an economic superpower. Napoleon now tried to bring Britain to its knees by waging economic war. Through threats, agreements and brute force, trade was to be steered to France's profit and Britain's loss. Through his Continental System, Napoleon forbade his allies and neutral countries from trading with Britain. The continental countries he had not conquered or allied himself with were bullied into submission: Russia, for example, was threatened with invasion if it didn't follow France's orders. Britain retaliated by blockading continental ports. Britain's allies and neutral countries were forbidden from trading with France and its allies. All ships trading with continental Europe had to anchor in a French port first, to check that they hadn't traded with Britain. While he was at it, Napoleon also punished his friends: he introduced an internal tariff favouring French goods and harming those from all the other continental countries.

Napoleon's economic warfare backfired badly. Without British and French colonial imports, the continent suffered a shortage of consumer goods. France, not having experienced the industrial revolution yet, was unable to make up for the shortages. Its friends were disgruntled about the deprivations and about France's unfavourable tariffs against their products. The Royal Navy dominated the seas, and France was only able to enforce its trade embargo on land. Portugal flatly refused to follow the Continental System, and the leaders of Spain, Westphalia and the German states were often in cahoots with widespread smuggling through faraway ports such as Salonica, Trieste and Venice. Napoleon set about punishing them through wars which he couldn't afford financially. In 1807, Napoleon invaded Portugal; one year later, Spain. Spanish soldiers and guerrilla fighters continued to fight the French until Napoleon was defeated in 1814. When Sweden refused to follow the System it was invaded by Russia. Russia's subsequent abandoning of the System and opening of trade links with England was the main incentive for Napoleon's disastrous invasion of that vast country.

Britain boomed in 1808 and 1809, despite suffering food shortages. Producers in France urged Napoleon to lift the food embargo, which he did in 1810. Still firmly deluded by old-fashioned mercantilist beliefs and blissfully ignorant of Adam Smith's teachings, he thought that the export of gold from Britain to France to pay for wheat would cause inflation and economic collapse. Nothing of the sort happened, and Britain's national income and output continued to increase.

The British trade which had not been made impossible by Napoleon was firmly put under the British government's control by way of twenty-four Orders in Council. The Orders declared France and her allies in a state of blockade, and banned all trade with them, including from the colonies. The Americans retaliated by closing American harbours to both British and French vessels in 1809. The termination of trade with America caused an economic crisis in Britain in 1810 and 1811, with rising prices, unemployment and bankruptcies. Citizens, manufacturers and merchants demanded the total abolition of the 'disastrous and stupid' Orders in Council. There were demonstrations everywhere. In 1812 the Orders in Council were abandoned, and Napoleon abandoned the Continental System. In a memorandum of December 1812 Napoleon stated that 'it is necessary to harm our foes, but above all we must live.'

The whole episode taught our ancestors a great deal. Even

though they realised that Britain's trade restrictions were retaliation against Napoleon's actions, those who suffered, such as the shopkeepers, the unemployed and the bankrupt traders, blamed the British government for making matters worse. They realised that if trade is reduced, both sides suffer. The deprivations incentivised both sides to demand peace and a return to normal trade. Later, Ludwig von Mises would state that: 'In an age in which nations are mutually dependent upon products of foreign provenance, war can no longer be waged.' The episode also showed that economics wins or loses wars: trading free market Britain was prosperous and able to support its Navy which guaranteed its survival and its trade; old-fashioned interventionist France did not have the economic strength to win the war. Napoleon disparagingly called Britain 'a nation of shopkeepers', unfit to wage war against France. The shopkeepers won.

‡

6. COMPARATIVE ADVANTAGE, FREE TRADE AND THE REVOCATION OF THE CORN LAWS

In the early part of the nineteenth century, governments continued to sweep away mercantilist controls. The Statute of Artificers, the enactment of crafts guilds' restrictive labour practices, was abolished in 1814. The Settlement Act, which had made it impossible for the poor to migrate and seek a better future, was repealed in 1834. Mercantilism was the economic policy of the *ancien régime*: Europe was drowning in well-enforced local privileges, tax exemptions, exclusive rights, monopolies, barriers to entry, regulations and occupational restrictions, all of which impeded economic growth and wealth creations.

However popular Adam Smith's *Wealth of Nations* may have been, occasionally there were relapses into attempts to 'improve' upon the market economy. One such example was the Corn Laws. The battle against the Corn Laws and their eventual revocation was epic, and inspires free marketeers right up to this day. Wheat prices in Britain had fallen as a result of cheap imports. The Importation Act 1815 introduced tariffs on cheap imported wheat, and became known as the Corn Laws. By increasing the price of imported wheat it guaranteed British producers a minimum price. It was sold to the public as a social measure to help farmers: the political economist Thomas Malthus had decided that £4 per quarter was a fair price to maintain decent wages for workers and a decent return for landowners. Those opposed observed that the special interest group of wheat producers had craftily captured the state's coercive powers to guarantee their own income. Rich aristocratic landowners, their agricultural labourers and tenant farmers benefited; consumers paid the costs through higher prices in the shops.

Riots duly ensued, but the Act stayed on the statute books for another thirty-one years. It was another example of concentrated benefits and dispersed costs: individual consumers only faced small increases in costs, making it difficult to rouse political action, whereas landowners gained enormously from the tariffs. Several politicians were landowners themselves. The campaign to repeal the Corn Laws gathered steam when Richard Cobden's Anti-Corn Law League came into being. Cobden rose from an impoverished farmer's background to become a successful Manchester businessman and self-taught economic politician and agitator. Inspired by Adam Smith, he looked forward to the day when all the great cities of England would have their Smithian Societies, to promulgate the truths of *The Wealth of Nations*. In 1842, Sir Robert Peel, who had gained his second term as Prime Minister on a protectionist platform just one year earlier, started to reduce tariffs on a number of products including grain. In the 1840s potato blight ravaged potato crops throughout Europe. It especially caused famine in Ireland, where one-third of the population was entirely dependent upon potatoes for food. This gave Peel the argument he needed to repeal the Corn Laws, against the wishes of many protectionists in his own party. In a three-hour speech in January 1846 he proposed abolishing the Corn Laws by 1849. After tremendous political upheaval, Parliament eventually abolished the Corn Laws with votes from free trading Tories ('Peelites'), Whigs and Radicals. The Peelites, including the later Prime Minister William Gladstone, left the Tory Party and formed the Liberal Party with the Whigs and the Radicals. But how were foreign imports in exchange for gold advantageous to the nation as a whole? In 1817 David Ricardo developed the theory of Comparative Advantage. Comparative Advantage shows that when a country produces a number of goods, it should focus on what it is most productive at and import the rest. There is even an advantage in doing so for countries which are less efficient at everything they do as compared to other countries. Comparative Advantage is one of the most important arguments in favour of free trade: it benefits every country, even if introduced unilaterally. It shows that protectionism is harmful.

‡

Ricardo's Comparative Advantage

If Britain can either produce one unit of wine by investing a labour cost of 110, or one unit of cloth by investing a labour cost of 100, it should produce cloth and not wine, as producing cloth requires fewer inputs of its scarce resources. Britain has a *comparative advantage* in producing cloth rather than wine. The wine it can import from, for example, Portugal.

If Portugal can either produce cloth by investing labour worth 90, or wine by labouring at a cost of 80, it is clear that it should focus on wine production, and import cloth (perhaps from Britain). Observe that Portugal has an *absolute advantage* in producing both as compared to Britain. It only needs a labour cost of 90 to produce cloth, whereas Britain needs to invest 100; and it only needs a labour cost of 80 to produce wine, when the British climate demands far more input of labour at 110. Yet Portugal has only a finite number of workers, so it must allocate them to the most profitable activity: wine making.

The message is that countries should focus on what they are best at, and trade their production surpluses with other countries which are better at other things. Both then end up better off than if they focus on less productive pursuits.

To use the Corn Law example: the government decided that its people had to use their scarce capital to pay for wheat. If they could have bought cheap wheat from abroad, they could have used the saved capital to invest into something more productive than British wheat production; e.g. industrial goods.

Comparative Advantage also illustrates that countries which attempt to become self-sufficient are misguided: they end up with less wealth than they would have had if they had let the market decide what it could produce most productively and imported the rest. Attempts at self-sufficiency are a constant concern; politicians regularly explain to us why it is important that this or the other industry is saved in this country *whatever the cost* (the latter part is rarely added to the discourse). They will invariably point at some higher political reason why the normal market allocation of resources should be overruled on this exceptional occasion. In the absence of objective grounds, emotive ones are used. How proud we are of this historic car industry; General Motors truly is one of our crown jewels, and should not be disposed of. And are we not afraid that we would become dependent upon the quarrelsome Middle East or a scary Russian leader for our energy supplies? Doesn't food security warrant the pumping of 50 billion euros into agricultural subsidies? Never mind that the soil is poor and produces little. The political friends who profit from the measures usually also go unmentioned.

Before Peel changed camps, he said that he favoured free trade but that corn was an exception as Britain needed to prevent negative social effects and needed to remain independent from foreign countries for its food supplies: 'We should tell ... the harsh, cold-blooded economist that there (are) higher considerations involved than mercantile profit.' In Nazi Germany the free market was pushed aside in favour of self-sufficiency for the 'higher' end of preparing for war.

Newly independent colonies protected 'industries in their infancy' and ended up with industries which never even evolved into infancy. Many developing countries were inspired by Raul Prebisch's new school of economic thought, which claimed that peripheral (poor ex-colonial) countries could only develop if they rejected the free trade system, stopped imports and industrialised domestically. In the light of Ricardo's Theory of Comparative Advantage, Prebisch must win the award for having done more than any other person in history to keep poor countries poor. In the 1980s Brazil was determined to have its own information technology industry and ended up with computers which were twice as slow and twice as expensive as those for sale on the world market.

‡

7. CONCLUSION

For the first time in 1,000 years, people believed that they could improve their situation through their own efforts. They threw off the shackles which had stopped them from prospering. The spirit of the Enlightenment, constantly questioning the existing order, set the whole country into motion. By the standards prevalent 100 years later, eighteenth-century growth was not actually that spectacular, but the fact that there *was* growth, and that it was sustained, was entirely novel and a complete break with the past.

In the seventeenth century, tyranny was defeated and England was spared French or Turkish-style absolutism. The finely balanced and venerated constitution that evolved was a bulwark of liberty. Checks and balances guaranteed that no one party or special interest group could monopolise power. There was no powerful bureaucracy and no state imperative to overrule common law or to intimidate judges and jurymen. There was no torture. The rule of law shielded individuals against encroachment by government. There was great hostility to special interest groups trying to use the law to reduce freedom.

The government meddled far less in people's lives than it does today. General legislation was not considered to be the most important occupation of Parliament. The government waged war and conducted foreign affairs and maintained law and order. Parliamentary debates concentrated on individual and civil rights, the handling of naval and diplomatic issues and taxation.

The end of arbitrary government for the few brought about economic freedom for the many. Instead of mercantilist privilege, the market treated everybody as equal. Hard work, saving, individual responsibility, intelligence and inventiveness could really improve your situation. Trading monopolies were outlawed or were outcompeted. The guilds' privileges, which had stopped people from moving into professions, were revoked, or outperformed by the new industries over which they had no power. Workers were free to seek higher income in the new factories. Merchants became free to sell where, when and at what price they chose. Domestic and national protectionism was thrown out of the window and free trade became fashionable.

The social mobility was tremendous. Hereditary aristocrats lost power when land ceased to be the main source of wealth. Old Money complained that 'new men' popped up everywhere out of nowhere. The frequency of the complaints proved that there was ample scope for what Adam Smith called 'the natural effort of every individual to better his own condition'. The poor no longer starved; small merchants became big merchants; big merchants bought land and were lifted into the gentry or married aristocrats. Millar claimed that 'every man who is industrious may entertain the hope of gaining a fortune.' Most people became better off than their ancestors.

All of this was identified by Adam Smith, who developed new theories as to how prosperity could be increased: through specialisation, which increases productivity and surpluses which can be sold, and through free trade, which benefits all. The free market's bounty allowed Britain to maintain a substantial army and to win wars against totalitarian neighbours with more tightly controlled economies.

Too often the industrial revolution is explained as a sudden explosion of miraculous inventions. Are we to believe that between 1700 and 1800 there was a sudden increase in brain capacity? Yes, there were large coal deposits – but they had been present before. Since the earliest times governments and special interest groups had tried to stop people from doing things their own way: for the glory of the King, in pursuance of the snake-oil ideology of mercantilism, to maintain the social order (i.e. to keep people small and in their place) and above all, to enrich themselves and keep others poor. The inventions and their commercial application took place when the oppressive forces and laws that stopped them lost their stranglehold over the country.

One country on the other side of the globe had neither democracy nor natural resources nor inventions. Yet it became immensely prosperous too; and in a far shorter time period than it took Britain in the industrial revolution.

FOUR

HONG KONG

I. 'IT WILL NEVER BE A MART FOR TRADE'

Before the British arrived, the island in the half-charted estuary of the Pearl River was part of southern China's defences. The district magistrate had his seat at a fort where Kowloon City is today. A shabby road ran to the quay. Government was sketchy and the administration notoriously corrupt. People lived on boats and in fortified towns. As long as they paid their taxes the Chinese Imperial administration left them alone. The population followed their ancestral, religious and Confucian rules; clan and village conflicts were a common pastime. One overenthusiastic district magistrate recorded his astonishment in 1744 on finding that 'culture has spread even to this remote place near the sea'.

Since the middle of the eighteenth century the belief had been gaining ground in Britain that free trade increased prosperity. Trade was also seen as a moral good and the only alternative to war. British traders had to compete with an increasing number of merchants worldwide, and the untapped Chinese market enticed them a great deal. Imperial China wasn't interested in trade – Britain's first embassy to Peking met with the retort from Emperor Qianlong that 'free trade is not in harmony with the state system of our dynasty and would definitely not be tolerated.' In the Confucian hierarchy, merchants were near pond life: just above beggars and prostitutes but below craftsmen and peasants.

Canton, at a mere seventy miles from Hong Kong, was the only port in China where foreign 'barbarians' were allowed to live – but only during the summer months. China maintained no diplomatic relations with foreign lands, as they were seen as mere tributaries. After the British East India Company lost its monopoly on trade with India in 1833, there were some thirty British firms in Canton. At the end of the 1830s, Dutch, French, British and American merchants occupied warehouses on the quays. In theory they were supervised by a Chief Superintendent of Trade, appointed by the British government. He was known as 'The Barbarian Eye' by the Imperial administration.

The Imperial administration treated the merchants with contempt. Strict rules applied: some seemed aimed at making life as unpleasant as possible. Traders were not allowed to enter the walled city, they could only deal with government-appointed merchants and they were forbidden from going out sailing for pleasure without express permission. They were also not allowed to learn Chinese – a state diktat which the indomitable human spirit solved by inventing a new common business language: pidgin English. Whenever the traders pressed for free trade, the Imperial administration reminded them that they were there at sufferance and that they had better 'Tremble and Obey'.

In 1833 Prime Minister Lord Palmerston sent Lord Napier to China to try to open up trade diplomatically. Lord Napier, who according to the *London Morning Post* knew as much about China as an orangutan, managed to land in Canton without permission from Peking, told the Chinese Viceroy that having made him wait was an insult to His Britannic Majesty and threatened force if free trade was not forthcoming at once. A military skirmish between the British Royal Navy and the Chinese Navy was engineered, and the Chinese Viceroy announced a boycott of British goods and promised death to any local who traded with the British. Napier left in a hurry.

As the Chinese were scornful of most other foreign products, opium had become the main trade. It was legally grown in British India. Selling the opium in China, where it was illegal, was highly profitable. Its use in China was as widespread as that of tobacco in Britain. The enforcement of the ban in China was half-hearted: with the possible exception of the addicts, everybody profited. Chinese officials were in the pay of the opium importers. In 1839 an attempt by the notoriously incorruptible Lin Zexu to stamp out the opium trade ended with the Royal Navy opening fire on Chinese war junks. William Jardine and James Matheson, the two most important Cantonese traders, were thrilled: they had been urging the British government to impose free trade through force for a long time. The Chinese were quickly beaten into submission and opened negotiations. Acting without authority from London, Captain Charles Elliot of the Royal Navy came up with a convention of his own design.

Instead of obtaining free trade in every major Chinese port, as ordered by Prime Minister Palmerston, Elliot obtained a piece of China which would henceforward fall under British jurisdiction, with a status similar to Macao (which was governed by the Portugese). The British traders in Canton had sought such a piece of territory 'to bring free trade and Christianity'. The treeless granite island of Hong Kong (Fragrant Harbour in Cantonese), seventy miles downstream from Canton, was only twenty-six miles square. Its population consisted of about 2,000 fishermen. Its hills were steep with virtually no flat land, and it lacked fertile soil and fresh water. At 8:15 a.m. on 26 January 1841, Captain Edward Belcher landed with a Royal Navy party on Hong Kong Island and raised the Union Jack at Possession Point. A gun salute followed. Admiral Sir Charles Elliot, aboard the HMS Wellesley, declared himself the First Governor of Hong Kong.

Everybody thought Elliot's venture was a joke. Prime Minister Palmerston pronounced it 'a barren rock with barely a house upon it', and predicted that 'it will never be a mart for trade'. Queen Victoria was surprised by Elliot's 'unaccountably strange conduct' and joked that the Princess Royal perhaps ought to be called Princess of Hong Kong as well. The *Canton Press* sneered that 'a street on a gigantic scale is already far advanced, leading from an intended public office to a contemplated public thoroughfare, and we now only require houses, inhabitants, and commerce to make this settlement one of the most valuable of our possessions.' The Chinese Emperor Daoguang concluded that 'these barbarians always look on trade as their chief occupation ... it is plain that they are not worth attending to.' As a punishment, Elliot was made a diplomat in the new Republic of Texas.

Hong Kong was set up as a free port without any duties to the British government. Both Britons and foreigners were subject to British law, and Chinese subjects to Chinese laws and customs, 'every description of torture excepted'. But all subjects enjoyed the British rule of law: due process and certainty of law, without retroactive changes or arbitrary decisions. The circumstances were perfect to encourage investment.

The first granite warehouse was built without permission by Jardine, Matheson and Co., and the first European house was James Matheson's colonial style bungalow. Land was sold by auction. Hong Kong Island was ceded to Great Britain in perpetuity by the Treaty of Nanking in 1842. Henceforward the British were no longer referred to as 'barbarians' in official documents, as Qi-ying confided to his Emperor in 1843: 'With this type of people from outside the bounds of civilisation one has to be diplomatic in the essential business of subduing and conciliating them.' After the second Anglo-Chinese war, the tip of Kowloon was added to the possession; the British knew it well, as it was there that they played cricket. Later the New Territories were leased from China for ninety-nine years, until 1997. This increased the territory tenfold, to 390 square miles (almost six times the size of Washington DC).

Merchants made great fortunes and lived in great style. The privately issued East India Rupee was legal tender in Hong Kong, though other currencies competed freely. In 1844 the Governor stated that anyone with money was either in government service or in the opium trade. There was also trading in cotton, sugar candy, salt, tea and rattan on a much smaller scale. The free port status meant that there were no duties whatsoever, and as most imports were smuggled out of China, there were no Chinese export duties either. The only deep-water port between Singapore and Shanghai, by the 1880s Hong Kong was the Empire's third port after London and Liverpool.

Nominally the Governor was in charge, subject to the instruction of the British government. As it took up to a year for messages to travel between London and Hong Kong, the Governor's decisions were law. In reality, the merchants, also called taipans (tycoons) had a great deal more power and money. Activist governors, especially those upsetting the free (opium) trade, were quickly told what's what. Governor John Davis started off by reducing the terms of the traders' land leases, which they thought had been granted in perpetuity. Next he imposed a property tax, and after that he set up government salt and opium monopolies to be sold by auction. The merchants lobbied their friends in London and treated Davis with boorish incivility. When he was to present the cup at the Happy Valley races in 1848, not a single horse was entered for the race. Davis eventually resigned. Subsequent governors learned the lesson. Davis's successor, Sir George Bonham, became the darling of the merchants: instead of raising taxes to increase the government's revenue, he reduced its spending.

After the opium trade was ended, the colony kept growing. As the movement of people between China and Hong Kong was free, there was a constant influx of runaways and capital. Gentlemanly it wasn't: the city was rife with European adventurers, Chinese paupers, confidence tricksters, sailors, triads, soldiers, pirates, racketeers, drug dealers and whores. From 1912 onwards the new Republic of China sought to abrogate the foreign treaty privileges. A boycott against foreign goods particularly harmed British trade. In the 1920s and 1930s Shanghai became far richer and more important, and Hong Kong was considered boring in comparison. In 1949 the Communists overthrew the Chinese government. Millions of refugees fled to the protection and rule of law which British Hong Kong offered. The numbers were so great that an economic and humanitarian catastrophe was expected. Trade suffered further when the United Nations embargoed trade with China and North Korea during the Korean War.

Population of Hong Kong		
1841	2,000	Hong Kong Island
1842	15,000	Hong Kong Island
1861	120,000	Addition Kowloon
1900	300,000	Addition New Territories
1941	1,600,000	Invasion Japan
1945	650,000	Japan surrenders
1950	1,630,000	
1960	2,615,000	
1970	3,458,000	
1995	6,224,000	
2010	7,552,000	

2. HONG KONG TODAY

The United Kingdom's Business Secretary Vince Cable arrived too late to hear Hong Kong's Chief Executive Donald

Tsang speak at a dinner organised by the Hong Kong Trade Development Council in London in September 2011. Some wondered whether it was diplomatic lateness: Tsang was elaborating on Hong Kong's HK $71.3 billion budget surplus while its former colonial master was still firmly engaged in deficit spending. In 2010, Hong Kong's economy grew by 6.8 per cent; the UK economy grew by 1.25 per cent.

In fact, from the end of the war until today, Hong Kong has been outperforming the United Kingdom in spectacular fashion.

Hong Kong vs United Kingdom – Average Annual Percentage Growth Rate of GDP		
	Hong Kong	United Kingdom
1961–1965	13	3.1
1966–1970	6.7	2.6
1971–1975	6.7	2.2
1976–1980	12	1.8
1981–1985	5.7	2
1986–1990	7.3	3.3
1991–1995	5.6	1.7
1996–2000	3.6	3.2
2001–2005	4.3	2.3
Source: NationMaster, Time Series. Annual percentage growth rate of GDP at market prices based on constant local currency. Aggregates are based on constant 2,000 US dollars.		

In 2011, Hong Kong's government had so much money in the kitty that they didn't know what to do with it. After all the public spending they could think of, Hong Kong sent all its 7.5 million residents who were eighteen and over a HK$6,000 cheque, and waived 75 per cent of the salaries taxes up to a maximum of HK$6,000 per taxpayer. It was a windfall other taxpayers in the developed world could only dream of.

The rebate came on top of some of the lowest tax rates

in the world. Corporations pay a flat tax of 16.5 per cent of profits. Individuals pay a salaries tax which is stepped from 2 to 17 per cent, with numerous deductions (mortgages, charitable giving, education, pensions, care of elderly relatives). But the total is capped at 15 per cent, meaning that one can choose to pay whatever is the lowest. Because of the deductions most employees pay little or no tax. The top 2 per cent choose the top 15 per cent rate – they account for half of all revenue from the salaries tax.

‡

Fact Sheet: What is the tax rate in Hong Kong?

- Profit tax for corporations: a flat rate of 16.5 per cent.
- Profit tax for unincorporated businesses: a flat rate of 15 per cent.
- Salaries tax: stepped from 2 to 17 per cent before deductions and allowances. Or, a flat rate of 15 per cent.
- No national insurance contributions, no sales tax, no tariffs on imports, no capital gains tax. There is a property tax.

‡

Ever since the city state was created, a whiff of profit has hung in the air. It is fired up by Chinese refugees, who work frantically never to be poor again. There are the expats, who can earn more in Hong Kong in ten years than in a lifetime in America, Britain or Germany. In fact, virtually everyone earns more than they would elsewhere: the street peddler, the taxi driver, the merchant banker and the tycoon. For a country so densely populated, Hong Kongers are remarkably happy. Even in the United Nations' happiness index, which is heavily weighted in favour of 'social values' such as education, health, gender equality and sustainability (apart

from income and economy), Hong Kong is thirteenth out
of 187 countries (United States fourth; France twentieth;
United Kingdom twenty-eighth). Hong Kong came first in the
World Competitiveness Index 2011, and it came first in
the Index of Economic Freedom 2012.

‡

Hong Kong in figures

	Hong Kong	United Kingdom
Population (2004)	7.764 million	61.417 million (8 times HK pop.)
Films produced (2003)	64	132
Mobile phones per 100 people (2002)	92.98	84.49
Numbers of daily newspapers and periodicals (1999)	48	106
Dependents to working population (2005)	36 per cent	51 per cent
Government spending per capita (2005)	$2,246.8	$7,951.9
Registered businesses (2003)	672,275 0.09 per person	2,016,770 0.03 per person
Total crimes (2002)	80,592	6,523,706 (80 times HK level)
Time required to start a business (2006)	11 days	18 days
GDP per capita (2011)	$36,956	$31,941
Life expectancy (2011)	82.04 years	80.05 years
Suicide rate (1995)	1.2 per 100,000	3.4 per 100,000

A Hong Kong government official told the writer Jan
Morris in the 1970s that Hong Kong was built on
'Victorian economic principles, the only ones that have ever

really worked'. And yet, at one point Hong Kong risked becoming a giant slum which would happily have been absorbed by Mao's China. The post-war period seemed grim indeed.

‡

3. OVERPOPULATION, COMMUNIST RIOTS AND BUSY SWEATSHOPS

Hong Kong's continued existence as a British colony followed from Roosevelt's early death in 1945. Roosevelt opposed all empires; he sought to dismantle the British Empire as a matter of principle and he told them to pack it up in Hong Kong. His fruitful imagination devised all sorts of schemes. At times he suggested to the British to sell Hong Kong to China at a price set by the United States. In Yalta he suggested to Stalin to internationalise Hong Kong. He annoyed Churchill by suggesting that Hong Kong should be given up 'as a sign of goodwill'. At the Cairo conference in 1943, FDR told Chiang Kai-shek that he was willing to force Churchill to cede Hong Kong to China if Chiang put it under international trusteeship to be operated as a free port. He shared the Chinese's view that the treaties handing over the territories had been unequal and imposed by overwhelming power. In 1943 all other concessions along the Chinese coast were ceded back to China, but Churchill stood firm and Hong Kong remained British. After FDR's death, orders for US marines to take Hong Kong from the Japanese and hand it over to the Chinese were aborted. On 25 December 1945, senior Japanese officers surrendered at Government House in Hong Kong to the British, headed by Admiral Sir Bruce Fraser, the 1st Baron Fraser of North Cape. With the outbreak of the Korean War in 1950 and the fight against Chinese Communists, America changed its tune: Hong Kong became vital for the army's logistics and to its soldiers for more prosaic purposes.

In 1946 Governor Sir Mark Young announced that Hong Kong would continue as a free port: there would be no export subsidies and no tariffs on imports (except for some commodities), and minimal restrictions on imports. On the Chinese mainland the battle between Chiang Kai-shek's Nationalists and Mao Zedong's Communists intensified, and hundreds of thousands of ordinary citizens fled to the safe haven of Hong Kong. When Chiang's army collapsed in 1949 the streams of refugees choosing to live under 'the yoke of colonial exploitation' increased further. Between 1945 and 1950 the population of Hong Kong more than quadrupled from 500,000 to 2.2 million people. Many refugees were merchants who moved their operations lock, stock and barrel to Hong Kong after Canton, Shanghai and Peking fell to the Communists. Others were peasants and soldiers from Chiang Kai-shek's army, often maimed and wounded.

All the efforts of the colonial government were geared towards coping with the overwhelming influx of refugees. In order not to provoke the new government in Peking into invading the territory, the colonial administration disparagingly referred to the refugees as 'squatters'. They feared that Mao or Chiang Kai-shek would urge their supporters in Hong Kong to rise up against their colonial masters. This fear wasn't far-fetched: in 1956 there were open battles between Chinese nationalists and Chinese Communists in the streets of Hong Kong.

The immigrants occupied every available piece of land. Shanty towns were built from 'packing cases, sacks, kerosene tins, linoleum, worn-out rubber tires, anything anyone could lay their hands on, tied together with bits of wire and even with rice straw'. The authorities provided standpipes and paved paths through the settlements.

Hong Kong had always largely been a clearing house for import into and export from China. The Communist army now closed the border with Hong Kong: air, steamer, and train connections were ended. On top of this came the war in Korea and the resulting trade boycott against China in 1951. Economic collapse and mass unemployment were forecast.

The human disaster the colony faced was of such magnitude that the colonial administration was too busy to start meddling in the economy. As the writer Austin Coates put it: 'Nowhere was the state of crisis more apparent than in the offices of the government, most of which were severely understaffed to meet the extraordinary conditions prevailing.' The fact that the colonial authorities did not have to face democratic elections, and were massively outnumbered by the ethnic Chinese, was a double blessing. The authorities didn't need to provide bread, circuses and bribes for short-term electoral gain and could take the long view. At the same time, in view of their overwhelming numerical minority, making the Chinese change their ways was out of the question. Socialism, which is the process of robbing Peter to pay Paul, is by its nature going to upset Peter. However popular it was in Britain at the time, the Hong Kong government was too astute to try it. Those in power had none, and those who weren't reigned supreme.

By way of production factors Hong Kong was not an entirely 'barren rock' as has often been claimed. It did enjoy some natural resources such as quartz, wolframite, silver, kaolin and feldspar. All of these were mined commercially at some point, but the reserves were small. Drinking water and food were imported. There was no timber as local farmers had eradicated trees for centuries as they used grasses, small shrubs and ferns for domestic fuel. But now the disaster in China landed an abundance of cheap labour on Hong Kong's shores. Many were experts in their trades, or professionals. Some businessmen who fled the Communists brought their entire workforce and machinery with them. Many more brought their money with them, and Hong Kong was flush with cash.

The mere presence of the production factor of labour does not suffice to make an economy grow. No refugee would have been spurred into action if the government had taxed it all away, or if it had made doing business difficult, or if it had limited the squatters' access to jobs. If tax or regulations had curbed their aspirations, the immigrants would probably have moved on to America. Hong Kong refugees realised that the British rule of law and laissez-faire economy meant that the fruits of their labours would be theirs to keep. They never wanted to be poor again – and Hong Kong allowed them to realise that dream.

Once they noticed that trade with China was no more, businessmen started to manufacture small goods for the international market. Initially the factories were hole-in-the-wall affairs. People produced sellable goods in their kitchens, basements and on sampans. Working conditions were harsh; the textile sweatshops were notorious. Occasionally a ramshackle warehouse collapsed. First the production of artificial flowers for export took hold, replacing Italy as the dominant producer. Other export products followed more and more quickly: toys, buttons, umbrellas, footwear, plastics and especially textiles. In ten years exports increased dramatically. Companies enjoyed colourful names such as the Flying Junk Industrial Company Ltd, the Joy and Happy Company, and the Ever Rich Industrial Company.

All along there were external and internal pressures to ditch economic freedom for socialism and interventionism. Hong Kong's freedom was not maintained automatically or by accident. The unlikely heroes of this battle for freedom were a handful of headstrong British civil servants who ran Hong Kong between 1945 and 1980. Free market economics were out of favour elsewhere, and at times it seemed as if the whole world was choosing between Keynes's or Marx's interventionism. Even in America both the left and the right often seemed to agree that keeping Roosevelt's interventionism of the 1930s in place was desirable. In Britain, post-war socialism was becoming firmly entrenched, and Prime Minister Clement Attlee wanted to extend it to the rest of the Empire. Fortunately for Hong Kong, he and his colleagues were kept extremely busy at home. As long as the colony didn't become a drain upon the mother country, it was to be left alone (the Hong Kong administration became self-sufficient in 1947). In the meantime, China sighed under the yoke of Mao Zedong's Communist tyranny. Though Mao didn't recognise Britain's rights over Hong Kong, he made no attempts to conquer the colony. But Communist China did support Communist agitators in Hong Kong, and was the main driver behind the leftist riots in the 1960s. After these riots some social protection was introduced by the cautious Hong Kong administration.

How did Hong Kong resist the outside pressures? The merchant class had always been powerful enough to do pretty much as it pleased and to block any attempt to reduce its economic freedoms. Since the interventionist Governor Davis had been sent packing in the nineteenth century, governors were careful to negotiate any change with the business community first. That said, if they had wanted to, the governors and financial secretaries could have imposed the state planning that dominated elsewhere. Only, they didn't want to do it. Both Governor Sir Alexander Grantham and Governor Sir Robert Black systematically rebuffed attempts by London to impose labour laws and other restrictions, and John Cowperthwaite, the Financial Secretary from 1961 until 1971, consistently refused to interfere in the economy or to increase taxation. He called this 'positive non-interventionism' – a policy which was continued by his successor Sir Philip Haddon-Cave.

4. BRITAIN'S ATTEMPTS TO INTRODUCE SOCIALISM IN HONG KONG

Hong Kong was portrayed as one big sweatshop with low wages and Dickensian working conditions. The reality was quite different. Pre-war Hong Kong regulated industrial employment by women and children and policed industrial safety. Many workers enjoyed customary and contractual rights from their employers, such as extra rest days for long working hours. In progressive firms, workers enjoyed sick, holiday and maternity pay and free or subsidised medical care. As there was full contractual freedom nobody was forced to work or prevented from working anywhere. When there was a labour shortage in the 1970s, pay went up and working conditions improved without any government pressure.

The Colonial Office in London, the British government and British MPs never tired of trying to impose British social policies and British tax rates upon the colony. Hong Kong's free market economy was undercutting British industries. In the 1930s the Colonial Office encouraged employers and unions to agree working conditions and minimum wages voluntarily. The colony was also urged to adopt British trade unions laws (including immunity from prosecution), to appoint trade union advisers, and to arbitrate during industrial disputes.

With the election of Clement Attlee's Labour government in Britain in 1945, the Fabian trade unionist Arthur Creech Jones became Colonial Secretary. He wanted to improve working conditions throughout the Empire. Hong Kong adopted its first trade union law in 1948. Labour officers encouraged the formation of trade unions and the Colonial Office in London sent a never-ending stream of advisers to urge for additional labour laws. In 1946, one Eleanor Hinder told Hong Kong's colonial administration to enforce labour laws and to encourage worker training. In 1947, E. W. Barltrop, adviser to Arthur Creech Jones, argued for wage boards, sick and maternity pay, compensation for injured workers and for employers to provide housing for their workers. In 1951, R. G. H. Houghton, on secondment from the Ministry of Labour, suggested setting up industrial courts and introducing an employment bill covering service contracts, child labour and wage dispute resolution. Most of these recommendations were royally ignored by the colonial government. Even if drafting on new laws started, it was done so with extreme reluctance and a studied lack of urgency. In 1955, Governor Grantham admitted the complete failure of voluntary collective bargaining and trade union laws as Hong Kong workers simply refused to join trade unions. The Colonial Office now urged the colonial government to impose core labour laws directly.

The overregulated and overtaxed British manufacturing industry was unable to compete with countries with fewer rules and lower taxes. From the mid-1950s onwards, workers at risk of losing their jobs, trade unions which wanted to keep protection and industrialists looking for profit started lobbying the British government to end Hong Kong's competitive regime. They asked it to impose labour laws and to introduce plain protectionism. When the outcomes of the 1955 and 1959 general elections depended upon a few marginal seats in industrial heartlands, both Conservative and Labour politicians jumped on this bandwagon. Under Conservative governments, Asian industrialists agreed to voluntarily reduce exports to Britain. Prices rose, the British manufacturers were able to sell their wares, and the Hong Kong businesses sold fewer goods for higher prices. The views of British consumers on this are not recorded. In Parliament, Barbara Castle, a Labour MP from Britain's industrial heartlands, quoted from a letter written by a textile worker in Hong Kong asking for relief from her '84-hour week' so that she, and the rest of the 'workers of Hong Kong', could 'enjoy a decent life'.

The Hong Kong government increased the number of health and safety inspectors, but only for registered factories (60 per cent of the total). The economy was growing so fast that inspectors could not keep up. Some factories were well established by the time the inspectors learned of their existence. When the Colonial Office tried to impose minimum labour standards upon all industries in Hong Kong (not just the registered companies), Governor Black testily replied that Hong Kong people were interested in survival rather than standards of living. Fearing the introduction of tariffs and quotas, the government of Hong Kong nonetheless implemented maximum working hours for the young and for women. When the Colonial Office asked to introduce paid annual holidays, sick leave, public holidays and maternity leave, the government of Hong Kong dragged its feet. Modest sick leave and paid holiday entitlements were introduced in 1962.

Hong Kong fought back. It started a public relations campaign overseas to shrug off the sweatshop cliché which was used by protectionists in Britain. The Hong Kong business community opposed new labour laws and tried to convince London that Hong Kong was an exceptional case. The Hong Kong Standard accused Lancashire textile interests of trying to 'break the rice bowls of HK mill workers and cause widespread unemployment in the colony'. The paper suggested that UK manufacturers needed to copy Hong Kong manufacturers, instead of the other way around. They should get rid of 'labour featherbedding' within their factories, including 'four-day weekends, two-hour lunch periods and endless breaks during the working day for tea and biscuits'.

What state regulations did not achieve, the free market did. Booming Hong Kong started to see skilled labour shortages. Competing to employ workers, companies increased salaries and fringe benefits. While millions were starving in neighbouring Communist China, wages increased by between 10 and 30 per cent in 1959. Between 1960 and 1970, while British socialists were expressing outrage about Hong Kong's nightmarish sweatshop conditions, Hong Kong wages rose on average by 50 per cent and the number of people living in acute poverty fell from over 50 per cent of the population to under 16 per cent.

The British authorities also undertook a relentless assault to have 'proper' (i.e. high) income tax introduced in Hong Kong. Before the Second World War, there was no income tax in Hong Kong. In 1940 the Colonial Office wanted to introduce an income tax on worldwide income to help pay for the war effort. Chinese businessmen and the expat community objected, and Governor Northcote asked businessmen to come up with a tax system themselves. Instead of a single income tax, they introduced a schedular system. There would be different taxes on different sorts of income: a property tax on the rental value of property; a salaries tax on income from employment; and a tax on business profits. The highest rate of the new tax was set at 10 per cent, with such generous deductions that 99 per cent paid nothing at all. It was supposed to be a temporary tax, which would be replaced by a 'normal' tax after the war; but that never happened and the 1940 tax remains largely in place today.

After the war, Colonial Secretary Arthur Creech Jones said that he wanted an income tax with rates 'as high as possible' – at the time this meant 50 per cent. The Chinese business community formed the Chinese Anti-Direct Tax Commission, marched on Government House and inundated the Colonial Office in London with protest letters. The 1940 tax was changed slightly: people now had the choice of either paying the different taxes separately, or going for a personal assessment: adding up all their income and paying a tax on the total (similar to normal income tax). Between 1947 and 1980, the British government continued to urge Hong Kong to introduce an income tax on worldwide income at British tax rate levels. Under pressure from London, each of the successive financial secretaries – Clarke, Cowperthwaite and Haddon-Cave – set up commissions to look into it. All three commissions failed. The business community convinced the governors during the first two commissions to so limit each commission's terms of reference that an income tax could not be the outcome. The 'failure' of the second commission is especially notable, as this was under Cowperthwaite's tenure. He was a domineering figure who always achieved what he wanted in Hong Kong. His 'failure' must have raised some eyebrows.

The third commission did propose a single income tax, but only on Hong Kong income, not worldwide income. Now it was the government of Hong Kong which rejected the proposal. They said they had just purchased a new computer and were therefore 'too busy' to deal with this tax reform. The business community had probably let it be known that they weren't going to have it. The Hong Kong government could have strong-armed the measure through the Legislative Council, as it held the majority there – but it chose not to. The token attempts at introducing an income tax worked for Haddon-Cave, though: in 1973 the British government had blocked his promotion because he refused to set up a steeply progressive income tax. His efforts with the third commission were sufficient for London to promote him in 1981.

The governors' and the Hong Kong administration's continued resistance to reducing economic freedom was extremely courageous. After all, they were in the employ of the British Colonial Office. They persevered because they strongly believed and saw that in doing so they were acting in the best interest of the millions of downtrodden people who had sought refuge in the colony. Occasionally, they had to cave in: some labour legislation was introduced, and Hong Kong also started a massive social house building programme. But even these concessions to diplomacy were small fry as compared to the increase in statism motherland Britain experienced during the same period.

5. JOHN COWPERTHWAITE

If one person out of the millions of individuals who have contributed to Hong Kong's success has to be singled out, it must be John Cowperthwaite. He could have been just one more colonial official who was quietly forgotten, but Cowperthwaite was of a different calibre. Not only did he have a brilliant insight into what creates mass prosperity; he also implemented it.

Just like Adam Smith, he was the son of a Scottish tax collector. He studied classics and economics at St. Andrew's University in Scotland and at Christ's College, Cambridge. His Scottish education imbibed him with the ideas of the Scottish Enlightenment, especially those of Adam Smith. While he was travelling to join the colonial office in Hong Kong he heard that the Japanese had taken it. He spent the war years in Sierra Leone instead, and eventually arrived in Hong Kong in 1946. He became Assistant Financial Secretary in 1952. When his boss retired in 1961, he succeeded him as Financial Secretary, and stayed in function until his retirement in 1971.

In theory, the Financial Secretary was the number three in the colonial administration, below the Governor and the Colonial Secretary. In reality, he was much more powerful, as he controlled the purse strings. Fortunately, Governor Black and Governor Trench were on the same economic wavelength as Cowperthwaite.

His brilliant mind furnished him with ready rebuttals to all attempts by interested parties to make the government interfere in the colony's economy. He assuredly rejected expert advice if it didn't convince him. As the former British Chancellor of the Exchequer Denis Healey admitted: 'I always retired hurt from my encounters with the redoubtable Financial Secretary.' He was a thinker: in his office he always kept a clear desk with no files. He was unrelenting in challenging his colleagues over all proposed public expenditures. He rarely compromised his philosophical beliefs. As an appointed colonial official he didn't need to bother about granting political favours to people who could be politically helpful.

He was 6 ft 4 in. tall, balding and gentle. He was shy in public and awkward in front of the cameras. Those who didn't know him personally often thought he was intellectually arrogant and aloof. Self-effacing and refusing to give interviews, he was certainly not a charismatic performer. Once, he was surrounded by journalists when he stepped off the plane in London. It went like this:

'Sir John, could you tell us about your talks in London?'

'I hardly think that is an appropriate question.'

'Well, Sir John, what do you think we should be asking you about?'

'It is not for me to tell you how to do your jobs.'

He was blessed with the old Protestant ethic of not wanting to waste other people's money. He was not interested in personal aggrandisement. As a senior civil servant he was entitled to have his residence upgraded, but he refused, saying that he could not accept a housing subsidy as the people of Hong Kong didn't enjoy one. His successor turned the residence into a palace because, as he told Cowperthwaite, he 'believed in luxury'. Cowperthwaite didn't – for him, his job was a duty, not a ticket to luxury and riches. After his retirement, he rejected offers to write an autobiography about his work in Hong Kong.

After the trade with China had stopped in 1949, Hong Kong had transformed from an entrepôt into a light industrial city. A number of government agencies had sprung up, including the Hong Kong Trade Development Council, the Hong Kong Export Credit Insurance Corporation and the Hong Kong Standards and Testing Centre. These gave businessmen the idea of asking for regulatory favours. John Cowperthwaite persistently refused. When an executive from a large British firm asked him to develop the merchant banking industry, Cowperthwaite replied that he'd better find a merchant banker, and asked him to leave. When the tourist industry asked for subsidies, they received them, but Cowperthwaite promptly recovered the costs through a tax on hotels – to discourage demands from other industries in the future.

When one legislator suggested that the government should prioritise the development of promising industries, Cowperthwaite replied that the government couldn't know which businesses had potential, and which one didn't. If an industry had potential, why would it need government subsidies anyway? He also rejected subsidies for start-ups, saying that 'an infant industry, if coddled, tends to remain an infant industry.' Hong Kong had accumulated financial reserves, and the incentive to spend them was great. Businessmen urged the government to subsidise the first cross-harbour tunnel between Kowloon and Hong Kong. Cowperthwaite said that if the private sector wanted a tunnel, it should finance it. After the 1967 riots he eventually relented, partly on the basis that it would be bad for the reputation of the colony if the scheme collapsed. The government did build piers for cross-harbour ferries, but the ferries and buses which used it were run privately.

Hong Kong did not regulate its financial sector. It even left the issuance of money to private commercial banks. Competition was fierce. When a bank collapsed in 1961, several bankers asked the government to introduce banking regulation and supervision. The colonial administration

ignored their request. The manager of the largest bank, the
Hong Kong and Shanghai Bank, started to draft legislation
himself and lobbied for the Bank of England to get involved.
Its representative, H. J. Tomkins, visited Hong Kong and
within no time he was urging the Hong Kong government to
restrict the number of commercial banks to prevent 'excessive competition'. He quickly clashed with Cowperthwaite,
who he described as 'near doctrinaire laissez-faire'. Tomkins
also expressed his exasperation over the fact that the Hong
Kong government regarded bankers' advice with such suspicion (perhaps Cowperthwaite remembered Adam Smith's
dictum that as soon as businessmen get together, they try to
restrict competition). A year later, when the crisis was over,
the bankers changed their view and now opposed regulation. A weaker version of the legislation was introduced.
Cowperthwaite still opposed the proposed spot checks
on banks to see whether they complied with the law – he
argued that this was contrary to the legal presumption of
innocence. The folding of two more banks in 1965 led to
demands to introduce deposit insurance, compensation of
the ruined depositors by the state, and the establishment
of a government-backed industrial bank. Cowperthwaite
rejected it all and said that depositors should bear their losses
resulting from the risks they took. Liquidity was provided
by the state to some banks, but in secret, as intervention
looked so bad. Hong Kong never had capital controls. To
use Cowperthwaite's words: 'Simply put, money comes here
and stays here because it can go if it wants to go.'

Cowperthwaite refused to collect all but the most superficial
economic statistics, as he feared these would give government the arguments and tools to interfere in people's affairs.
The economy would grow through businessmen not wasting
time filling in statistics about it. He thought such statistics were academic anyway, as, for example, tax revenues
came in well before any plausible GDP estimates could be

compiled from which to estimate the tax revenue. Hong Kong did organise a census in 1961 (the last one having been carried out thirty years earlier), but as soon as the data were collected the department was closed down. The absence of statistical information caused disquiet in Whitehall – when they sent a delegation of civil servants to Hong Kong to find out why the facts were not being collected, Cowperthwaite sent them home on the next plane. Asked what poor countries should do, Cowperthwaite replied that they should abolish their Office of National Statistics. He also refused to draft five-year plans for the colony.

Cowperthwaite's successor estimated that the size of the Hong Kong government as a percentage of GDP was 13 per cent. Government employment stood at 2 per cent of the population, or about 5 per cent of the workforce. At the end of Cowperthwaite's tenure there was no government debt. Cowperthwaite opposed borrowing, as he believed it meant passing on the burden of today's development to the next generation. The government ran surpluses virtually continuously from 1945 until the handover to the People's Republic of China in 1997. But even the surpluses weren't planned: the government was constantly surprised by the amount of revenue it raised. The economy grew faster than anybody expected.

Right up to this day, some do castigate Cowperthwaite for social and infrastructure under-spending. In Jonathan Dimbleby's book *The Last Governor* it is claimed that Cowperthwaite left 'Hong Kong's basic services woefully underfunded. Health and education languished far behind what the developed world would regard as appropriate for a thriving society.' This is a value judgment rather than fact: whether this assertion is true or false depends upon whether you believe that the state should provide a social hammock rather than a social safety net. Employment legislation and health and safety rules were in existence in Cowperthwaite's days. The difference from today's level of social legislation in most Western countries is that its level was far lower, and limited to the poorest in society. There was some, limited, state healthcare, subsidised education and help for the physically impaired, and many charities provided an assortment of welfare services. Most schools were privately run and charged low fees. In 1971 Cowperthwaite announced the abolition of school fees, even though he was personally opposed to it, as it also subsidised the rich who could afford the fees. In addition to social legislation, the government of Hong Kong provided water and owned the Kowloon–Canton railway, the airport and the post office.

Hong Kong also provides social housing for 40 per cent of its population. Its interference in the property market is not just the one truly great exception to its general laissez-faire attitude, but also its one unmitigated disaster. There was always a shortage of building land, as the Hong Kong government rationed it. Apart from the Anglican Cathedral, all property is held on long leases from the government. As land was released for development at a snail's pace, there was a permanent shortage – the high population growth was only part of the story. In the 1950s the government enforced rent controls on pre-war buildings and increased the building density for new plots. Old buildings were rapidly replaced by taller new ones, resulting in the government reducing the building density in 1962. There was a tremendous building boom in the three-year transition period before the density was reduced. The glut resulted in a collapse in property prices and a five-year crisis in the property market. After Cowperthwaite left the Hong Kong stage, Governor Maclehose perpetuated the shortage by designating 40 per cent of the territory as park land. Today, more than two-thirds of Hong Kong land remains undeveloped thanks to restrictive planning policies. These planning policies have also created a class of property owners with a vested interest in restricting development so as to keep property prices high.

The social house building scheme went wrong, too. After the war, immigrants had built wooden shanties on a hillside of the Sham Shui Po area. A fire in 1953 made 53,000 people homeless. Citing an assortment of laudable reasons such as fire risk, the unsanitary conditions and the risk of social unrest, the government started building social housing. Between 1954 and 1965, 607,673 people were rehoused. The figure is odd, because in 1954 only 300,000 people were officially squatting, and by 1965 there were still an estimated 600,000 squatters left. What happened? By providing housing at one-third of the market rent, the government incentivised people to apply for it – including those who weren't poor. People quickly left their private accommodation, went squatting on the hill, and received a flat. When those living on boats received priority on the housing list, many left their house to live on a boat. After Cowperthwaite was gone, the 'progressive' Governor Maclehose announced hundreds of thousands of new social housing units. The whole system became riddled with abuse. People living in social housing were not poorer; many of them were simply better at playing the system. This may sound familiar to readers in many Western countries where the government provides social housing.

Occasionally, Cowperthwaite's detractors accused him of 'doing nothing'. In his usual self-deprecating way, Sir John once quipped to Yeung Wai Hong, the editor-in-chief of *Next* magazine, 'I was just damn lazy.' In reality, stopping government interference from going ahead was a labour-intensive activity – Cowperthwaite was constantly on the warpath. The later Governor Trench coined the phrase 'positive laissez-faire', and Cowperthwaite implemented it for a decade. Government would not interfere in business and commerce as it was judged not competent to do so. Government would only introduce a legal framework to ensure that business operated in as fair and public-spirited a way as possible.

Cowperthwaite's successor Philip Haddon-Cave called this 'positive non-interventionism' in the 1970s.

When Sir John stepped down in 1971, he left his successor HK$2.1 billion of reserves and an economy growing at a pace of 13.8 per cent a year. Nobel Prize Laureate Milton Friedman said that 'it would be hard to overestimate the debt Hong Kong owes to Cowperthwaite.' Cowperthwaite's successors continued his policies. Hong Kong's growth continued to be very high right up to the time the British government started to negotiate the handover to the People's Republic of China. Afterwards it declined slightly, but growth was still much higher than in its overregulated and overtaxed motherland. More and more regulations and social legislation seeped into the system, though it still showed its resilience and illustrated the principle of 'creative destruction' – the positive effect of more efficient companies displacing the stale ones. After the People's Republic set up the special zone of Shenzhen, Hong Kong could no longer compete in manufacturing goods. The market economy simply adapted by focusing on the services industry. Cowperthwaite's principle of a balanced budget was written into the Basic Law of Hong Kong, which governed Hong Kong after the handover to the People's Republic.

6. THE MEANING OF HONG KONG

When, in the late 1970s, Nobel Prize laureate Milton Friedman produced *Free to Choose*, his famous documentary on free market economics, he started the first episode with a visit to Hong Kong because 'It's a place where there is an almost laboratory experience of what happens when government is limited to its proper functions and leaves people free to pursue their own objectives. If you want to see how the free market really works, this is the place to come.'

Hong Kong's glittering skyscrapers and 21st-century lifestyle show those who want to see it what a free market economy can achieve. In 1960, Hong Kong's per capita income was a quarter of Britain's. In 1997 it was a third higher, even though Britain experienced sizeable growth over that period. The traditional Chinese New Year's greeting in Hong Kong translates as 'respectfully hope you get rich'. This wish was granted to very many indeed. Hong Kong inspired the Reagan and Thatcher revolutions of the 1980s. It even inspired the People's Republic of China to introduce free market reforms.

When considering Hong Kong's success, two vital features emerge: positive non-interventionism and the rule of law. John Cowperthwaite explained Hong Kong's policies in the following way: 'I still believe that, in the long run, the aggregate of the decisions of individual businessmen, exercising individual judgement in a free economy, even if often mistaken, is likely to do less harm than the centralised decisions of a government, and certainly the harm is likely to be counteracted faster.'

Between 1945 and 1997, Hong Kong's policies could be narrowed down to a few basic rules:

- Equality before the law, without privileges for specific groups.
- Low taxes which remain the same in the long term.
- Some basic employment and health and safety protection (but no minimum wage).
- Freedom of employment.
- Unilateral free trade with the world; no export subsidies.
- Basic government support for the less well-off, but not 'on demand'.
- No government financing of private expectations, services or infrastructure.
- No financial sector regulation.
- Private issuance of currency.

The last Governor or Hong Kong, Chris Patten, wept when
he stood in the rain on the day Hong Kong was handed over
to the People's Republic of China. Many free marketeers
were weeping, too. In her later days, former Prime Minister
Margaret Thatcher admitted that she regretted handing over
Hong Kong – she had hoped to be able to extend its lease.
Is there cause for regret? Did the People's Republic conquer
Hong Kong? Or was it the other way around?

FIVE

CHINA

I. THE MOST TOTALITARIAN STATE IN HISTORY?

Cowperthwaite's Hong Kong was as close to a comprehensive free market with free individuals as Mao's China was to a totalitarian state with quasi-slavery. At one point there was even an attempt to replace people's names by numbers: in Henan and other communes, people worked in the fields with a number sewn on the back of their jacket.

The monstrosity of Mao's rule meant that, for most Chinese, any desire for Communism died with him. There were the tens of millions who starved through Mao's Great Leap Forward. There were the eye-watering numbers of people who were discredited, imprisoned, and whose families were destroyed during Mao's many revolutionary campaigns. There was the mass destruction of morality, tradition and culture. And worse: as Dr Tom Palmer stated in a lecture in 2005: 'When Mao collectivised agriculture and abolished all private property, people started to eat each other.' I thought it such an extraordinary assertion that I did some research on it. Dr Palmer was absolutely correct. In her epic work *Mao, The Unknown Story*, Jung Chang mentions how a subsequently repressed study listed sixty-three instances of cannibalism in Fengyang county (Anhui province) in the spring of 1960. In one county in Gansu province where one-third of the population had died from hunger during The Great Leap Forward, a village cadre told journalists that many had eaten human flesh. For his book *Hungry Ghosts*, the journalist Jasper Becker conducted hundreds of interviews. According to several interviewees, cannibalism had been widespread.

Permanent crisis is a characteristic of totalitarian government: if government tries to dictate everything, the smallest discontent becomes a political act, and everyone becomes a potential dissident. Apart from causing tremendous suffering, Mao's policies also failed. Regulatory failure spiral went into overdrive: if everything is regulated, everything fails. The chief Soviet economic adviser in China, Ivan Arkhipov, once stated that Mao 'had no understanding, absolutely no understanding at all, of economics'. Mao's philosophy was unable to produce the material goods needed to improve the living standards of his people. That is what ended radical Communism in China.

Most leaders who came after Mao had suffered from his totalitarian mania. It made them lose their faith in the ideology they had supported before. Most still wanted to make sure that nobody was left behind – but the monstrosity of Maoism meant that they had no time for non-evidence-based ideological fairy-tales. Hence their successors' focus on Mao's forgotten principle of 'seeking truths from facts'. (There are so many Mao quotes that one can always be found to suit any situation.) Or, as Deng Xiaoping said: 'It doesn't matter if a cat is black or white, as long as it catches mice.' Freshly rehabilitated from Mao's purges, China's leaders were willing at least to consider free market alternatives. And when they saw how successful those were, little remained of their erstwhile beliefs.

2. MAO'S COMMUNISM

Since the Communist takeover in 1949 the desires, beliefs and hopes of the Chinese people have been irrelevant to the direction of the country. The absence of a free media, a free political opposition and democratic participation means that for over sixty years China's history has been the stamping ground of a few thousand well-connected politicos who can more or less ignore what the 1 billion others think about it. What goes on at the top is veiled in almost complete secrecy.

To discuss the period between 1949 and the free market reforms from 1978 onwards, it is necessary to focus on the person of Mao Zedong, who was the absolute leader of China until 1976. The few courageous individuals at the top of the party who spoke out against him were swiftly dealt with. He is therefore solely responsible for the disasters which befell China. Officially, the People's Republic maintains that Mao was a brilliant leader, even today – though it is admitted that he sometimes made mistakes. Few Chinese leaders still believe in Mao's greatness, but as they owe their position to Mao's takeover in 1949, they are not about to question him. Official communications still use Mao quotes; but in post-Mao 'newspeak', Mao's 'wisdoms' have been carefully altered to support free market reforms. The gloss applied over the Mao Zedong era is a worldwide phenomenon. All over the west, post-modern relativism portrays Mao as somebody 'who did a lot of good, and a lot of evil'. Researchers may struggle to find what the good part consisted of.

Mao is often praised for 'unifying the country'; and for being such a brilliant strategist in the war against Japan. In fact, it was Generalissimo Chiang Kai-shek who did away with the warlords, unified the country and led the war against Japan. It was Chiang who convinced the US and Britain to retrocede their territorial concessions (apart from

Hong Kong). It was under Chiang that China obtained its permanent seat and veto on the United Nations Security Council. Official Chinese post-1949 history books are careful to omit it all.

Mao kept China in permanent turmoil. Grand revolutionary campaigns would rejuvenate socialism, rid it of capitalist corruption and lead the now reborn property-less and unselfish workers to the socialist paradise. Just as in sects, the people had to forget and reject their past, including family ties and traditional morality. If all else had gone, they would come to rely entirely upon the messianic Great Helmsman. The campaigns also allowed Mao to get rid of his political competitors.

From 1947 onwards, even before Mao became the undisputed master of China, he started to confiscate land and redistribute it to poor farmers. At the time, about 80 per cent of the population were peasants. The party dictated that 10 per cent of the population was to be classified as 'landlord' or 'kulak'. Unlike Russia, China never had very big landlords, and the eradication of 'landlordism' turned into the eradication of the better-off in general. The campaign went hand-in-hand with executions of 'counter-revolutionaries'. Every village had an Order Keeping Committee, which consisted of the local hotheads. They kept an eye on everybody, and forced all peasants to register for a fixed home and fixed place of work. The better-off were dragged before village meetings which everybody was forced to attend. There the peasants were encouraged to shout abuse at them, usually followed by gruesome physical abuse. Many peasants took part out of fear that they would be next. Several million people perished through violent death or suicide.

With his First Five Year Plan (1953–7) Mao hoped to achieve military superpower status. The whole economy was to be planned along Soviet lines to achieve this. Private businessmen were 'induced' to sell or cede their companies to the state. Workers were not allowed to move away from their work units. By 1956, 67.5 per cent of companies were state-owned, and 32.5 per cent were under joint public–private ownership.

After land had been redistributed to them, the peasants were only allowed to keep enough produce to survive; all the rest was requisitioned to pay for the superpower programme. When people were reduced to eating tree bark, Mao laughed, and said that 'the state should try its hardest ... to prevent peasants eating too much'. Provincial leaders were told to expect deaths and riots in 100,000 villages. The requisitioning failed partly because many peasants underreported their harvest. To make underreporting impossible, Mao forced all peasants into communes during the Great Leap Forward. They had to hand over all their land, animals and equipment to the commune, and lost all their rights as independent farmers. Charters laid down every aspect of the people's lives in the commune. People were only allowed negligible amounts of cash. Their woks and stoves were smashed; they now had communal canteens where theoretically one could eat as much as one wanted. When the peasants moved to the communes, their mud houses collapsed or were used as fertiliser. Farmers were not allowed to move away from the land and attempts were made to double working hours. One of the Communist Party of China's ruling elite admitted in 1998 that peasants were treated as slaves in people's communes. It failed: not enough grain was produced.

Cadres had a vested interest in flattering the disastrous agricultural production figures, so Mao probably only ever received reports of bumper harvest. As the media was strictly controlled by the state and intellectuals were eliminated, there was no scope for dissension. The Agricultural Ministry forecast a 70 per cent increase in the grain production in 1958. As a result, exports were increased by 80 per cent while the population starved. Eventually grain was imported in 1961; but by that time between 15 million (government figures) and 45 million (highest independent estimate) had died from hunger. There were rebellions and raids on granaries in Honan, Yunnan, Fujian, Sichuan, Gansu, Qinghai, Shandong, Szechuan and occupied Tibet. Party cadres were attacked.

When all private ownership in industry and agriculture had been abolished, Mao announced that they were living through 'the high tide of socialism'. In reality, the collectivisation illustrated the flaws of socialist central planning: together with private property, incentives to work disappeared. Instead of resources being allocated towards the most productive activities, state planning steered them towards political aims or crony interests. Where previously individual mistakes had only harmed the few parties involved, now centrally guided mistakes harmed the whole country.

In a fashion not exclusive to tyrannies, Mao tried to remedy state failure with more failure. With the demise of private property, the power of bureaucrats had grown, resulting in abuse and inefficiency. 14.3 million state employees were now put through remorseless vetting, denunciation, forced confessions and physical abuse. Offices, sports halls and universities were turned into detention centres. Mao declared that 5 per cent of those vetted were 'counter-revolutionaries' who were to be punished and executed. Next, Mao encouraged intellectuals and party members to comment on and to suggest ways of improving government. When they did, they were labelled 'Rightists', and rounded up in the Anti-Rightist Movements. Henceforward, anyone who dared to take another line than the government's was eliminated. An estimated 550,000 educated people were purged.

Apart from agriculture, Mao saw steel production as firm evidence of successful development. As Stalin had promised to out-produce the United States, Mao promised to outperform Britain. As China aimed to double steel production within the year, steel mills alone wouldn't do the job. The entire rural population was drafted into producing steel in backyard furnaces; quite often grain was left to rot in the fields while the peasants were busy making steel. The population was coerced into donating every piece of metal they had. The steel produced in the primitive furnaces was of low quality and often unusable. The number of state workers involved in industrialisation increased rapidly, but productivity did not.

After the failed Great Leap Forward, Mao suspected that his party colleagues wanted to replace him. To return to the fore and to dispense with his party opponents, he launched the Cultural Revolution in 1966. The mass upheaval this revolutionary campaign created lasted for ten years, until Mao's death in 1976. Mao's militia, the Red Guards, which mainly consisted of school kids, were to destroy the 'Four Olds': old customs, old habits, old ideas and old culture. In a sort of latter-day iconoclastic fury, temples, artefacts and non-Communist books were destroyed. Intellectuals were accused of being Rightists, humiliated and imprisoned. In many areas, descendants of the old landowning class were buried alive – the landowners being dead already. Many party members suffered, especially party veterans. The terror brought the country to a standstill and living conditions deteriorated.

3. THE CLASS OF '76

After Mao's death in 1976, a number of party cadres who had been purged as 'anti-socialist elements' and 'capitalist roaders' during the Cultural Revolution returned to power: Deng Xiaoping, Hu Yaobang and Zhao Ziyang, to name but a few. By 1982, 3 million people had been rehabilitated. It resulted in leadership reshuffles at all levels with a strong bias in favour of reformers.

The post-Mao leadership wanted to improve people's living conditions after Mao's catastrophe. But how? Political economic debate had been ruthlessly suppressed under Mao: those with knowledge of free market economics had either left the country or died in terror campaigns. After Mao's class struggle, the new leaders turned away from ideological purity and sought answers in empirical success. They were open to all ideas. Some remembered success stories of tentative returns to private agriculture during the famine caused by Mao's Great Leap Forward. Some knew about timid attempts of (illegal) free market enterprise in their provinces. Others lived in coastal areas close to capitalist Hong Kong. Some travelled to the West to see how things were done there.

After Mao's terror campaigns they craved stability, and few favoured the uncertainties of Western-style democracy. They wanted to remain in the driving seat. Deng Xiaoping, the paramount leader between 1978 and 1992, was firmly in favour of economic reform, but when he talked about political democracy, he meant debate *within the Communist Party*. When Prime Minister Zhao Ziyang attempted to introduce some democratic notions into the report for the 13th Congress of the Communist Party in 1987, Deng repeatedly warned Ziyang that: 'The idea of political reform must absolutely not be influenced by Western parliamentarian political ideas. Let there not be even a trace of it.' The leaders remained reluctant to criticise Mao openly, as Mao's takeover was the only reason they were in power. The continued presence of Mao's portrait and mausoleum on Tiananmen Square has nothing to do with adoration and everything to do with self-preservation. As they don't want there to be an impression that they were wrong, the leadership also continues to use socialist rhetoric to describe the return to capitalism. The reforms are explained as a natural continuation of socialism, rather than a clean break with the past.

Lacking a democratic mandate, the Chinese Communist Party leadership holds on to power through both repression and persuasion. The latter is done in three ways: by asserting that the reforms merely continue Mao's revolution; by claiming credit for starting the economic reforms after Mao; and by ensuring that the economy continues to enrich the Chinese people. The claim of continuity is untrue, the claim of starting the reforms is an invention and the claim of persistent economic growth is a wish. Even so, the Chinese people are now infinitely better off than under Mao. If the Chinese leaders had not allowed the reforms, that would not have happened.

4. OFFICIAL REFORMS

At the tail end of Mao's reign there were already some official attempts at free market reform. These often failed as they were too timid, and were undone by socialist hardliners. During Deng's brief period of rehabilitation he relaxed foreign trade and reintroduced some incentives, including the establishment of private plots. After the bloody suppression of mass demonstrations in Tiananmen Square in 1976, Deng was purged again.

After Mao's death, Hua Guofeng, his chosen successor as Paramount Leader, ended the Cultural Revolution and introduced a few reforms. Sadly those were dominated by a continued belief in Soviet-style central planning. His plan, nicknamed 'The Leap Outward', launched 120 new industrial projects, including oil and gas fields exploitation and the building of power stations. The unwanted side effects soon outnumbered the main aims. Central planning remained blissfully unaware of demand as there was no free market price mechanism to signal it. Steel production was increased on the assumption that it sufficed to produce it to sell it abroad. The bureaucracy was unable to provide efficient management.

But there were good free market reforms as well: private commerce was legalised at the end of 1976. Before, monetary rewards had been seen as a capitalist relic; now bonus and piece rate payments were reinstated. The price mechanism was reintroduced in labour management, even though labour mobility continued to be controlled. The class background system, which legalised employment discrimination against those who were alleged to have belonged to the former 'landlord class', was abolished.

The most important change was that China opened up to the outside world. Mao had pursued a policy of isolation. The perceived exploitation, humiliation and undermining of sovereignty during the Qing Dynasty had strengthened hostility to and suspicion of foreign powers. Mao feared the lure of Western lifestyles and ideas and pursued a policy of self-sufficiency. Instead of producing what China was good at, and importing the rest from countries which could produce more cheaply, huge resources were allocated to unproductive sectors to ensure that everything was made in China. In the event, little was made at all.

Economic necessity forced China to open up to the West. Huofeng's Stalinist Leap Outward was financed with foreign capital. The leadership learned fast and foreign investment would continue to finance many reforms. Senior party members travelling abroad were shocked when they realised how economically backward China was. They reported back on what they had seen, and so inspired a new generation with the fire of free market economics. Foreign experts were hired by state companies to teach them Western managerial skills. In 1980 Milton Friedman taught a one-week intensive course on the price mechanism to senior apparatchiks.

Macao and Hong Kong were top destinations on the travel itineraries of the Chinese officials in 1978. The idea of setting up special zones with free market policies in China was suggested by their hosts. Deng Xiaoping, Paramount Leader since 1980, who had ensured that sound economic reformers such as Zhao Ziyang and Hu Yaobang were appointed in senior posts, went to see Lee Kuan Yew of Singapore. Yew later recalled how he had told Deng that Singaporeans descended from poor Chinese immigrant farmers and that China could achieve everything Singapore had achieved, and even better. Deng later stated in a speech that China intended to outperform Singapore.

The official mythology claims that China's boom sprouted from the Wise Decisions of its Enlightened Leaders at the Third Plenum of the Eleventh Communist Party of China Central Committee (1978). In reality, free market change had been going on for quite a while before this without the official stamp of approval. The Plenum's communiqué praised Mao while admitting that mistakes had been made. In the future, material remuneration would be accepted – or, as Xiaoping put it: 'Let some people get rich first.' Agriculture would be reformed, though the only measure the Central Committee came up with was to increase the official prices which farmers were paid for the mandatory procurement of their produce. The Central Committee expressly outlawed the privatisation of land (this is especially relevant, as one of the main engines of early economic growth was precisely private farming).

Economic success started *before* the third Plenum, in the private sector: private agriculture, village businesses and self-employment. The economic growth was fuelled by the self-interested ordinary people – despite the Communist laws and officials who tried to stop it. The fourth early success story, the special economic zones, were sanctioned by a few reforming party leaders who constantly had to fight their colleagues. The government-planned reform of the state sector was a complete fiasco.

Under Maoist agriculture, a quota was imposed upon the

collective farm and the peasants working there were paid according to production costs and work points. There were no incentives to work harder or to produce extra, and famine ensued. A number of production teams illegally introduced private property to try to escape famine. Under the household responsibility system, an individual family would contractually obtain a separate plot of land to cultivate. They delivered their grain quota to the state, paid the (collective) production team an agreed amount and could sell the remainder on their own account on the open market at unregulated prices. The system appeared repeatedly in famine-stricken provinces between 1953 and the early 1960s. Mao was viciously opposed to the household contract responsibility system as he thought it would lead to the destruction of the commune system. Its instigators were persecuted remorselessly. In the early 1960s more than 100,000 agricultural office holders were persecuted in Anhui province alone. The system returned in 1976, and possibly even earlier, long before the supposedly crucial Third Plenum. Those engaged in it kept their actions secret as the practice was entirely illegal; it directly contravened the 1975 Constitution and the Agricultural Policies of the CPC Central Committee.

Ronald Coase's book *When China Became Capitalist* recounts one specific early example. In September 1976, Party Secretary Deng Tianyuan of the village commune of Nine Dragon Hill in Sichuan Province called an evening meeting to discuss what to do about the poor agricultural returns. The village was one of the poorest in the area, and widely known as 'the village of beggars'. After a heated debate they decided to introduce incentives by allowing some marginal land to be farmed privately. That year, private land produced three times more than fertile communal land. They immediately privatised more. When the secret was revealed, the county secretary endorsed it. When a delegation from the Ministry of Agriculture visited Nine Dragon

Hill it condemned private farming, while at the same time congratulating the village for its increased production.

Similar secret experiments took place in other villages. In the official history books, the example of the Xiao Gang Production Team in Anhui Province is the earliest one, its 1978 start date happily coinciding with the official start of free market reforms at the instigation of the Third Plenum. The land in Anhui was assigned to twenty households. They promised to deliver the quota to the state, as well as to look after the children of the team leaders, should they be persecuted. The latter provision shows it was clearly understood that the officials who sanctioned the illegal practice risked a great deal.

Instead of introducing free market reforms in agriculture as the official history claims, the Third Plenum in 1978 singled private agriculture out as a criminal activity. Even at the Fourth Plenum in 1979, private farming and contracting output quotas to each household was expressly declared illegal. Many cadres knew that private farming had lifted agricultural output but kept their counsel. On 15 March 1979, a letter to the editor of the *People's Daily*, along with a supporting editorial, sparked a crusade against the household responsibility system. In July 1979, Deng Xiaoping visited Anhui and told the local officials to encourage the peasants to get rich – the sooner the better. In September 1980 the party reached a compromise: it allowed private farming in mountainous, poverty-stricken regions (inhabited by about 100 million people). This was easy politically: where socialism had failed, resistance to the reforms would be smallest, and if the experiment failed the economic impact would not be too dramatic. It was the thin end of a wedge: the poverty-stricken regions which practised private farming rapidly became more prosperous, and the practice was copied elsewhere. By 1983, 96 per cent of agriculture had been decollectivised.

Three other reforms came in its wake: the freeing of production choice, the freeing of job choice and the abolition of mandatory procurement. Central command dictating the growing of grain irrespective of local soil and climate had resulted in double efforts yielding half the results. Now farmers could grow what they were best at, and the rest was imported – a direct application of Ricardo's theory of comparative advantage. When farmers were no longer chained to the land and banned from leaving their villages, many left, and agriculture became more profitable. Until 1985, farmers were forced to sell their produce to the state at set prices; now the state bought a quota at set prices, and farmers could sell the surplus on the free market. The success of freeing agriculture was spectacular. Between 1979 and 1984 the output in agriculture grew by 6.7 per cent annually.

Private agriculture was not the only part of the economy which started to revive the Chinese economy well before the party approved of it. So-called village businesses achieved even more spectacular results than private agriculture. A number of local enterprises had survived Mao's violent distrust of non-state enterprise. Commune and Brigade Enterprises had been set up between 1958 and 1961 to offer the rural community something else besides agriculture. They produced iron, steel, cement, fertiliser, tools and hydroelectric power. Because their activities were not included in the state plan, they were quasi-illegal. Their second-rate status was both a disadvantage and an advantage. Their competitors, the state companies, benefited from all the privileges. Central officials in charge of economic policy, who often had financial ties with the state companies, were hostile to village enterprises. Village enterprises had to pay bribes to obtain raw materials or to circumvent legal and administrative constraints. At the same time, they were forced to be inventive and entrepreneurial: they had to obtain production factors such as capital, raw materials and labour through the market forces of supply and demand, and they were responsible for their own profits and losses. And most important of all: unlike state companies, they were not subject to the state plan and had little government interference and red tape to submit to. After Mao's death they began to thrive. Officially, the Brigade and Commune Enterprises were owned by local villages and production teams; in reality, some were managed by just a handful of people. Some individuals also set up entirely private companies without any political permission.

Change of Industrial Ownership 1971–1886 Proportion of Gross Industrial Output										
	1971	1975	1978	1980	1981	1982	1983	1984	1985	1986
State-Owned Enterprises	85.9	81.2	77.6	75.1	74.3	73.8	72.6	67.6	64.9	62.2
Urban Collective-Owned Enterprises	10.9	13.7	13.7	14.4	14.1	14.2	14.4	15.9	15.5	15.3
Others				0.5	0.6	0.8	0.9	1.3	1.6	1.7
Rural Non-State-Owned Enterprises	3.2	5.1	8.7	10	11	11.2	12.1	15.2 (TVE)	18	20.8

In 1984 the government recognised Brigade and Commune Enterprises and private companies under the name 'Township and Village Enterprises' (TVE). Still the government couldn't quite bring itself to recognise that there was such a thing as 'private companies'. The private companies brought under the TVE banner were therefore labelled 'self-employed' people. They could employ up to five employees. How did private companies with more than five employees circumvent the regulations? Some simply concealed the true number of employees, and some used the practice of 'carrying red hats'. This consisted in paying a fee to collective enterprises or local government so they could register as collective or cooperative enterprises. A study of Wenzhou showed that

71 per cent of purely private enterprises were registered as collective, and 29 per cent as self-employed individuals. In 1989, private companies with more than five employees were legalised and 'carrying red hats' was no longer necessary.

Because of their flexibility and competitiveness, the TVEs out-competed state companies and poached their best employees. In 1978, 28 million people were employed in village enterprise; 1996, there were 135 million (one fifth of the total labour force). Its share of GDP grew from 6 to 26 per cent. By the mid-1990s, township and village enterprises contributed 40 per cent to China's industrial growth, and 40 per cent of China's exports.

The success of rural village enterprises took the Communist leadership by total surprise. With great honesty, Deng Xiaoping admitted that 'in the rural reform, our greatest success – and this we had by no means anticipated – has been the emergence of a large number of enterprises run by villages.' In 1987 he said that they had 'appeared out of nowhere'.

In urban areas, self-employment blossomed too. The absence of unemployment in Mao's China had been achieved by sending surplus youths to the countryside to work in the fields and by forcing schools, factories and hospitals to employ more people irrespective of the productivity. When 20 million returned to the cities after Mao's death, many became unemployed. After demonstrations the government legalised self-employment in 1981. Despite the limiting rules which forced the self-employed to bribe officials, and despite the social stigma, self-employment flourished. The socialist state had always focused on heavy industry; the self-employed spotted the gap in the market and focused on consumer goods and services. There was, for example, an acute shortage of restaurants. Many started small street eateries, some of which developed into successful food brands, turning the self-employed businessmen into million-aires. The earnings of the self-employed rose much faster than the salaries in unproductive state companies: street vendors earned more than nuclear scientists, taxi-drivers more than doctors. Many state employees left their jobs to start their own businesses.

	Self-employed x 1,000
1978	140
1979	310
1980	806
1981	1,600
1984	3,295
1985	9,253
1986	12,332
1987	14,730
1988	16,091
1989	16,081
1990	16,071
1991	16,788
1992	18,487

Special economic zones obtained political approval and support from reforming party chiefs from the very beginning. For decades the coastal regions had seen their citizens flee to the 'hell-holes' of capitalist exploitation, Hong-Kong, Macao and Taiwan. In some villages on the border, more than half of the working population had left. When local authorities urged Deng Xiaoping in July 1977 to increase border patrols to stop Chinese citizens fleeing to Hong Kong, he lucidly replied that, 'This reflects problems in our policies. There is nothing the army can do.' In How China Became Capitalist, Ronald Coase recounts how refugees from the Chinese village of Luofang had set up a new village in Hong Kong's New Territories, across the Shenzhen River, which they also called Luofang. In 1979 the annual per capita income of capitalist Luofang was 100 times that of their families in Communist Luofang. Leaders from Taiwan, Hong Kong, and Singapore told travelling Communist party leaders that they could achieve precisely the same on the Chinese mainland. Hong Kong businessmen asked to invest in China, and the issue was hotly debated. The reformers pointed out that the investors had far more to lose than China, but the hardliners continued to oppose foreign investment for decades. A few projects went ahead; others were thwarted by old-school Communists.

The Party Secretary of Guangdong Province, Wu Nanshen (the man who had earlier investigated the phenomenon of the two Luofang villages), was born in the coastal town of Shantou. Once it had been called 'little Shanghai' for the buoyancy of its economy, but in Communist China it had become a provincial backwater. A friend from Singapore suggested transforming it into an export processing zone. The leaders of Guangdong Province made the counter-proposal to turn the whole province into an experimental economic zone. Deng Xiaoping heartily approved, and suggested the name 'Special Economic Zone'. But why stop at one? On 15 July 1979 the State Council (the council of ministers) approved four Special Economic Zones of Zhuhai, Shantou, Shenzheng and Xiamen. The zones would attract foreign investment for export-led trade. They would provide commercial, legal and government services to support manufacturing and trade. More special zones were added later. The gradualism was Prime Minister Zhao Ziyang's brainchild: instead of a 'big bang' of sudden economic change as in former Communist Eastern European countries, areas were reformed one by one, and sector by sector – so as not to provoke opposition and unmanageable discontent. To avoid too much national debate and compromise, faraway regions obtained zones first. Between 1979 and 2012, Shenzhen grew from a fishing village of 30,000 people into the third largest Chinese city with almost 14.5 million people. Today it is the largest manufacturing base in the world.

The four Special Economic Zones were followed by fourteen further areas being opened up for foreign investment in 1984. The setting up of new zones was delayed because of the absence of recognised property rights. The Chinese Constitution forbade the selling or leasing of land (private property only became a constitutional right in 2004). Leasing land to foreigners in particular raised suspicion – had not Macao originally been leased out to foreigners to dry their fishing nets, and never been returned? Shenzhen had been the first land to be leased to the Hong Kong businessman Gordon Wu. The leasing issue was hotly debated. Economic necessity forced change. The Chinese government didn't have the money to build infrastructure, and foreigners wouldn't invest without it. When Zhao Ziyang raised the issue with Hong Kong tycoon Henry Fok in 1985, Fok replied: 'How can you not have money, if you have land? Municipalities should get permission to lease out some of their land for rent, and let others develop the land.' In 1987 a Chinese-American investor leased Pudong, across the river from Shanghai's City Centre. He asked for a lease of between thirty and fifty years. He asked for property transfer rights, so investors could obtain mortgages from the bank. The Pudong Development Zone was established in 1990, and within a short time it revived Shanghai as the economic heart of China.

Only one sector of the economy was directly reformed by Beijing: the state sector. The leaders considered this to be the family silver. They attempted to reform it and failed: over the next decades the state sector persistently lost terrain to the emerging private sector.

State companies were subject to myriad rules and needed to obtain clearance for virtually every decision from a large number of state bodies. Companies received different subsidies and bought raw materials at different prices set by the state. Neither state production nor state prices bore any resemblance to market demand. Coal prices were set low, even when demand was rising. As wages were set nationally irrespective of productivity, it didn't pay to work harder. Companies couldn't fire workers.

From 1981 onwards, a system akin to the household responsibility system in agriculture was introduced in state companies. Companies now had the choice: either they stayed within the state plan and produced all the state demanded, or they could sign a contract to produce a certain quota for the state and keep the surplus and sell it for profit on the market. It was hoped that this would incentivise them to produce more and to be more inventive. The employees could also sign performance contracts with their companies. State planning continued to allocate resources in a planned way, while at the same time a parallel for profit market production emerged.

Applied to state companies, the household responsibility system immediately produced unwanted side effects: (1) The contracting employees or the contracting companies soon realised that far greater profit could be had from renegotiating terms with the authorities than from trying to make profits in an uncertain market. (2) As they realised that their companies' success had nothing to do with profitability and everything to do with political bargaining skills, the employees bargained for higher salaries irrespective of productivity. This created inflation. (3) The price system for raw materials encouraged widespread fraud. As state companies could sell their production above quota at much higher prices on the market, many underperformed their quota in order to make a quick buck in the market. State companies were allocated raw materials cheaply below market prices – so many managers fraudulently sold such raw materials in the market

for profit. (4) And last but not least, the rights granted by the
state were not transferable. Whenever managers wanted a
change to the contract (e.g. extending its term), the state was
called back in, opening the door for additional interference
or changing of the rules. This made long-term decisions or
investment difficult.

The continued failure of state planning forced the Chinese
leadership into more reforms. After 1978 the government
ran out of money. When the state reduced agricultural
production quotas, it had to import grain from abroad.
The foreign currency it needed for this it could not spend
on buying machinery for its heavy industry state sector.
Autonomous state companies increased wages, resulting
in higher state spending. Revenue declined in proportion
to the declining GDP, and spending increased, resulting in
deficits. The government was forced to cut spending on the
military, infrastructure projects, iron and steel production
and machinery. The private sector grew – while the public
sector shrank.

1984 saw the re-emergence of joint stock companies.
Milton Friedman suggested a method to Prime Minister
Zhao Ziyang to make state companies more profitable without causing unrest among the workers: the issuing of shares
to employees. Shares in state companies were sold to employees and to the public. By the end of 1986 there were 6,000
joint stock companies. Both the Shanghai Stock Exchange
and the Shenzhen Stock Exchange were established in 1990.
In 1986, employment legislation was changed: jobs in the
state sector were no longer guaranteed for life. From now
on, companies could freely decide wages and bonuses, and
companies became entitled to take on contract workers.

Under Mao, law had ceased to exist. When he took power
in 1949 he abolished the existing legal system. The law was
not to restrain his Communist revolution. The new Chinese
law consisted of general principles and shifting policies,

rather than constant rules. The Soviet Constitution was translated into Chinese and became law in 1954. The same year,
a judiciary was set up and the law developed. This 'golden
period' of Chinese Communist law came to an abrupt end:
in 1957 Mao purged the judiciary of its last remaining independent voices when they criticised the Communist leaders
for holding themselves above the law. Law schools were
closed, and from now on most civil disputes were resolved
by non-judicial mediation committees. From then onwards
the Chinese legal system steadily declined in importance.
During the Cultural Revolution (1966–76), the personality
cult surrounding Mao turned him into a virtual deity and his
word became law (Mao said: 'Depend on the rule of man,
not the rule of law.') Lawyers were forced to work in the
countryside, kangaroo courts condemned people for political rather than legal reasons and the Red Guards terrorised
the population with impunity. In 1978 a court system was
reintroduced. The reintroduction of law was forced upon the
leadership for economic reasons: foreign investors needed to
feel safe. A new law on joint ventures was adopted. In 1979
and in 1980, special regulations for the Special Economic
Zones in Guangdong were passed. Later, new contract law,
trademark law, civil law, law on wholly owned foreign
companies and bankruptcy law saw the light of day. At the
same time, the number of lawyers grew from virtually none
in 1979 to 200,000 in 17,000 law firms at the end of 2011.

Unfortunately, government continued to interfere in the
legal process. Protection of property rights largely depended
upon bribing the right authorities. Anyone who wants to
read a vivid illustration of how far this intervention can go
should read *China Cuckoo* by Mark Kitto. Mark founded
a magazine in Shanghai which became highly successful.
When he stopped paying bribes to the officials, local party
chiefs just changed the locks. When he went to court the
judge ruled against him: the evening before her verdict she

had received a call from local party chiefs to tell her what her verdict was to be.

5. THE RUN-UP TO TIANANMEN

In the mid-1980s, inflation rose rapidly: 9.3 per cent in 1985, 6.5 per cent in 1986, 7.3 per cent in 1987, 18.8 per cent in 1988 and 18 per cent in 1989. It is important to consider this in some detail, as Communist hardliners used it to attack the free market reforms. The high inflation was all the more remarkable as it was 'official' inflation. Between 1950 and 1978, China's official average inflation had been 1.3 per cent. Communist countries traditionally showed lower inflation because they used a different formula from Western countries to measure it. These lower inflation figures in turn flattered real GDP growth figures (that is, GDP adjusted for inflation). Real inflation was a great deal higher than China stated, as state figures only reflected the fixed official prices and not the prices which existed on the black market. At those cheap official prices, demand was so great that there were permanent shortages of consumer goods, queues, rationing, black markets and, the scourge of all authoritarian governments, corruption and special treatment for the privileged.

Inflation started to rise rapidly. Communist hardliners blamed the abolition of price controls, even though the increase in the money supply by the banks was a far more important factor. From 1979 onwards the government had gradually reduced price controls. When the household responsibility system was introduced in state companies, the companies had to provide a quota production for the state, and could sell the surplus on the market at free market prices. There was therefore a dual pricing system: the official state prices and the market prices (added to by black market production). In 1985, for example, market prices for capital goods were on average 2 to 2.6 times higher than the state prices. When price controls were gradually abolished in the 1980s the high market prices replaced the low state prices. For some goods the state set prices were actually higher than the market prices, but it was politically impossible to free those prices as this went against the interests of the state companies. So prices only went up, and never down.

Other factors contributed to rising inflation. The household responsibility system in factories caused wage inflation, because employees renegotiated their contracts and company directors easily conceded to higher bonuses as their careers depended upon the evaluation by their current employees. The increased bonuses were largely spent on food and clothing, as the state companies provided virtually everything else to state employees (flat, pension, leisure activities) – so when the prices for those goods were freed, demand made them rise rapidly.

What caused more harm than anything else was the ill-judged banking reform of the early 1980s, which resulted in a massive increase in the money supply. Deposit-taking and lending became a monopoly in the hand of four state banks, which each catered exclusively for clients engaged in specific activities: foreign trade and investments; agriculture; industry and commerce; and construction. They saw the government's investment target as a common pool, and they each tried to obtain as big a share as possible to increase their bank's prestige. With no shareholders to hold them to account, and without personal financial stakes, they had no incentive to monitor the projects they financed with state money. In 1984, the government capped the loans each bank could make. The 1985 cap was to be based on loans provided in 1984. There was immediately a rush to agree as many loans as possible. This increased the money supply by 160 per cent in the fourth quarter of 1984, resulting in several years of high inflation.

When, in the mid-1980s, the government once again

announced that it would liberate prices further, all hell broke loose. The expected price rises, combined with the high infla-tion and the below-inflation interest on bank deposits, led to a run on the banks and panic buying and hoarding of commodi-ties. Prices sky-rocketed. The banks printing money to pay out their deposit holders led to inflation being pushed up to 20 per cent. Fearing social unrest, the government stopped economic reform and almost all the old price controls were reinstated. Within a year there was a recession and a market slump.

On 15 April 1989, former General Secretary Hu Yaobang died. A quixotic maverick, he had always opposed purges, had defended reform-minded officials and liberal intellectuals and had never been tainted by rumours of corruption. The hard left in the government had disliked him, and he was purged during the Anti-Bourgeois Liberalisation Campaign of 1987. So it was fitting that protest against the stalled economic reforms, the profiteering from the half-baked reforms by those in power, and the absence of political democ-racy, crystallised around the period of mourning for Yaobang. The demonstrators in Tiananmen Square were careful not to mention inflation as they did not want a reversal of economic liberalisation. Started by students, the demonstrations were soon widely supported by the general population.

For Chinese leaders, protest on Tiananmen Square was traditionally seen as a bad omen. The Emperors were believed to rule with a Mandate from Heaven. If the moral bonds between ruler and ruled were violated, the mandate would be revoked and the dynasty would collapse. Disasters and disorder would signal the mandate slipping away. Reaching Tiananmen Square and *zai fotou dongtu*, or 'digging up the earth right under the Buddha's nose', was always seen as the yardstick to evaluate the strength of dissent. Mao tried to make reaching the square impossible. After he had destroyed a number of historic buildings to allow for Moscow-style parades, had lined the square with Stalinesque official buildings and hung his image on the Tiananmen Gate, he made sure that possible sources of dissent such as Beijing University and all major higher institutions of learning were moved far away to the suburbs. In the future their malcontents could be stopped along the miles of roads they had to traverse to reach the square. Tiananmen Square was now used to hold ostentatious mass spectacles of obedience to Mao. Ironically, he himself reintroduced the tradition of protest on the square in 1966, when he noticed that his co-leaders were unwilling to follow his mindless class struggle and were trying to oust him, his own private militia, the Red Guards, used the square to show their allegiance. Standing on top of Tiananmen Gate, he harangued his entranced followers to 'oust the capitalist roaders from the headquarters'.

At first the Communist Party leadership allowed the 1989 demonstrations on Tiananmen Square to take place. But when Communist hardliners started to report the more extreme views of some of the students, including direct criticism of the party leaders and allegations that their family members were using public resources to land lucrative business deals, even more moderate party leaders felt threatened. Li Peng, who from the start had been intent on a crackdown, inflamed the situation by leaking internal discussions in which Deng Xiaoping had called the demonstrations 'anti-party, anti-socialist turmoil' and a 'premeditated plot' which needed to be dealt with quickly in the manner of 'using a sharp knife to cut through knotted hemp'. The allegation of a conspiracy was far-fetched, as the students had no clear leadership, no unified command and no clear plan. Martial law was imposed on 20 May 1989, but the protests continued. Wherever the students went, crowds applauded and encouraged them. The police made only token attempts to stop them. There were no established channels to hold political negotiations and neither side was willing to back down.

Some in the party hierarchy urged the arrest of hundreds of thousands of people; other urged the Establishment to listen to the students. Fifty thousand troops were stopped by Beijing residents and students from marching into Tiananmen Square. Believing that the presence of the world media for Gorbachev's state visit would prevent a crackdown, they increased their demonstrations. Holding a megaphone and almost in tears, Premier Zhao Ziyang pleaded with the students to disperse, as he could no longer protect them. Two hundred thousand demonstrators now occupied Tiananmen Square, and a hunger strike took off. Employees from government departments and ordinary citizens joined the crowds. On the night of 3 and 4 June 1989, Deng Xiaoping sent in the tanks. Hundreds and possibly thousands of unarmed demonstrators were killed when the People's Liberation Army opened fire. The student leaders were hounded, arrested and killed in the years afterwards. Zhao Ziyang was stripped of his functions and became a 'non-person' – he was never mentioned again and lived under house arrest.

After the Tiananmen Massacre and the demise of the Soviet Bloc, the left exploited the leadership's fear of unrest with a campaign against 'bourgeois liberalisation'. Inflation was blamed on the reforms. Li Peng proposed measures to – in effect – re-nationalise privatised industries. The number of private enterprises fell. Fortunately, the victory of market-hostile forces was short-lived. The fear of losing power may have incentivised Deng Xiaoping to smash the Tiananmen rising, but he had not given up on economic reform.

6. AFTER TIANANMEN

Deng Xiaoping broke with Chinese Communist tradition and retired instead of staying in power for life; Jiang Zemin succeeded him as paramount leader. Xiaoping was nevertheless still influential, and decided to re-ignite economic reform. Under the banner of Mao's dictum of 'seeking truth from fact' the 88-year-old undertook a tour of the southern coastal regions, where the success of the reforms was most visible. In a number of speeches he urged the party chiefs to speed up reforms and ignore ideology. Gradually the theme was taken up by newspapers. Reformist party leaders hailed his efforts. Deputy Prime Minister Tian Jiyun said in a speech to the Central Party School in 1992 that leftists 'should go and live in a special Leftist Zone, with a purely planned economy and shortages and rationing everywhere.'

It worked. President Jiang Zemin announced in 1992 that the market economy was the ultimate goal of China's reforms. Ten million government officials took unpaid leave to start their own businesses. Price controls were abolished. The greatest shifts concerned the reform of the tax system, privatisations, and the increase of competition between regions.

China did not have a unified tax system. Under the responsibility contracts, each state or private company owed different levels of tax. This falsified competition and encouraged favouritism. In 1993, taxes were simplified and unified for the whole country. Instead of a tax on turnover, irrespective of actual profit, a value added tax of 13 or 17 per cent was introduced. Services became subject to a business tax of 3 or 5 per cent on turnover. Tax revenue rose from 10 per cent of GDP to the current level of between 15 and 20 per cent of GDP.

Local government was incentivised to create an attractive business climate when land rent and value added tax became their main source of income. In addition, government promotions were increasingly dependent upon proven economic performance. The national government gave tax credits to those who invested in neglected regions. In order to increase their competitiveness, some businesses moved away from the long-developed coastal regions, where wages and property costs had increased, to inland regions with lower production costs. Regions and local authorities typically set up industrial parks, where they built the infrastructure and set up a business-friendly administration. They offered tax and regulatory inducements which allowed companies to compete against overregulated and over-taxed companies abroad. Deng Xiaoping identified the Hayekian Knowledge Problem when he admitted igno-rance as to how best to reform the economy – therefore local governments were encouraged to experiment on their own. If things went wrong, the negative effects remained local instead of causing nationwide catastrophe as under central planning in the 1950s and 1960s. A process of crea-tive destruction – inefficient methods being out-competed by better ones – did the rest. Sometimes local governments were too helpful. They would, for example, create specific industrial hubs (e.g. little 'Silicon Valleys'), instead of letting the market decide for itself which industry should go where. Often the infrastructure which the government built had to be changed because it didn't fit the purposes of the businesses.

State companies remained a drain on public resources. State employees had a job for life with benefits such as housing, health insurance, cultural and recreational facili-ties, restaurants, labour insurance and pensions attached to it – why go the extra mile and be competitive? But how to end the cash injections without causing mass protests? Milton Friedman's method of giving employees shares in their freshly privatised companies remained the most popu-lar. In 1992, the small city of Zhucheng, south of Beijing, realised that two-thirds of its revenue was being eaten by the corporate losses of its state companies. Shunde, a small city north of Hong Kong, was in a similar position, with crippling debts. The state bank was unwilling to grant more loans. Zhucheng and Shunde were quietly allowed by Beijing to ignore forty years of failed policies and to find a better approach. *The Economist* describes what happened:

Put more simply, in words that even now the Chinese government cannot bring itself to utter, they started to privatise
many of their companies. At first Shunde and Zhucheng
turned their firms over to employees (and became stock
cooperatives). In 1997, again before a broader shift in
national policy, the two began selling companies directly to
existing managements. Shunde, in particular, thrived. Two of
the companies that emerged, a maker of bottle caps and a
trader of duck feathers, are now among the world's largest
appliance manufacturers, Midea and Galanz. Other factories
have spread like wild flowers among what were once rice
fields and fish farms.

In 1997, ownership of many state companies was transferred
to local government in order to privatise faster. The State
Asset Management Company took ownership of all the
state companies which up to then were run by government
departments. Instead of having to submit to red tape from a
myriad of departments, they now became solely answerable
to the State Asset Management Company. Some remained
in state asset companies; in some the state merely kept a
majority share; some were turned into freely tradable joint
stock companies; some were liquidated. The 'iron rice bowl',
the promise to the Chinese that the state would take care of
them, was broken. Unemployment insurance was introduced
in 1993, and state housing attached to the state companies
was sold below market price to the occupants. Between
1995 and 2001, the number of state-owned companies fell
from 1.2 million to 468,000.

7. THE CONTINUED EFFECTS OF STATE INTERFERENCE

The remaining state companies have monopolies over
sectors which the government believes are of strategic

importance, or because public sector provision is seen as more virtuous than private sector provision (a mindset not unknown in the West). They include communication, banking and oil and gas. These monopolies are massive: in 2010, forty-two Chinese companies featured in the Fortune 500, only two of which were private. They try to look like normal businesses, but look and feel like ministries. A small share may be sold on the stock market. To keep a firm grip, the government appoints their senior managers, including a Communist Party Committee and a party secretary. The state companies are above the rule of law. They use their political clout to buy small private companies or force them out of the market. The state companies enjoy privileges such as land obtained cheaply or subsidised loans which make it impossible for private companies to compete. The government's neo-Keynesian stimulus programmes since 2008 have mainly been directed towards the state sector. The monopolies get away with lousy customer service, monopolistic profits, preventing private competition and fixing prices. Unsurprisingly, their productivity remains much lower than similar private companies elsewhere in the world. This explains why Chinese state companies' brands are virtually unknown outside of China. Milton Friedman's dictum that the surest way of destroying an industry is to protect it with a state monopoly certainly rings true.

State interference is not limited to state companies. The government also has also a substantial amount of influence over joint ventures, investment funds and even private companies. The sole aim of joint ventures between Chinese state companies and private foreign companies seems to be obtaining the know-how, after which the foreign partner is squeezed out. The state often keeps a share in privatised companies and exerts influence through its appointment of a party secretary. Often these largely private companies benefit from subsidies, protection against foreign competition and purchases subsidised by the state. Because of these advantages, they are often the only ones who are in a position to bid for government contracts. The fully private sector thrives where the state fails, such as in anything to do with the internet. Competition is strong and employees are incentivised with share schemes. Often, local authorities set up investment funds to invest in promising private companies. Often they are chosen because they provide jobs for local people (including for the children of the local party elite). They enjoy privileges from the local governments, making them less responsive to market demand.

But there is more: the excessive power of government comes with its twin brother: graft. It takes many forms: embezzlement, nepotism, patronage, backdoor deals and direct bribery. It is almost impossible to do serious business in China without engaging in corruption. Nor is it limited to business: corruption subverts the whole of society. As Murong Xuecun wrote in an article in the *New York Times*:

> Corruption is the norm, it has become the unwritten law, an article of faith. It is everywhere. You don't have to engage corruption, corruption engages you. It follows you, no matter where you go. No one can stay clean. Journalists take 'travel expenses' for writing articles. Professors ask for a 'consulting fee' to go to doctoral seminars. Doctors expect red packets of cash for performing operations. Even donations to charities and temples are subject to corruption. Good luck to the person who tries to stay clean.

According to Minxin Pei, an Expert on Governance in the People's Republic, corruption in China has evolved in two new directions. More and more corruption takes the form of legal office expenditure, e.g. office buildings that resemble mansions. There is also an increased collusion with the criminal world. Some join the Communist Party for financial gain only. For obvious reasons it is difficult to ascertain the magnitude of the problem.

Why is corruption so prevalent in China? The finger-wagging bureaucrat needs to approve virtually every economic activity. When the law is highly elastic, a friendly interpretation by a state operative can make all the difference. The high economic stakes in transforming a developing into a developed country with 1.3 billion customers has made a number of officials extremely well-off (some whisper that Hong Kong is merely maintained to serve as a conduit for officials' unexplained cash). The risk of being caught is minimal: journalists who report corruption are at serious risk from the officials they are reporting on. If need be, the corrupt can always pay a bribe themselves. There is no recourse to an independent judiciary; indeed, the judiciary is corrupt too. Less than 3 per cent of officials suspected of corruption end up in prison.

The public disquiet about corruption is well known, and occasionally the Communist Party leadership launches high-visibility anti-corruption campaigns. It is not easy, as those who are in a position to cure society of corruption benefit most from it. The purges often have more to do with one political faction fighting another than with fighting corruption effectively. A new phenomenon is the denunciation of corruption via the internet. A businessman admitted on a website that he had paid bribes of $463,000 to win contracts, including taking a planning officer on a ten-day tour of Europe. One internet activist posted photos of officials with expensive watches which they could not possibly have afforded with their official salaries. With 300 million users and tens of millions of bloggers, the power of the internet in China is not to be trifled with. Or is it? There is a lot of self-censorship, as the government can trace and monitor all online activity (the slang word for state internet monitoring is 'harmonising'). The government has used internet protest against corruption to its own advantage. In 2009, it set up a site where citizens could report corruption – it immediately attracted so many hits that it crashed. Later, conversations disappeared after a while so as not to create too great a critical mass. When Bo Xilai, a member of the 25-strong Chinese Politburo and Party Chief of the megalopolis of Chongqing, became implicated in a corruption scandal (including a homicide), the internet accounts of a raft of commentators were deleted. When it suits the Chinese leaders, internet protests are used to identify and remove local officials who stain the Communist Party's image. Several officials have been sentenced to death for bribery. Some Chinese citizens use foreign servers to post their complaints, e.g. on the Indian website ipaidabribe.com. The self-censorship and the careful monitoring and use for its own purposes means that the internet is no threat to the Chinese leadership.

In the last thirty years the expansion of corruption was regularly invoked by Communist hardliners to demand a return to the planned state. In his excellent book, *Prisoner of the State*, the erstwhile Prime Minister Zhao Ziyang thought that this 'would be like never eating again for fear of choking'. Indeed, corruption is the enemy of the free market, not the friend. Corruption distorts prices. The cost of the bribe will be passed on by the paying business to its consumers (e.g. higher tolls to use a bridge) or to the taxpayers (if the use of the bridge is free). Bribes are a tax on the poorest, who cannot set off the bribes they pay against the bribes they receive. Bribes reduce economic growth, as less money remains to reinvest – not just by the payee, but also by the recipient, who will consume it, or put it in secret foreign bank accounts, or keep it under the mattress to avoid detection. There is ample evidence that corruption goes hand-in-hand with low economic growth. While in office, Ziyang asked for the phenomenon to be studied. His solution is an open democracy: decentralisation; an end to monopolies;

transparency and public accountability; democratic checks on power; a multiparty system; an independent judiciary and a rule of law.

8. CONCLUSION

When the people starved, Mao's Communism died. China's leaders knew that to stay in power they had to improve people's living conditions. They didn't know how to do it, but they were fast learners: the free market was already creating prosperity through private farming and private enterprise. The leaders visited Hong Kong and Taiwan and Singapore, and wanted to copy their prosperity in China.

As the Chinese leaders want to stay in power, they are still not attacking socialism openly. After all, they owe their position to Mao's victory against the Kuomintang. They want to keep a firm grip on all economic activity. They cannot bring themselves to trust their people and introduce a free market economy. Instead, they try to find a 'third way'. The system whereby market capitalism is allowed to progress but only in the way central command allows it to, has now become known as state capitalism. Deng Xiaoping called it 'socialism with Chinese characteristics'. Through sheer size and mind-boggling figures, the achievements of state capitalism look very great indeed. Political commentator P. J. O'Rourke is correct when he calls China's success 'the miracle of the zero baseline, as everything looks good if you start from nothing'. China has achieved a lot and created wealth like never before. But when China under state capitalism is compared with free market economies, China still lags behind by a mile. It has huge state companies, but few have heard about these outside of China. In 2011, China's GDP per capita was $5,430; America's was $48,442.

What China has achieved is a fantastic improvement,

but it will remain second best for as long as the state keeps interfering in the market. The 'third way' is scattered with the skeletons of those who have tried it all over the world and throughout history. A market economy is superior to all other systems because it allows the greatest number of people to experiment in ways to improve their circumstances. Through trial and error, maximal growth is achieved. Whenever central planners try to improve on this, they fail. The economically free will always prosper more than the economically unfree. The Chinese leaders want to harvest the free market's bounty, but are hindering its growth. Many Westerners express fear for China's economic might. For he who believes in the free market, the economic 'threat' from China under state capitalism is non-existent. Or is it? After all, most Western countries can't stop themselves from interfering in the free market economy, either.

Can authoritarian regimes introduce free market economics? Most certainly: many have done it. The problem is that an authoritarian government is a permanent threat to prosperity as strong politicians can rarely resist the temptation to meddle in economics. Without free speech, the failures will not be exposed and cannot be rectified. It also results in graft, which is widespread in China. Authoritarians usually can't stop themselves from interfering in the rule of law if it disagrees with them, e.g. by interfering in court cases. All of this makes investors nervous and reduces the growth opportunities. Who will make long-term investments if the government can take it all away at the snap of a finger?

One serious international issue with China's state capitalism is that it tries to export its system abroad. Central planners in China are suspicious that the free world market will not provide them with the raw materials they need. They therefore go and extract it themselves from everywhere they can. State companies and private companies with state finance buy mines and factories, sign contracts and bribe local leaders. Labour is imported, including in Africa, where labour is abundant. As China's foreign ventures are not steered by sound market imperatives, and are usually performed by state companies, they result in huge misallo-cations of resources and huge waste. The Chinese investors promise the local leaders that they will not intervene in their internal affairs. This means that those leaders can quietly continue with their tyrannical rule, their human rights abuses and their atrocities. Now that authoritarian China provides the dollars, they can safely ignore the West's insistency on human rights.

Then there is the prickly issue of democracy. The present Chinese leaders seem to think that their staying in power is anathema to introducing democracy. Arrests and indict-ments on state security charges remain high. This is strange: if the economic success is so great, people would surely vote for them? The answer lies in the deceptive nature of the impressive economic figures. On the ground, people know about the abuse of power, the graft, the privileges and the petty bureaucrats who keep them away from reaching their full potential. The regime remains in place, but at sufferance: as soon as there is a severe economic crisis, its hand will be forced into allowing democracy. The only way in which they can ever hope of winning an election is to ditch the 'third way' of state capitalism and opt for a fully-fledged free market economy right now.

This can be done. In fact, it has been done, by another country on the other side of the world. Just like China, it went through thirty years of economic reforms. Today it is a successful democracy, and those who brought the reforms were duly returned to power by the electorate.

SIX

CHILE

I. WHEN THE GENERALS MARCHED IN

At 9 a.m. the army controlled the country, except for a small area around the La Moneda Presidential palace in the capital Santiago. The President refused to resign and refused to leave the palace to organise a counter-coup. He called upon workers to support his government, but none turned up. After the snipers from the President's Communist militia repelled the infantry troops, they were machine-gunned by Puma helicopters. The Air Force's Hawker Hunter jets attacked the palace with rockets and bombs. At least one was a direct hit. At 2:30 p.m. the defenders surrendered. Thirty-eight years later, an independent enquiry confirmed that President Allende killed himself with an AK47 which he had received as a gift from Fidel Castro.

After the coup, all the leftist political parties were banned, and their followers persecuted. According to several studies carried out after Pinochet had left power, more than 2,000 people were killed for political reasons by both the left and the right, almost 1,000 disappeared, more than 30,000 were tortured and 1,313 were exiled. It was a gruesome start for South America's greatest economic success of the modern era.

One hundred years earlier, Chile had been one of the most prosperous countries of South America. Republicanism and the rule of law were firmly established. The government's main adviser, Jean Courcelle-Seneuil, had been a follower of Adam Smith. In the early twentieth century, socialist and nationalist ideas gained ground. Protectionism and import substitution became popular. The resulting misallocation of resources, lack of competition and low productivity rapidly reduced economic growth. The market was blamed and greater state intervention was requested. Higher public spending, higher taxation, and higher inflation further reduced growth.

From the mid-1960s onwards, Chilean society became increasingly polarised between the left and the right. Several left-wing groups openly pursued Che Guevara's call for an armed struggle to take power. Other left-wing parties believed in gaining power democratically, including President Allende himself. In the 1970–73 period, more left-wing groups were drawn into the armed struggle. From 1972 onwards, centre-right and right-wing politicians and groups advocated a military coup to end the chaos in the country. There was a cold war side to the conflict: Allende's presidency was seen as a victory for the Communist camp (Fidel Castro made a month-long celebratory visit to Chile after Allende's election). The KGB and CIA were heavily entwined in Chile's affairs.

The result of the Presidential election of 4 September 1970 was inconclusive. Salvador Allende, the candidate of the Unidad Popular coalition of Socialists and Marxists, obtained 36.6 per cent; Conservative Jorge Allesandri Rodriguez obtained 35.3 per cent; and Christian Democrat Radomiro Tomic 28 per cent. Allende in fact obtained just 40,000 votes more than Allesandri out of a total of 3 million. Two-thirds of the voters had not voted for a Marxist government. Wealthy Chileans readied themselves to leave the country. On the black market the dollar tripled in value. As there was no absolute majority the National Congress had to elect a President out of the two candidates with the most votes. The Christian Democrat votes were key. Ideologically, they were probably closest to the Socialists. With his expropriation of farms, introduction of a wealth tax, greater progressivity of property taxes and dramatic increase in public spending, the outgoing Christian Democrat President Eduardo Frei was very much Allende's precursor. In the end the Christian Democrats followed tradition by voting for the candidate with the most votes. But first, Congress made Allende sign a promise that he would not abandon democratic methods and that he would not form a workers' militia. They had reason to be suspicious: Allende was an avowed lifelong Marxist; he was President of the Latin American Organization of Solidarity, which attempted to export armed Castro-like revolutions, and had on numerous occasions expressed his sympathy for the armed Marxist guerrilla organisation MIR. His Socialist Party supported the destruction of the 'democratic-military apparatus of the bourgeois state' to achieve the socialist revolution.

Allende immediately used all his powers to turn Chile into a socialist country as his party had promised. The opening sentences of the economic statement of the Unidad Popular were: 'The central objective of the United Popular Forces is to replace the current economic structure, ending the power of national and foreign monopoly capitalists and large landowners, in order to initiate the construction of socialism.' Allende's predecessor Frei had already expropriated thousands of agricultural properties without fair compensation; now Allende went further. As his party only held slightly more than one-third of the seats in Parliament, he circumvented the need to obtain parliamentary approval by using legal loopholes and obscure laws. For example, under a 1932 law, the government could impose an intervenor upon any private company which did not meet its obligations or which was accused of financial irregularities. Private banks and US-owned companies were seized through this method, without needing further legislation from Parliament and without compensation. Other businesses were seized as well. When Allende came to power in 1970, the state owned sixty-seven enterprises; by 1973 it owned or had seized 592 firms, and state companies alone accounted for 40 per cent of GDP.

Already under President Frei the government had stopped protecting private property rights. He had allowed de facto expropriations of universities, municipalities, agricultural land and real estate, companies and even the Cathedral of Santiago by groups of agitators. Allende now sanctioned replacing the judicial system with 'socialist legality', through which neighbourhood tribunals could seize property. The administrative authorities deliberately failed to enforce court orders of restitution. The owners received no help to recover their property rights.

The weakening of private property rights was probably the most economically harmful aspect of Allende's time in office. As the economist Hernando de Soto often observes, it is the absence of legal property rights in developing countries which prevents houses and land from functioning as capital does in the West – as assets which can be borrowed against to create more wealth. Who will accept a piece of land as collateral for a loan to buy a tractor if the land can be occupied and taken away at any moment?

As they received no help from the authorities or the police, the victims, often small shopkeepers or farmers, started to arm and defend themselves and their property. Sometimes strikes were used to put pressure on the government to counter the illegal confiscations. When Allende announced the creation of a state transportation company, 23,000 truckers went on strike. Housewives protested by banging their empty pots and pans during Fidel Castro's visit in 1971. The ever increasing numbers of killings, kidnappings and woundings resulting from the clashes between armed citizens and Communist militias were treated as political crimes and usually went unpunished.

The most notorious Communist militia was the MIR. This guerrilla movement aimed to establish a socialist state through violence: strikes, the setting up of 'popular militias' in cities, and guerrilla activities. Allende was close to them, and several of his bodyguards were MIR members. By mid-1972 the MIR had built up a substantial powerbase by way of communal governments and militias in nationalised industries. When these started to evict property owners from their land, the government told the police to stand aside.

Society became increasingly polarised. Some elements from the right encouraged disorder to provoke a military intervention. The politicians were unable to control the situation. At the Congressional elections of March 1973, the Allende coalition obtained 44 per cent of the vote, and the centre-right 56 per cent. Therefore, the right fell short of the two-thirds majority needed to impeach Allende. Allende had boosted his vote by reducing the voting age and by buying votes: spending on social programmes had almost doubled. Former President Frei – once nicknamed 'the Chilean Kerensky' for his expropriation of farms – was re-elected to the senate and became Allende's leading adversary. His Christian Democrats made common cause with the Conservatives to oppose the destruction of private property, and champion the free market, law and order and the rule of law.

Allende's extremism incentivised politicians and businessmen to look to polar opposite policies for solutions. On the right, radical free market thinking became mainstream. This differed from the corporatism, conservative status quo and social teachings of the Catholic Church which had dominated centre-right thinking before Allende. Politicians took advice from the free market economists who were known as 'Chicago Boys'. It was 'all hands on deck' against socialism. One group, the Monday Club, met in secret and drafted an economic plan for the post-Allende era. The existence of this plan, which was called '*El ladrillo*' ('The brick'), only became publicly known after 1992.

On 26 May 1973 the Supreme Court unanimously denounced Allende's disruption of the rule of law, especially his failure to permit police enforcement of judicial decisions. In a public speech a few days later, Allende counter-attacked, saying that 'In a time of revolution, political power has the right to decide whether or not judicial decisions correspond with the higher goals and historical necessities of social transformation ... consequently, the Executive has the right to decide whether or not to carry out the verdicts of the Judicial Branch.'

In September 1973 Allende was considering holding a referendum to increase his powers in order to overrule Congress. The Christian Democrat Patricio Aylwin, who would become the first democratically elected President after Pinochet, stated that Allende's friends planned 'a coup d'état which, with the aid of armed militias and the military power at the government's disposal, and with the collaboration of no less than 10,000 foreigners in the country, would have established a Communist dictatorship'.

On 22 August 1973, after a day-long session (interrupted for a six-hour lunch break), two-thirds of the members of the Chamber of Deputies passed a resolution asking the President, ministers and armed forces to put an immediate end to the breaches of the Constitution and the rule of law. It contained the statement that 'a government that assumes powers not granted to it by the people engages in sedition', and observed that Allende had not been elected by a major-ity of the popular vote, but by Congress. It accused Allende of trying to set up a totalitarian regime in which citizens would be subjected to the strictest political and economic controls by the state. The resolution then set out twenty direct violations of the Constitution and the law, in a list not unlike the accusations against King George III set out in the Declaration of Independence of the United States of America. The most important one was Allende's usurpation of powers which legally belonged to Congress, the Treasury and the Judiciary through the use of decrees. (According to the great philosopher John Locke, tyranny is precisely 'the exercise of power beyond the bounds of the law'.) Allende replied that the resolution was a call for a military coup; and that he would not obey the rule of law because '[in] the expression "Rule of Law" is hidden a situation of economic and social injustice among Chileans that our people have rejected. They are trying to ignore that the Rule of Law can only fully exist in such measure as we can overcome the inequalities of a capitalist society.'

Eighteen days later, the army, headed by General Augusto Pinochet, removed Allende from office by force. An editorial in *The Economist* regretted the temporary death of democracy in Chile, but pointed out that Allende and his followers were to blame as they persistently overrode the Constitution. The military stayed in power for seventeen years. Augusto Pinochet declared himself President in 1974.

2. THE CHICAGO BOYS

The generals wanted to rebuild the Chilean economy, but didn't know how to do it. Their views didn't go beyond an instinctive liking for the free market and a dislike of Communism. The Conservative and Christian Democrat Parties had supported the coup; but they were equally muddled as to what needed to be done. Their views ranged from a desire to restore pre-Allende corporatism to the necessity of building a mixed economy. Christian Democrats believed social injustice had to be put right by the state, but even for them Allende had gone too far. In any event, the generals had no confidence in the political class, which they held responsible for the crisis. They turned to expert advice from free market economists instead.

In late 1972, about ten months before the coup, naval sources asked Roberto Kelly, a former naval officer who had become a journalist at the right-wing broadsheet *El Mercurio*, for an economic plan to ease the way for a coup. To their surprise Kelly told them that a post-Allende blueprint was already being drawn up.

Out of fear that the agrarian expropriations and loss of property rights during the Frei government would escalate towards the expropriation of businesses, Chile's businessmen and self-employed workers had increasingly united in business associations and ventured into the political sphere. One such group was the CICYP, which mainly consisted of internationally focused business leaders. They stood up for private enterprise in a much more clear-cut manner than other business organisations. They saw their colleagues' support for a mixed economy as weakness. From the early 1960s onwards, they had supported the Chicago Boys: a group of academics at the *Universidad Católica de Chile* who taught free market economics. The CICYP also wrote a regular column in *El Mercurio*. Recurring themes were the efficiency of the market, state overspending causing inflation, the disruption of the economy through inefficient state intervention, and the desirability of replacing social policies with a determined liberalisation of the economy and the tackling of inflation. A group of economists and journalists, many of whom were CICYP members, started to meet every Monday to discuss the political emergency. They set up an office near the La Moneda Presidential palace where a group of economists, mainly Chicago Boys, but also Christian Democrats, carried out daily analysis of the economic situation and provided the Conservative and Christian Democrat parties in Congress with ammunition to fight Allende's policies. It was here that they

started working on *El ladrillo*, although at this point they had
no idea yet how it could be achieved. When the parliamentary
elections of March 1973 destroyed the hope of impeaching
Allende, the group sped up its activities, suggesting that they
were aware of the army's planned coup. Christian Democrats
continued holding discussions with Allende right up to the
coup, in an effort to reach agreement, while keeping their
economists' participation in *El ladrillo* secret. Money came
in from everywhere and its origins weren't questioned. It was
mostly business money, but also included some CIA funds.
Huge sums were not needed as many worked at the centre for
free. From May 1973, gradually finalised chapters of the plan
were transferred to the navy. As quoted in the book *Pinochet's
Economists*: 'On September 11, 1973, the photocopying
machines at *Editorial Lord Cochrane* (the parent company
of *El Mercurio*) worked non-stop to duplicate copies of this
long document ... Before midday on Wednesday, September
12, 1973, the General Officers of the Armed Forces who
performed governmental duties had the plan on their desk.'
The coup was already in full swing. A few hours later, the
Presidential palace was bombed.

Seven of the ten main authors of *El ladrillo* were 'Chicago
Boys': a group of radical free marketeers who had been
trained at the University of Chicago. Initially, economic
reforms were timid, but when the Christian Democrats
started to withdraw their support for the coup, the Chicago
Boys became more influential. Several Chicago Boys were
appointed to important government posts. Sergio de Castro
became Economics Minister from 1975 to 1976 and then
Finance Minister until 1982. He appointed a large number
of Chilean alumni of the University of Chicago to posts
in the ministries, the Central Bank, the Budget Office and
government planning departments.

The free market policies which the Chicago Boys introduced in Chile had been almost absent from the pre-1973

discourse. The most radical reforms took place between 1974 and the democratic elections of 1989. They encouraged free trade, individual responsibility and economic growth through the reintroduction of incentives to a population which had become too dependent on the state. The Chilean free market revolution predated Thatcher's and Reagan's by five years. When democracy returned in 1989, the democratic centre-left and the democratic centre-right took turns in power. Both continued the reforms, albeit in a more moderate form. The transformation of the Chilean economy continues right up to this day.

‡

The Chicago Boys
In early 1953, Albion W. Patterson was appointed director of the US Agency for International Development in Chile. The organisation channelled American aid to developing countries. He noticed that there was little reliable economic data available as the few economists were either socialists or poorly trained, or both. One day in late 1953, Theodore W. Schultz walked into his office. He was the Dean of the Department of Economics of the University of Chicago. They met every day for two weeks. Schultz and Patterson discussed the idea of educating people as a means to economic development.

Schultz was enthusiastic about Patterson's idea of establishing contact between the Economics Department of the Chicago School of Economics and the *Universidad de Chile*. Sadly the *Universidad* refused to work with the University of Chicago with its messiah status in the field of free market economics. Laissez-faire classical liberalism was miles away from the Keynesianism and Marxism taught in Chile at the time, and from Raul Prebisch's development economics, for which the *Universidad de Chile* was renowned throughout Latin America.

In 1954 Monsignor Alfredo Silva Santiago, rector of the *Pontificia Universidad Católica de Chile* asked Patterson for help. The university did not yet have an Economics Department. Some on the *Universidad Católica*'s Superior Council objected to teaching 'a brand of conservative economics where social justice considerations do not exist'. One year later the two universities signed a three-year cooperation contract. The programme was funded by the US Agency for International Development, and a number of charitable organisations including The Rockefeller Foundation and the Ford Foundation. The rest is history: between 1956 and 1964, twenty-six Chilean economists were intensively trained in Chicago. They were given a great deal of attention and followed a graduate course, including classes and workshops by Milton Friedman. When they returned to Chile, the first three became professors at the *Universidad Católica* and started to teach free market economics. One was Sergio de Castro, who became Dean in 1964. He became the leader of the group which drafted *El ladrillo*.

The three trailblazers didn't have it easy. The academic rigour they introduced displeased the sitting academics and the students, who were quite content with the status quo. The opponents questioned the relevance of free market economics for Chile's developing economy. It was the 1960s, and students more or less decided which academics were allowed to teach. When four students broke a strike against the Chicago Boys' courses, their hair was cut by their fellow students, much as the collaborators with Nazi Germany had their heads shaved after the liberation of France. Several protesters were subsequently expelled from the university (they moved to the state-run *Universidad de Chile*). The incident strengthened the Chicago Boys' authority and returned discipline and vigour to the *Universidad Católica*. Gradually the mood changed, and the students began to see that the high-quality courses improved their knowledge and reputation. The number of students steadily increased. They formed strong bonds with the academics – the 'mission' feeling took hold.

Dean Chana and some other faculty members were unhappy about the Chicago Boys' influence in the Faculty and tried to have other academics appointed whose economics were more in tune with the social teachings of the church. The Chicago Boys were often excluded from the *Universidad Católica*'s economic conferences and discussions. Funding came almost exclusively from outside Chile; local right-wing politicians and businessmen were too busy trying to profit from the status-quo to support the new radical economic teachings. In 1964 the Dean hinted that the Chicago Boys' future at the *Universidad Católica* was in doubt. Salaries were increased below inflation and some academics moved to the private sector. The Chicago Boys decided to 'risk everything'. Through concerted action between students and Chicago Boys, the Dean resigned and Chicago Boy Hugo Hanisch became acting Dean. After that, the Chicago Boys' position was never again in doubt. They started to export the rigorous Chicago teaching all over Latin America; and to challenge Raul Prebisch's development economics directly.

‡

3. REFORMS UNDER PINOCHET

The economic situation of Chile in the early 1970s was catastrophic. Chile's GDP declined in 1973 as a direct result of the government's nationalisations. When agriculture and industries were nationalised, their productivity declined. For example, between 1967 and 1973, employment in mines increased by 45 per cent, while production decreased by 28 per cent. By 1973, government spending reached 70 per cent of GDP. The rising state spending mainly favoured workers

and middle-class interest groups. The social policies for
health, housing and education failed to help the more than
20 per cent of Chileans who lived in extreme poverty. When
the economy declined, the tax take declined. The deficit
reached 30.5 per cent of GDP. This was paid for by borrowing abroad and by printing money. Inflation reached 605
per cent in 1973: prices doubled every two months. When
people complained about the unprecedented inflation, the
President of the Central Bank replied that money supply
was a bourgeois variable irrelevant in the construction of
Chilean socialism.

In a classic case of regulatory failure spiral, the Allende
government tried to master inflation by fixing prices for
basic goods. Few producers were willing to sell at those low
prices, and hoarded goods to sell on the black market. Long
queues formed in front of shops. To make matters worse, the
Allende government introduced tariffs on foreign imports of
between 105 per cent and 750 per cent.

Chile had followed an economic path of heavy-handed
interventionism for decades. High import duties, protectionism of Chilean industries and regulatory favouritism
towards well-connected business interests were sold to the
public as being 'in the common interest'. The policies were
based on development economist Raul Prebisch's Import
Substitution Industrialisation theory. This held that governments in developing countries were to encourage their infant
industries by blocking imports from industrialised countries and by offering subsidies and other legal preferment.
Developing countries were trying to become self-sufficient
the world over. The Import Substitution Industrialisation
theory rejected David Ricardo's Law, which had proved that
countries should focus on producing what they are most
efficient at, and import the rest. In his 1850 essay 'What is
seen and what is unseen', the political economist and politician Frédéric Bastiat explained what was really happening

when Chile and so many other countries tried to become self-sufficient. What was seen by all was the attempted achievement of the political goals; what remained unseen was what could have happened if politicians had not intervened: the opportunity cost. The resources which Chile diverted to its pet political projects could not be used by the private sector to increase productivity. When competition was reduced, better and cheaper products never came to the market – but this remained unseen.

‡

Import Substitution Industrialisation and Raul Prebisch

One of the most famous development economists was the Argentinian Raul Prebisch who, as Director of the United Nations Commission for Latin America, was very influential in Chilean economic thinking. According to his Singer-Prebisch Thesis, developing countries produce primary goods (e.g. food, minerals), which are exported to developed countries. Developed countries produce secondary goods (e.g. radios, cars), which are exported to developing countries. Prebisch observed that over the longer term, the prices of primary commodities tend to decline.

As productivity increases, the developed countries can retain the extra savings: in developed countries, unions ensure that wages remain high, and companies are astute at retaining profits. In addition, when incomes rise, demand for secondary products will rise (the potential demand for luxury goods is endless). In contrast, developing countries cannot retain surpluses, because they are weaker. They will have to pass on the savings to their customers in the developed countries. When incomes rise, demand for primary goods will not significantly increase (we can only eat so much food). Therefore developing countries' terms of trade constantly worsen: they constantly have to export more goods to pay for the same amount of imports. All savings accrue to the developed countries.

From this Singer-Prebisch Thesis, Prebish developed his Import Substitution Industrialisation policy. As their terms of trade will continue to decline, the only solution for developing countries is to start producing secondary goods instead of primary goods. An activist government must intervene to industrialise the country. It must close off its markets from imports (e.g. through tariffs), and produce substitutes. Infant industries must be built up through protection, subsidies etc. When the industries have built up enough knowledge, capital and comparative advantage, they will be able to trade on the world market. Development economists pointed out that all developed countries went through such periods of high protectionism to develop their industries. The Nobel Prize winner Hernando de Soto rightly equated imported substitution industrialisation with mercantilism.

Prebisch's success brought about a massive misallocation of scarce resources. In a direct negation of Ricardo's Law, instead of using its scarce resources to produce what it was best at, Chile used them for the political goal of becoming auto-sufficient. For a small country with a small population far away from world markets, protectionist policies were nothing short of suicidal.

‡

With a small internal market of 10 million people, the only way to increase employment and prosperity was by focusing on exports. According to the 1975 Cato Institute and Fraser Institute Annual Report, Chile was the second most protectionist country in the world. Quotas and non-tariff barriers were abolished in 1974. Import tariffs were gradually reduced – even when that meant that there was a fiscal shortfall. In 1979, a simple flat tariff of 10 per cent became standard for all imports. Later, tariffs were further reduced until they reached 6 per cent in 2003. The cheap imports increased competition in the domestic market. This forced Chilean companies to become more competitive. Consumers benefited from a greater variety of goods and from lower prices. It also made Chilean secondary goods made from imported primary goods more competitive. When all sectors of the economy faced the same treatment, politicians could no longer offer special deals to special interest groups. Exports diversified; the share of copper exports decreased from 76 per cent of total exports in 1970 to 38 per cent in 2001. Exports increased tenfold in twenty-five years. Free trade agreements were signed with the United States, the EU, China and many others.

The international economic crisis of the early 1980s caused high unemployment. The private sector was encouraged to create jobs. Labour taxes were reduced, VAT in the construction industry became refundable and large investments could be deducted more quickly from profits for tax purposes. From 1985 to 1989, annual job creation averaged 239,000: the highest number ever. By 1989, unemployment had come down to 5 per cent.

By 1975 most of the companies which Allende had seized were returned to their rightful owners. Farms were privatised. Other companies were sold without open auctions and with little information to the public. Initially, the capital market was insufficiently developed to finance large privatisations. When the pension funds were privatised from 1980 onwards, the accumulating capital in the pension funds became available for investment. This allowed the privatisation of the electricity and telecommunications sectors. The privatisations created 50,000 new direct shareholders and millions of indirect shareholders through the pension funds. In the end, 350 state companies were privatised. In many cases employment increased post-privatisation.

In 1971, Allende had nationalised all foreign mines in Chile, including copper mines. The 1980 Constitution declared the copper resources to be inalienable. The mining code did however allow the government to grant concessions, and this is how mining was shifted to the private sector. Investment by foreign companies was encouraged. Today the majority of mining companies are in foreign ownership, and they are much more productive than the state-run CODELCO copper company.

The hostility towards foreign investment of the previous decades was completely reversed. Chile withdrew from the Andean Pact, a protectionist regional treaty hostile to foreign investment. In 1974 Chile introduced one of the most foreign-investment-friendly frameworks in the world. The decree guarantees non-discriminatory and non-discretionary treatment of foreign investors. The investor agrees a contract with the state which neither the state nor regulation can change unilaterally. If more favourable regulations are introduced, the investors can request their insertion into the contract. The Chilean peso is freely convertible and profits are freely transferable abroad. As a result, foreign direct investment more than tripled.

There were three major tax reforms. A flat tax of 18 per cent was introduced in 1975. In 1984, corporation tax was simplified and reduced to 16 per cent. Corporation tax was changed from a tax on profits to a tax on distributions of the profits to the shareholders, to encourage companies to re-invest. From 2002 onwards, the top income tax was gradually reduced from 45 per cent to 40 per cent. According to the *Centro de Estudios Publicos*, a Chilean think tank, tax evasion in Chile is today about 22 per cent of potential tax revenue – the lowest in Latin America and smaller than the black economies in developed countries such as Sweden, Belgium, Spain and Portugal.

The reduced import duties and the tax cuts initially

reduced the total tax take. This was accepted on the basis that it would make the economy grow sufficiently to catch up the shortfall later. The tax cuts were partly funded by reducing state spending. Privatisations reduced the bill for the losses which the state companies had previously made. State spending as a percentage of GDP went down dramatically: from 70 per cent in 1973 to 21.1 per cent in 2011.

All price restrictions were abolished in 1974, so market price signals could once again guide supply and demand. In the Allende period, labour had become immobile through minimum wages and labour laws such as unlimited compensation for dismissal. Now, collective bargaining was decentralised to company level, and employment terms were negotiated between employer and employee. Apart from setting a minimum wage, the government did not interfere. Flexible conditions for hiring and firing employees, as well as restrictions on severance pay were introduced.

The state's spending spree financed by money printing had led to extremely high inflation. After 1973, state spending and money printing was curbed. Banks were privatised and interest rates freed, but capital flows remained strictly controlled. By the mid-1970s, inflation remained in the triple digits. Desperate to bring inflation down, Minister of Finance Sergio de Castro abandoned freely floating exchange rates, and introduced a fixed exchange rate between the peso and the US dollar in 1979. Milton Friedman criticised him for this in his memoirs. The overvalued peso decreased international competitiveness, and when the Chileans tried to buy goods with their strong pesos, asset price bubbles emerged. The crisis of 1982 was exasperated by serious financial problems in the rest of Latin America. GDP dropped by 14 per cent, and half the Chilean banks went bankrupt. A number of banks were liquidated and the state supported two important ones. The Chicago Boys put together an adjustment programme. The peso was devalued. Banks were privatised and recapitalised. State spending was cut, the budget was balanced and the Central Bank was made independent, so it would no longer print money as and when the government needed it. Unemployment halved, GDP grew by 8 per cent, and by 1989 Chile had the lowest inflation in South America. A lot of credit must go to Hernan Buchi, who became Finance Minister in 1985.

The most important achievement of Chile's reforms was the introduction of a private pension system. It has been copied by at least twenty other countries. How was the pension system privatised without causing mass unrest in a country as polarised as Chile?

From the 1920s onwards, Chile provided retirement benefits for the elderly. Different pension schemes catered for different groups of employees. By 1979 there were thirty-two schemes. All were pay-as-you-go systems, whereby the current contributors pay for the pensions of the current retirees. Initially the surpluses (contributions minus payments) were transferred to the government for investment. The surpluses encouraged demands for increasing the benefits. This led to shortfalls, which were met by raising the contributions. Over the decades, ever fewer contributors paid for ever more pensioners. By 1974, pension contributions reduced the average worker's pay by 50 per cent, and the evasion of social security contributions was massive. Benefits and contributions were not linked; the system was essentially a progressive tax on labour. The upper and middle-class employees with the best lobbying power obtained the highest pensions. The taxpayers had to fork out ever larger amounts to cover the shortfalls.

In 1980 the Chicago Boys introduced a new pension system. Individuals could either continue to pay into the state pay-as-you-go system or switch their contributions into individual capitalisation accounts managed by private joint stock companies. To encourage people to switch to the private system, the state subsidised the contributions so they were lower than state pension contributions. The state paid compensation into the private pension funds for those who made the switch and would otherwise have lost the years they had already paid into the state system. The new private and the old state system continue to exist side-by-side right up to this day.

Paying into a private pension system is compulsory for new employees and optional for the newly self-employed. Employees can choose their private pension fund and can move between them. The low contributions increased voluntary participation and decreased evasion. Contributions are tax deductible.

The pension funds invested the contributions and, as the private economy prospered, the employees enjoyed dramatic increases in their pension accounts. The funds can freely charge administration costs, but to encourage competition they cannot charge exit fees. Sadly, the administration charges are high – partly to pay for marketing to entice people away from rival funds. The funds are required to make maximum and minimum returns to contributors, based on the average performance of the system over twelve months. If they fall short, they have to make it up by using their compulsory reserves of 1 per cent.

Is the private pensions system fair? Critics argued that anything different from everybody paying for everybody was immoral. In a lecture to the Atlas Foundation, former Treasury Minister Hernan Buchi recounted how he put the fairness question to Singaporean Prime Minister Lee Kuan Yew. Yew replied: 'Westerners have turned morality upside down. How can it be moral that you decide how your kids will pay your pensions? That is immoral. What is moral is that you take responsibility, you save for your own pension.' Indeed, under a traditional pay-as-you-go ('repartition') system, current taxpayers pay for the pensions of yesterday's employees. This 'solidarity between generations' is essentially an obligation put upon the young by and for today's elderly. In most pay-as-you-go countries with an ageing population, the younger generation are sceptical about the likelihood that they will ever receive a decent state pension themselves.

A second moral issue is that some pensioners receive much less than others because they earned and therefore contributed less. The Chicago Boys who devised the system see this as a virtue: the potential higher pension encourages people to save extra (above the minimum imposed by the state). If the final pension was equal for all, everyone would save the absolute minimum. The state guarantees the private pensions of the poor and the unlucky. It guarantees a minimum pension for those who contributed for at least twenty years but fall below the minimum pension, and for those whose pension fund underperforms or goes bankrupt. The minimum pension reduces the incentive to contribute.

The fiscal costs of the transfer from a state to a private pension system are high. There is the subsidy to entice people to switch; the compensation for people who switch but who had already paid into the state system; and the fact that as more people switch, the state system has fewer contributors but the pensions still need to be paid out. In addition, the state guarantee of a minimum pension is a serious risk as investments may turn sour in an economic downturn.

The cost is borne in a number of ways. The government anticipated the changes by building up a war chest before the private pensions came into existence. It refused to borrow and raise taxes, reducing public spending and public sector wages instead. The introduction of a uniform retirement age for men and women meant that the average employee has to work five years longer. Notwithstanding the high pension costs, the Chilean government managed to achieve significant budget surpluses throughout the 1980s and 1990s.

The reform was a roaring success. The private pensions system was maintained after democracy returned. People now hold a reasonable hope that their contributions will entitle them to a pension. In addition, the system funded massive economic growth. The holdings of the pension funds increased dramatically over the years, from 0.81 per cent of GDP in 1981 to 59 per cent of GDP in 2005. The average return was 12.8 per cent in real terms between 1981 and 1996. In fact, there was so much capital that they often found it difficult to find investment projects in Chile. The funds allowed the development of important economic sectors, such as the mortgage market, the newly privatised state companies, and public works.

4. REFORMS UNDER DEMOCRACY

When the new democratic government of Patricio Aylwin took office in 1990, free marketeers feared that the reforms would be reversed. The Christian Democrats had been highly critical of the free market reforms. Aylwin's and the subsequent governments left most policies in place and continued the reforms. A lot of credit must go to the think tank *Libertad y Desarrollo*, created by Hernan Buchi, which developed new policy ideas and built direct ties with the new governments. In 1990, Chile ranked twenty-sixth in the worldwide Index of Economic Freedom; by 2012, it ranked seventh.

Increasingly, basic public infrastructure was provided by concessions. Chile privatised more than most other countries in the world. Ports, airports, highways, public services, health, pensions, water, gas, waste disposal and telecoms are all in private hands. The share of public enterprises as a percentage of GDP declined from 40 per cent in 1973 to 9 per cent in 1998. Some state companies remain: the largest commercial bank, one energy company, one mining company, the post; the Metro, part of the public railways and the principal oil company. It is believed that the centre-right government which was elected in 2009 will privatise the copper company CODELCO.

When democracy returned, rates of corporation tax and

value added tax rose; but personal income tax rates and tariffs decreased. In education, freedom of choice was reduced, with more centralised planning. Labour regulation increased, leading to higher unemployment and lower growth in the last decade.

5. CHILE TODAY

Chile's GDP per capita is the second highest in South America, only just behind Argentina. It is still a long way behind other developed countries, but higher growth of just a few per cent annually will make up the shortfall very fast. In 2011 Chile's economy grew by 6.5 per cent notwithstanding the country suffering one of the strongest earthquakes on record in 2010. The size of the state is a mere 20.3 per cent of GDP. Chile has the lowest inflation in South America. Chile has become a destination for immigrants.

The benefits of the Chilean free market reforms have been durable, and all parts of society have prospered. The number of people below the poverty line dropped from 40 per cent to 20 per cent between 1985 and 1997, and to 15.1 per cent in 2009. Chile has a higher life expectancy, lower infant mortality and lower unemployment than other South American countries.

	Chile	Brazil	Argentina	Venezuela	Bolivia
Population below poverty	11.9% (2009)	26% (2008)	30% (2010)	27.4%	51.3% (2009)
Life expectancy at birth (years)	78.1	72.79	77.14	74.08	67.9
Infant mortality rate /1,000	7.36	20.5	10.52	20.18	40.94
Inflation	3.3%	6.5%	22%	27.6%	6.9%
GDP per capita	$17,400	$11,900	$17,700	$12,700	$4,900

Figures are for 2011, unless otherwise indicated. Source: CIA Factbook (online)

Internationally, Chile outperforms some of the biggest players. As Margaret Thatcher observed:

> Chile's economy is better balanced and more diversified and so more able to withstand adverse conditions: almost complete reliance on copper export has given way to the export of computer software, wine, fish, fruit and vegetables, to such an extent that the European Community is clamouring to keep Chile's products out.

Chile has more free trade agreements than any other country, and is one of the most open economies in the world. It was the first South American country to join the OECD.

	Chile	UK	USA	EU
Growth	5.9 per cent	0.7 per cent	1.7 per cent	1.6 per cent
Govmt spending (per cent GDP)	24.4 per cent	51.2 per cent	42.2 per cent	n/a
Budget (per cent GDP)	1.5 per cent	−8.3 per cent	−8.6 per cent	n/a
Unemployment	6.6 per cent	8.1 per cent	9 per cent	9.5 per cent
GDP per capita	$17,400	$36,600	$49,000	$34,500

Year is 2011. Source: CIA Factbook (online) and 2012 Index of Economic Freedom, The Heritage Foundation.

6. WHY DID THE REFORMS SUCCEED?

The alarming economic situation Chile found itself in on the eve of the military putsch was followed by a determined economic liberalisation. Despite the human rights abuses during the Pinochet-era, the economic reforms were continued long after the dictatorship disappeared. Even when left-wing governments tweaked the reforms, they never went back to the suicidal economics of the Allende years.

Why did the reforms last for almost forty years and why did they succeed? Former Treasury Minister Hernan Buchi gives a few reasons:

- At the outset there was a crisis atmosphere and sense of urgency. Those who introduced the reforms feared that they would be undone after the 1988 democratic general election. So they wanted positive economic results: that is, job creation and wealth creation for the many, as soon as possible. There was a sense of mission: several hundred people agreed to work long hours for a salary far below what they could have obtained in the private sector.

- The reformers had a clear eight-year run. The 1980 Constitution, which was approved by a controversial plebiscite with 67 per cent of the votes, gave Pinochet powers until 1989, when he would be succeeded by a democratically elected President. The reformers were able to take the long view, rather than having to think about immediate popular democratic appeal.

- The reforms were deep and coherent as opposed to partial and haphazard. This was achieved by employing a large team of dedicated Chicago Boys. When the centre-left gained power, the centre-right opposition remained strong enough to prevent a return to the socialist economic destruction of the past. When democracy returned, free market reformers built bridges with centre-left political parties and advised them.

- Great effort was put into tackling poverty. Job creation was the main method of achieving this. As human capital is more evenly distributed in society than capital, jobs help income redistribution. Although social programmes such as pensions were available under Allende, the payments were inflated away. The pensions system was technically bankrupt; most state money for education subsidised universities attended by the rich; the middle classes benefited from housing subsidies and left the poorest out in the cold. Notwithstanding the extremely high government spending on social programmes under Allende, 20 per cent of Chileans lived in extreme poverty in 1974. After Allende, state spending was increasingly targeted at the poorest in society.

- Most of the stable institutions set up under the 1980 Constitution still exist today. Private property rights were better protected. The Constitution limited state spending, and changes to the cap on that provision require a special majority in Parliament. Money printing at the behest of the government was made impossible when the Central Bank became independent in 1989.

- After thirty years of reforms and open markets, Chileans no longer associate with strong ideologies or with economic or ethnic nationalism. The division into two ideological opposites, which reached its apotheosis during the Allende government, faded away. Chileans see themselves as actors in a globalised world.

Buchi also detects some failures:

There still persists a trend towards socialism that claims success for the government and its policies when the country grows and employment rises, but blames businessmen for economic downturns and unemployment. A persistent demagogy wrongly stresses that the luck of the workers can be changed by simply changing a law or regulation, when we know that only a dynamic economy will continually create more and better jobs.

Today, Chile is one of the best examples of successful long-term economic reform leading to prolonged growth and the creation of mass prosperity. Some countries launched successful reforms, but started slacking after a few years because the reforms had not been profound enough. For one such example we turn the globe, but stay in the southern hemisphere.

SEVEN

NEW ZEALAND

I. A POLITICIAN WHO KNEW HE WAS WRONG

Have you ever heard a politician say that he was wrong? They occasionally say 'sorry', standing next to their long-suffering wives and in front of flashing cameras, for having been found in the wrong bed. Ideologically, politicians rarely apologise. There is usually no point, as they will be gone by the time their policies derail.

New Zealand had one exemplary Labour Party politician who, aged forty-six, dramatically reversed from most of his previously held views. At the end of 1983, Roger Douglas drafted an 'Economic Policy Package' for the Labour Party in which he more or less abandoned everything he and his party had said before. It called for a market-led restructuring of the economy. In his maiden speech back in 1969, when he was freshly elected, he had made the case against foreign investment in the domestic economy. In May 1983, he wrote a paper arguing that an unregulated market led to unhealthy concentrations of market power; a few months later he called for massive deregulation. Labour's Economic Committee did adopt Douglas's free market paper, but not unanimously – his fellow Labour Member of Parliament Stan Rodger called the paper 'an unacceptable leap to the right'.

What made one courageous Labour politician change

his views to such an extent that his politics were dubbed Rogernomics, after Ronald Reagan's Reaganomics?

2. WHAT WENT WRONG

Douglas changed his views because he realised that New Zealand's policies of the previous decades hadn't worked. New Zealand had turned into the poor relation of the developed world. As with Germany after the war, China after Mao, Hong Kong faced with mass immigration, and Chile's quasi-civil war, New Zealand's zeal for reform materialised during an emergency. It wasn't the proliferation of Hayek's, Popper's or Friedman's writings which made Douglas and many others abandon their Keynesian beliefs in growth through deficit spending: it was the simple realisation that those beliefs didn't produce the goods.

In the 1950s New Zealand had a higher living standard than Australia and Western Europe – its income per person was in the top ten in the world. In a typical year between 1920 and 1950 over 90 per cent of its exports were meat, dairy and wool. Subsequently, economic growth slowed down. Between 1950 and 1984 New Zealand grew at half the average OECD rate. The seeds of decline had been sown even earlier.

From the 1930s onwards New Zealand provided cradle-to-grave welfare. Both parties maintained a structural shortage of labour – the labour market was tightly regulated and wages were kept artificially high. The first Labour government of 1936 introduced high levels of protection in order to shield the country from outside economic competition. Just like Australia, the economy was kept 'judiciously insulated and shielded from the international system'. Subsequent governments maintained and added to these often inconsistent, erratic and arbitrary policies. Imports were restricted through import duties and licensing. Price controls kept prices artificially high and reduced competition from more efficient producers. The protection allowed domestic producers to stay aloof from consumers' expectations. It also prevented exporters from buying cheaper components. Any dealings requiring foreign currency involved a government-licensed cartel of banks which charged high margins. In order to buy a subscription to a foreign magazine you needed exchange control approval. Producers were state subsidised through cheap export loans from the Reserve Bank.

The distortions in markets which the intervention created led to side-effects which the all-powerful government tried to remedy through new interventions. By the 1980s prices, interest rates, dividends, wages and rents were controlled by the government. Before the price controls on bread were abolished in 1979 it was impossible to find any speciality breads.

Special interest groups dictated daily life. Shopping, drinking and dining were limited to hours which suited the retail industry rather than the customers. In order to buy margarine you needed a doctor's prescription – this protected domestic butter production, care of good lobbying by the dairy industry. (New Zealand was not alone. Margarine was illegal in Canada until 1948, where large amounts of fish, seal, and whale oil margarine were smuggled in from Newfoundland.)

The public sector was large and inefficient. Both parties used it as an employment agency. Public sector employees knew that their jobs were for life and that there would always be more of them. The journalist David McLoughlin captured the spirit:

> Anything approaching the definition of real work was regarded, particularly in government departments, as a form of perversion; turning up for an eight-hour day ... was all that was required; the *Dominion* crossword would see an

army of grey-cardiganed clerks through nicely until morning tea … and the first edition of the *Evening Post*, to help while away the afternoon, was on the streets at 1 p.m.

The government lived above its means as a matter of course: fiscal deficits became the rule; carefully hidden under high inflation. Inflation stood at more than 10 per cent through-out the 1970s. When wages were frozen, compensations were introduced through the tax system; thereby further reducing state income and increasing the deficit.

Homemade economic mismanagement was exacerbated by international factors. When the United Kingdom joined the European Common Market it ended Commonwealth Preference (the successor of Imperial Preference), and New Zealand's export market reduced substantially. By the end of the 1970s New Zealand was in an economic depression. Living standards fell. The 1973 and 1979 world oil crises made matters worse. Prime Minister Muldoon had the bright idea of trying to remedy this through state enterprise: his Think Big programme borrowed heavily abroad to pay for large-scale industrial investment in the petrochemical and energy sectors. By 1982 New Zealand had the lowest per capita income of developing countries. As is usually the case in countries where people's income goes down, the state had never been so bloated: in the ten years before 1984 the size of state spending as a percentage of GDP had gone up by 10 per cent up to 45 per cent. A quarter of the workforce worked in the public sector.

‡

Imperial Preference
Imperial Preferences were the protectionist policies by which the British Empire tried to shield itself from foreign compe-tition. It was promoted by the British politician Joseph Chamberlain at the beginning of the twentieth century

and bitterly opposed by free traders. It proposed recipro-
cal low tariffs between the colonies and dominions of the
British Empire, combined with high barriers against outsiders. Latter-day mercantilists fancied that this protectionism
would sustain Britain as a global power. New Zealand
applied the lowest customs duties for British imports, and
low tariffs for other members of the Empire for decades.

In the 1920s, the idea was revived. Free trader Winston
Churchill was a strong opponent. Public opposition to
protectionism led to two Conservative Party election defeats,
and to the election of the first two socialist governments.
The 1930s Great Depression inspired Britain to abandon
free trade. Warmly supported by the special interest group
of British manufacturers, Britain abandoned free trade and
introduced tariffs on manufactured goods in 1932. Food
and British Empire imports were excluded. The tariff for
steel reached 50 per cent in 1935. Britain hoped to offset
the effects of increasing trade barriers and shrinking world
trade by agreeing Imperial Preferences within the Empire.
The Ottawa Conference of 1932 only achieved limited
results, as Britain insisted on protecting its farmers (the
entire Conference was Keynesian in its outlook: it declared
the gold standard had failed, and advocated increasing the
money supply and increasing government spending).

When the colonial era ended, Imperial Preference became
Commonwealth Preference. It declined: Commonwealth
countries bargained hard for every concession. Britain's
entry into the Common Market effectively ended the system.
New Zealand now had to pay the higher Common Market
duties to enter the British market.

Both the advocates of Imperial Preference and the opponents claimed to be in favour of free trade. The former
wanted free trade with the Empire, the latter with the world.
Today advocates of the European Union point at free trade
within Europe, whereas those opposing the EU aim for free

trade with the world. Advocates of trading blocs persistently fail to appreciate that the advantage of free trade within the bloc is often offset by the economic cost of the bloc's protectionist policies towards third countries.

‡

3. THE REFORMS UNDER THE FOURTH LABOUR GOVERNMENT (1984–1990)

Roger Douglas had been arguing for economic reforms from the early 1980s onwards, though he only switched to a radical pro-free market position in 1983. Given his background – one grandfather, his father and his brother were all Labour Party Members of Parliament, and firmly rooted in the trade union movement – it was certainly an exceptional change.

As a Labour Party Minister he had been highly interventionist between 1972 and 1975. In his 1980 book *There's Got to Be a Better Way*, he argued against Prime Minister Robert Muldoon's (National Party) tinkering with the economy to the advantage of vested interests. In fact, the book hinted in equal measure to the Rogernomics of the mid-1980s and to the remnants of interventionism; for example, he advocated a scheme for country-wide carpet companies. Labour leader Bill Rowling saw the book as an attack on Labour policy and demoted Douglas from the front bench. Instead of being a party that promised anything to get elected, Douglas wanted Labour policies which reflected reality. His persistent and open disagreement with Rowling made him look like a maverick in the eyes of the political class.

After Labour's 1981 defeat Douglas's views became more popular. One fellow Member of Parliament, Mike Moore, said that Labour was seen as a party which rewarded the lazy. Fortunately for Douglas, Rowling was deposed as Labour leader by David Lange in 1983. David Lange put Douglas in charge of Labour's economic policy.

Prime Minister Muldoon has received a lot of bad press over the years. When he was first appointed to the finance portfolio in the late 1960s, he was seen as a radical. As is so often the case with politicians, his reforming zeal waned when ambition called for moderation. In 1979 he opened up foreign exchange dealings and inland freight restrictions favouring the state railways were dropped. Trade with Australia was freed. After talking about it for forty years and after numerous last-minute withdrawals, the National Government repealed compulsory union membership. But his reforms remained too hesitant – and later, when Ruth Richardson tried to advance further reform – he opposed them.

Douglas had assembled a group of policy makers from the Treasury, think tanks and politicians around him. When the Treasury issued 'Economic Management', a briefing paper for the incoming government, it closely resembled Douglas's radical paper. He wanted to end New Zealand's problematic consensus model, whereby special interest groups participated in policy making, and replace it with market forces to revive the economy.

Labour did not use Douglas's Economic Policy Package for its election campaign. Rowling and others had issued an alternative paper, which urged Keynesian fiscal and monetary policy. It stated that the state in consultation with social partners was better equipped than the private sector to steer development. A compromise was drawn up which was so vague that it often had two meanings. For example, it promised both cuts in protectionism and the set-up of a state investment fund. It didn't satisfy either side but it became party policy when Muldoon called a snap election. The proposal of devaluation was not mentioned at all, out of fear that speculators would take money out of the country beforehand. When Labour won the election, the manifesto's vague parts were interpreted by those in charge of the economic leavers.

Prime Minister David Lange appointed three reformers in essential posts. They became known as The Troika: Roger Douglas became Minister of Finance, Richard Prebble, the most right-wing of the three (although in an earlier life in opposition he had advocated government intervention in transport), became Minister of Transport and Associate Minister of Finance, and the unassuming David Caygill, a Monetarist who, unlike the other two, had a degree in economics, became Minister of Trade and Industry. Economic commentator Brian Easton observed that previous Trade and Industry Ministers always had their anteroom filled with those who wanted hand-outs, but that 'Caygill's soon became empty because he refused to offer lobbyists any special concessions.' There was a general acceptance that radical reforms needed to take place, and many other senior politicians helped the Troika succeed. One example was Stan Rodger, Minister of Labour. He became known as 'Sideline Stan' because he systematically refused to intervene in labour disputes.

The first of Douglas's proposals was more or less forced upon the outgoing and incoming government. As soon as the election was called, speculators started buying foreign currency, causing a currency crisis. Even though the devaluation was not official Labour Party policy, during the election Muldoon had obtained a copy of Douglas's Economic Policy Package and distributed it to the media. One day after the election, the Reserve Bank suspended trading in foreign currency. The government had to act fast. Outgoing Prime Minister Robert Muldoon almost caused a constitutional crisis when he initially refused to devaluate when the newly elected government asked to do so. Two days after the election, but before the new Labour government was sworn in, Muldoon buckled and the New Zealand dollar was devalued by 20 per cent. This decisive action improved Douglas's standing: economic measures were called for, and Douglas had thought them through.

Douglas's 1984 Budget owed almost nothing to the Labour Manifesto – and it is an open question whether Labour would have been elected if it had spelled it out. The introduction of a consumption tax (GST) and the floating of the Kiwi dollar had not been in the manifesto. Douglas denied that this made his Budget right-wing – he said that his budget remained true to the original aims of the Labour Party, and that only the methods to achieve those aims had changed. He said that he preferred the Treasury's advice to the Labour Party manifesto as the former was in the interest of the country as a whole without party-political considerations or ideology.

The New Zealand reforms were comprehensive and offer numerous benchmarks for wannabe reformers elsewhere. While the first steps towards reform were taken by Douglas, the subsequent National Party government expanded and intensified the reforms between 1990 and 1999. The Labour and National governments after 1999 did not. The best-known reforms are the trade liberalisation, the privatisations and the removal of all subsidies to industry. But there were many more: the flattening and lowering of taxes; the introduction of private sector methods and efficiency in government departments; the contractualisation of employment agreements and many more. First place must go to the marketisation of agriculture; New Zealand was the pioneer in abandoning protectionism unilaterally.

Before the reforms, taxes used to be high and complicated. The high tax rates incentivised avoidance and evasion, caused the misallocation of capital towards tax shelters instead of towards production, and disincentivised work and businessmanship. Income taxes were simplified, flattened and lowered in 1984. The five tax brackets were reduced to three. The highest tax bracket of 66 per cent was effectively halved. A number of deductions were abolished. Despite the lowering of the tax rates, tax revenue started to increase:

from an average of 30 per cent to 33.2 per cent of GDP. There was a wholesale sales tax with rates differing from low to 50 per cent for confused reasons; a raft of special interest groups had over the years been successful in influencing policy to favour their products. This was replaced by a new sales tax on all goods except financial services at 10 per cent (today 15 per cent). The simplification and lowering of taxes reduced distortions as well as compliance and collection costs. Corporation tax was reduced from 48 to 33 per cent (28 per cent today). The public sector was made more accountable. Departments are now headed by Chief Executives on term contracts with pay based on performance. They can hire, fire and promote staff. Departments manage their own finances and contract with government ministers to achieve specific measurable results instead of vague political goals. The departments have great autonomy in deciding how to achieve the outcomes and can, for example, outsource services to the private sector. If they obtain services from other departments, they are invoiced and have to pay for it. Increasingly, market prices were charged for public services (e.g. market rent for state housing). Public sector accounting now include amounts owed but unpaid, such as pension liabilities. This gives a fairer view of the public sector's finances.

When Douglas came to power in New Zealand, the state companies provided mediocre services and were a drain on public finances (the state coal companies had made a loss in each of the previous twenty years). The state owned the only domestic airline, the largest bank and several quasi-banks, the only telecommunications company, the only railway, an international shipping line, the dominant coal producer, the Post Office and many others. The state companies were transformed into State-Owned Enterprises (SOEs), which operated like private companies. They would not be bailed out by the state, but they were allowed to borrow. A board of directors was answerable to the Minister for State-Owned Enterprises, who was the sole shareholder. The companies' performance improved. When the Shipping Corporation went nearly bankrupt its directors reflagged the ships to Hong Kong and gave the crew four hours to accept internationally competitive levels of staffing or face being replaced by Filipinos. The company recovered its profitability and was later sold. In three years, Telecom reduced its tariffs by between 20 and 30 per cent and increased profits threefold. Railways cut freight rates by 50 per cent and made the first profit in six years. Monopolies were abolished by law and all companies became subject to light-touch regulation to encourage competition. All along, corporatisation was seen as a precursor to privatisation.

From 1987 many SOEs were fully privatised and freed from political interference. Both the Bank of New Zealand and Petrocorp, a petroleum exploitation company, were eventually sold to the private sector. All the shares in New Zealand Steel were sold. The Treasury was helpful again, with 'Government Management', its briefing after the 1987 elections, strongly arguing in favour of privatisations. Politicians would no longer have to 'pick winners' and be held responsible for their inevitable failure; the market, rather than politicians, would steer investment decision; the poor growth of state companies was seen as a direct result of managers seeking subsidies instead of profitability by following market signals; the state would no longer have to subsidise the privatised companies and the private sector would achieve the public objectives at a cheaper price.

By mid-1995, the Labour and subsequent National governments had privatised twenty-seven companies. As the companies were deemed to be the property of the taxpayers, they were sold to the highest bidder, with no preference for any foreign or domestic buyer. Air New Zealand was only privatised after the domestic skies had been deregulated. New Zealand's ports were put into the hands of local authorities, headed by commercial boards. The Waterfront Industry Commission had previously employed all port staff. A productivity agreement had remunerated workers on the basis of tonnage handled; this discouraged them from investing in more efficient cargo-handling equipment. Now the WIC was abolished. The same day, port companies made 50 per cent of the workers redundant and only kept those they needed. Ship turn-around times dropped dramatically: for example, in Tauranga it used to take twelve days and forty-four workers to load 27,000 cubic metres of logs onto a vessel; after the changes it took thirty hours and four men.

Most subsidies to New Zealand's industry were reduced or removed. Foreign investors obtained equal access to New Zealand's markets. Producers became more productive and focused on what they could sell on the world market instead of relying on subsidies. Internal monopolies and competition-reducing restrictions were prohibited: licences in trades and professions, quantitative restrictions (e.g. for taxis), restrictions on road transport to protect the railways, the prohibition of private sector electricity generation and private courier services, shop trading hours – all were abolished.

In the mid-1980s, New Zealand's inflation stood at 15 per cent, one of the highest levels in the OECD. In the past, the government had manipulated the money supply to increase state spending to win elections. Douglas was determined to make the currency 'Muldoon-proof'. The Reserve Bank was made quasi-independent. A contract tabled in Parliament set out the objectives, and the bank was left free in its choice of methods to achieve the objectives set by Parliament. Monetary policy cannot be used to increase employment levels or economic growth, and inflation cannot be above 2 per cent. The Act was passed unanimously by government and opposition. Between 1991 and 2000, inflation was between 0 and 2 per cent. The fact that the money supply cannot be manipulated for political goals such as employment and growth is interesting. It is not just a matter of 'it must not be done' but also of 'it cannot be done'. Indeed, no government has ever managed to increase growth or employment sustainably by increasing the money supply – it can be achieved in the short term, but in the long term the bubble always bursts.

Overregulation and overprotection meant that there was only a stale offering in financial services by just one state bank and three foreign banks. Competition was thrown wide open, with serious deregulation and a return to the vigours imposed by a free market. All controls on credit, dividends, wages, prices and investment abroad were removed. Licensing for banks to be allowed to deal in foreign currencies was abolished. How much banks could lend was no longer controlled by government. They were no longer forced to hold specific levels of government securities. Supervision of banking prudence was changed from secretive reporting to the Reserve Bank to quarterly public disclosure statements. Instead of government-prescribed internal control mechanisms, directors must attest that the internal controls are appropriate. There are now twenty-one registered banks in New Zealand.

Steps towards free trade were made even before the reforms. The 1983 free trade agreement with Australia brought complete free trade and free flows of investment. Subsequently, quantitative import restrictions were abolished generally, and import duties either removed or significantly reduced. Most of this was done unilaterally. It is worthwhile considering unilateral free trade. New Zealand politicians often said that they had to do it unilaterally, as they were too small to request equal treatment from other countries (this is not entirely correct; many small countries in the world have free trade agreements with large ones; e.g. Iceland with China). Professor Razeen Sally has observed that, since the Second World War, there has been an international presumption that agreements between several countries are best steered by international organisations. This would reduce conflict. Trade liberalisation is now seen by many as only achievable by an 'outside' international body's endless haggling rounds with a large number of countries. It favours international regulation and intervention over a rule telling states not to intervene and to allow individuals to trade freely. There are compelling reasons for countries to bring about free trade unilaterally. For starters, it's much quicker than waiting until the world agrees in an international trade round. A country benefits greatly from letting imports come in freely: cheap imports allow the reallocation of resources which would otherwise have been spent on expensive domestic production towards more productive sectors; skills and technology are acquired; cheap components help produce cheaper goods for export. A country on its own can tailor its policy along the specific characteristics of its case, instead of using an international 'one size fits all' approach. When they see the benefits, other countries are likely to follow the example. According to the World Bank, between 1983 and 2003, around 65 per cent of the developing world's trade liberalisation came about unilaterally, whereas 35 per cent was the result of international agreements. Britain unilaterally freed its trade in the second half of the nineteenth century – its economy boomed. Ludwig Erhard did the same in Germany after the war.

Among New Zealand's many reforms, one stands out. New Zealand is the only country in the world which has unilaterally abolished all subsidies and all protective measures for its farmers. Most developed countries have been intensively subsidising their farmers for the last fifty or sixty years. In Europe, protectionism was widespread in the Middle Ages.

England improved on it with the Corn Laws. In the United States it started in earnest under the New Deal, quickly followed by many other developed countries. The subsidising of Europe's Common Agricultural Policy was one of the reasons why the European Common Market, precursor to the European Union, was set up in the first place (President De Gaulle needed the farmers' votes – at the time they constituted 25 per cent of France's population). In developed countries, protection of farmers has led to waste (too much food produced), environmental damage (intensive farming through fertilisers and pesticides), high taxes (to fund subsidies to farmers) and artificially high prices for consumers (as cheaper food imports are blocked). Subsidies distort price signals which would otherwise inform producers of what the market requires: consumer preference is replaced by political preference. As the protection guarantees their income, farmers have no incentive to innovate or to become more productive. For developing countries, protectionism means poverty, as their food is blocked from developed countries' markets. Developed countries dump their food surpluses below production cost on poor countries' markets, thereby destroying local farming. In a perverse guilt-trip, developed countries then grant development aid to those same countries. The development aid is sometimes used to buy food surpluses from developed countries. Development aid could be slashed if rich countries stopped subsidising their own agriculture. It seems as if, under a subsidy system, everybody loses out except the subsidised farmers. Or do they? When New Zealand abolished protectionism, its farmers did just fine.

Traditionally, agriculture was New Zealand's main export product. Through much of the nineteenth and twentieth centuries, New Zealand was Great Britain's agricultural hinterland, supplying grain and wool. Later, after the development of refrigerated shipping in the 1880s, meat and dairy products were sold to Britain and other parts of the British Empire. Imperial Preference protected the British Empire from outside competition. Disruptions of New Zealand's agricultural trade during the First and Second World War led to more protectionism. After the Second World War, agriculture continued to thrive. In 1964, for example, 94 per cent of New Zealand's butter and 87 per cent of its cheese was exported to the UK. From the 1970s onwards, decline set in. Islands producing cheap phosphate became independent; the oil crisis of 1973 increased transport costs; and when Britain joined the European Common Market in 1973, New Zealand lost the preferential access to British markets which it had enjoyed under the system of Commonwealth Preference.

Quite a few economists have said that the oil crisis, the Common Market and cheap phosphate were merely scapegoats for the rot created by decades of disastrous state interventionism. As an important electoral constituency, farmers received subsidies to increase production through fertilisers, and tax breaks to increase herds. This glut in supply decreased prices, which in turn increased the political pressure to subsidise farmers. Farmers received low-interest loans, price supports, weed eradication subsidies, training and disaster relief. Almost half of sheep- and beef-farmers' gross income came from subsidies. The cost of all the subsidies put pressures on the government's budget, thereby increasing inflation.

Prolonged inflation cripples any nation. Farmers had great difficulty doing business in a climate of rapidly devaluing currency, and found it difficult to sell their produce abroad. In 1982, the main farmers' organisation, the Federated Farmers of New Zealand, submitted a paper urging the government to tackle inflation rather than compensating them for the effects of it. They understood that the root cause of inflation was budget deficits – partly incurred by doling out subsidies. Prime Minister Muldoon rejected their demands, but the debate was thrown wide open. The subsidies caused the most resentment: taxpayers derided the farmers for being subsidy-grabbers; subsidies to increase production on marginal land caused ecological harm; subsidies appeared to benefit suppliers and related enterprises rather than the farmers; and the subsidies and the cheap loans caused a spike in land prices. Consumers resented the higher food prices in the shops. Central command failed miserably: ailing state policies caused mistakes such as paying to rip out hedgerows and paying to put them back in a decade later, while those who had preserved the land obtained nothing.

The cost of subsidies had spiralled out of control. Prime Minister Robert Muldoon had introduced Supplementary Minimum Prices in 1978. Government planners stated that fluctuating market prices held agriculture back. The government guaranteed a minimum price for agricultural produce, irrespective of rise or fall in demand or supply. The minimum prices were set to safeguard an adequate return, allowing farmers enough room for living, operating, and development expenditure. Initially, the total subsidy was not high as the guaranteed prices were set below the high world food prices. But in 1980/81, world market prices for wool, meat and dairy dropped; and the government set prices above market rates. The total subsidy rose to NZ$1 billion, or one-third of the government's deficit. The Reserve Bank basically printed the money to pay for it, and inflation went up. The banks were happy to lend to farmers, thereby further increasing the money supply and inflation. After the guaranteed prices were introduced, production increased by 10 per cent in four years. Unlike the National Party, the Labour Party didn't rely on farmers' votes; and when it came to power in 1984 it abolished about thirty production subsidies (including SMPs) and export incentives early in its term. Price controls for food were abolished.

Initially the abolition of agricultural protectionism caused hardship. Sheep farmers, who had received the highest subsidies, were hardest hit. Farmers suffered a triple whammy: apart from the withdrawal of subsidies, interest rates rose to historic highs for several years, and when the New Zealand dollar was floated it appreciated in value and made New Zealand produce more expensive abroad. The intermediary sectors of food processing, farm equipment, farm chemicals and transport all suffered. Some transitional measures were taken by the government. The bad patch lasted for about six years.

From 1990 onwards the tide turned. Food prices, land values and farm profitability indices started to rise. In fifteen years the value of agriculture grew by over 40 per cent in constant dollar terms. Agricultural production as a percentage of GDP rose. Productivity went up fivefold. In 1980 New Zealand exported agricultural produce to ten countries; by 2002, it exported to 102. It had been predicted that 8,000 farms would fail – but only about 800 did (1 per cent of the total). The numbers of traditional family farms held steady and the rural and urban population growth was similar. Farming land slightly reduced because some marginal unproductive land was allowed to return to bush. The number of people employed in agriculture fell slightly, but that was more than compensated for by a rise in rural tourism jobs. Farmers gained a new self-worth as businessmen, instead of recipients of state hand-outs. The state was no longer there to tell the farmers what to grow, and instead they started to look at what people really wanted to buy. It was a process of trial and error. New kiwi fruit varieties and vegetable crops saw the light of day. The world's wine drinkers also have to thank the abolition of all subsidies for the boom in New Zealand's wine production: in 1986, it exported 1 million litres of wine; by 2009, it was 105 million litres.

One positive side-effect which everybody profits from is

that New Zealand farmers have become ardent supporters of the abolition of farm subsidies worldwide. In 2001,
New Zealand's government assistance to agriculture (mostly
support of research and development) amounted to 1 per
cent of the agricultural output; whereas the average for
the developed world is 31 per cent. New Zealand is part
of the Cairns Group, an organisation of nineteen food-
exporting countries which campaigns against agricultural
protectionism. It was set up as a response to the spiralling
subsidies of the Europe's Common Agricultural Policy and
America's Export Enhancement Program. Today, the cost
of the European Union's Common Agricultural Policy is 42
per cent of its total budget, or £42 billion. Countries like
the United Kingdom contribute £4.7 billion directly to the
budget, but increased food prices, increased social welfare
costs, the regulatory burden, and duplication of food safety
agencies mean that the real cost is £10.3 billion, or £398
per household.

The privatisations, increased efficiency in the departments, and the abolition of subsidies helped to reduce the
deficit. Tax rate cuts were offset by the abolition of most
avoidance methods. The government's deficit, which had
been 7 per cent of GDP in 1983/84, went down to 1.3 per
cent in 1989/1990. Total government spending went up to
41 per cent of GDP because of increased spending on welfare
payments, health and education.

The transformation did not immediately yield positive
results. Just as with agricultural reform, the economy as a
whole took some time to adapt. The over-subsidised and
overprotected industries lost their privileges and had to
swim or sink – about 76,000 manufacturing jobs were lost
between 1987 and 1992. For a while, below-inflation wage
increases were common. Between 1984 and 1993, inflation
averaged 9 per cent per year, New Zealand's credit rating
dropped twice and foreign debt quadrupled. Between 1986

and 1993, the unemployment rate rose from 3.6 per cent to 11 per cent. Poverty increased marginally in the 1980s, if one uses the Benefit Datum Line method to measure it (a method which is disputed). The small increase was well below the increase in poverty which had been foretold by the critics of reforms.

But people realised that the reforms were essential, and that the growing pains would lead to a better future with more jobs and less state dependency. If the electorate may have been largely in the dark about its economic plans when it elected Labour in 1984, there was no such doubt at the 1987 general election. By then, the privatisations and the removals of subsidies and protectionist tariffs were widely known. Support for the measures had built up, including among the self-employed and businessmen. Douglas personally had received large amounts of money from business for his campaign. Prime Minister Lange's official election campaign was lacklustre, and one can say that the election victory was largely Douglas's success. As the economic figures looked weak, the campaign itself – the ideological defence of what was being attempted – must be credited for Labour's election victory. The total number of seats each party obtained showed only slight changes.

After the 1987 general election, Douglas continued the reforms, even though Lange tried to stop him. The Labour Party had had enough of the reforms. Douglas's radical ideas had put him on a collision course with Lange. When Douglas suggested selling off more state assets, introducing a guaranteed minimum family income, increasing charging for public health and education, and introducing a flat tax of 15 per cent, Lange complained that 'it was an unaccustomed addition to the burdens of office to have the finance minister take leave of his senses'. Lange declared that the bulk of the reforms were over; Douglas promised more. At the end of 1988, Douglas was replaced as Minister of Finance. The

Labour government and subsequent governments largely kept the reforms in place: free open markets with little protectionism, sound monetary and fiscal policies, few interventions in the economy and a deregulated financial sector.

‡

What happened to Roger Douglas?
The remarkable Roger Douglas remained a Labour Member of Parliament from 1969 to 1990. He realised that neither the Labour Party nor the National Party represented his ideals of freedom. He founded the ACT Party (Association of Consumers and Taxpayers) together with Derek Quigley, himself an ex-Cabinet member who clashed with his own National Party. The party obtained eight seats in the 1996 election. ACT is a pro-free market party, which advocates Rogernomics: individual responsibility, a prosperous economy through smaller government, and individual liberty. After the 2008 and 2011 elections, ACT joined the government, although it only obtained one seat in 2011.

‡

4. THE REFORMS UNDER THE FOURTH NATIONAL GOVERNMENT (1990-1999)

When the National Party took office in 1990, it continued the reforms for a number of years. It reduced excessive welfare payments, reformed public housing, abolished inheritance tax, brought public spending down, introduced fiscal discipline, reformed the health system and attempted to reform the labour market. The pace was kept by another formidable Minister of Finance, Ruth Richardson. Her policies were dubbed 'Ruthanasia' by those opposed to change; but in fact she revived the economy, rather than killing it.

While in opposition, she had actively been involved in the Reserve Bank Act of 1989 which had introduced institutional autonomy on the central bank and which had introduced the single focus on maintaining price stability. During the 1990 election campaign she persistently quipped that a strict monetary policy needed mates to succeed – in particular, fiscal discipline and labour market flexibility. Within six weeks of taking office in 1990, Ruth Richardson initiated a major public expenditure reduction round and sought far-reaching deregulation of the labour market.

Just as the Labour Party had found it easy to reform agriculture as it didn't rely on farmers' votes, so the National Party had no qualms about reforming the labour market as it didn't need trade unionists' votes. The general intention was good: the old Labour regime, which dated back to 1894, by which the heavy hand of government tried to protect employees and reduce industrial conflicts through the protection and regulation of trade unions, was replaced by contractual freedom between employer and employee. Sadly, the legislation fell short of introducing a free market for labour as it also introduced minimum standards and maintained separate labour law as distinct from general contract law.

Trade unions lost a number of rights. The trade union monopoly on workers' representation was abolished. Henceforward, an employment contract could be either individual or collective; if it was collective, the employee could choose his bargaining agent freely. By 2003, only 15 per cent of the workforce was on collective contracts negotiated by unions. The government stopped intervening in major labour disputes: procedures for labour disputes were available, but contract parties could agree other methods. Working days lost through strikes declined dramatically. Rises in productivity did not come at the expense of employment: between 1991 and 1996, unemployment fell rapidly and the numbers of people employed increased by an average of 3.3 per cent annually.

Ruth Richardson's fiscal strategy was first to take the axe to public spending in real terms, followed by legislation to preserve the continuation of fiscal discipline in the future. She proudly recalls how she secured fiscal surpluses for the first time in her adult lifetime, and how she brought New Zealand back from the brink of fiscal ruination. The economic success of the measures she introduced was such that subsequent governments were unable to reverse them.

A lawyer by training, Ruth Richardson proposed to impose fiscal discipline by law. She had to fight hard with the Treasury to convince them that a set of fiscal rules was appropriate and that they would have real utility. She first ambushed the Treasury with the idea, followed by her colleagues, who, while they indulged her, had no real conception of how important a policy innovation this would prove to be in years to come.

A fiscal responsibility act enshrines quantitative fiscal rules in law. Governments have to publish long-term economic aims. This stimulates debate and forces the government to be responsible. Many countries have introduced a fiscal responsibility law to prevent a reversal of improvements in the fiscal position. Countries which currently have a fiscal responsibility law include Australia, the United Kingdom, Mexico, Hungary, Brazil, Argentina, India and Pakistan.

New Zealand's Fiscal Responsibility Act 1994 tried to make sure that the public liabilities could not accumulate undiscussed at the expense of the future generations. Basic principles included maintaining a prudent level of debt and maintaining net worth (gross debt minus government financial assets) in order to absorb shocks and to provide stable and predictable tax rates in the future. The regular publication of the projected budgetary position allowed society to focus on the long term. Government spending as percentage of GDP fell by a quarter, fiscal surpluses were achieved, and debt levels fell dramatically.

Instead of having to accept what the state provides, the poor were increasingly given help in cash, to allow the recipients to make their own choices. The belief held by many welfare bureaucracies that the poor are too stupid to make their own decisions had not spread to New Zealand. The subsidised housing and subsidised mortgages low-income people received were replaced by cash grants or housing vouchers, irrespective of whether they lived in state-owned housing or rented or bought privately. This offered greater choice for low-income people. Notwithstanding the allegation that 'New Zealand abolished the welfare state', spending on income support as a percentage of GDP increased.

Another new policy was the conversion of hospitals into private businesses. Instead of health services being commissioned by the state, healthcare began to be funded by contributions and private insurance. The vested interests of health professionals, voluntary sector workers and intellectuals mounted a formidable campaign. One group which opposed the reforms, the Coalition for Public Health, was funded by doctors and trade unions. Nevertheless, the state-provided healthcare purchaser and healthcare provider were separated. Four public health authorities now buy health services. Any public or private sector provider, including the government-owned hospitals, can tender for the contracts. Hospital outpatients pay similar rates to patients of private GPs. Prescriptions are part-charged, though high-frequency users and low-income users (half the population) pay $3 ($5 from 2012), and the charge is waived for them after a number of prescriptions. Charges are made for visits to general practitioners and family doctors – the fee is set by the GP and can differ from place to place. Again, high-frequency users and low-income users pay less. The health reforms were implemented half-heartedly and were easily undone by the Labour government afterwards. The government started to lose its stomach for reforms at the end of 1991. Prime Minister Jim Bolger limited Richardson's opportunities for changing policy unilaterally.

At the time of the 1993 general election, New Zealand also held a referendum about the voting system. A majority voted in favour of replacing the first-past-the-post system with the German Mixed Member Proportional system. The system was first applied in the 1996 election; since then, neither National nor Labour Party have been able to secure an absolute majority and have always had to form coalitions. One of the reasons for introducing electoral reform was to fetter future policy reform adventurers such as Roger Douglas and Ruth Richardson. Bolger and his crew reverted to type and broke with market radicalism in favour of the National Party's more traditional managerialism. The National Party lost seats, but scraped back into power. Bolger announced that reform was over and that it was time for a quieter life. He offered Richardson a lesser role. She resigned from Cabinet but stayed on as Chairman of the Finance and Expenditure Committee long enough to see the Fiscal Responsibility Act passed into law in 1994. The next day she resigned from Parliament, considering that her policy work was done.

Once the growing pains of the dramatic economic reforms passed, New Zealand's economic recovery was impressive. Government spending fell from 40 per cent of GDP in the late 1980s to below 31 per cent by 2001, and large fiscal surpluses were achieved. A concerted effort was made to reduce the size of the debt while other countries continued to increase their debt levels to produce instantaneous growth at the expense of future growth. The net government debt fell from 52 per cent of GDP in 1992 to 33 per cent in 1996.

Mainly as a result of the simplification and reduction of taxes, prolonged economic growth was achieved. When the

National Party was in power in the 1990s, the increased economic growth produced such budget surpluses that it was possible to increase people's disposable income by between 6 and 8 per cent through tax cuts in 1996 and 1997.

New Zealand is ranked fourth in the world in the 2012 Index of Economic Freedom.

Real GDP growth	NZ	Australia	USA	Japan
1990	0.4	4.4	3.2	4.3
1991	0.1	0.4	0.9	6
1992	–1.3	–0.6	0.7	2.2
1993	1.1	3.7	3.6	1.1
1994	6.4	3.9	2.9	–1
1995	5.2	4.4	4	0.3
1996	4.5	3.9	2.3	2.7
1997	3.7	3.5	4.3	2.7
1998	1.8	4.8	4.5	0.1
1999	0.7	4.9	4.5	–1.5
2000	5.2	3.9	4.6	0.5

5. WHY DID IT SUCCEED?

Over a period of fifteen years, from the Labour government of 1984 onwards, and throughout the subsequent National government, New Zealand was transformed. State-led development was abandoned and replaced by people-led development. Inflation disappeared; New Zealand became part of the world economy. Old-fashioned industries were replaced by new ones, including an expanded financial and services sector (the latter created a new 'café society'). Foreign investment flooded into the country.

New Zealand is an example of dramatic economic reforms carried out by democratically elected governments.

What the Labour government started was completed by the National government. Powerful industrial, agricultural and trade union interests, which up 'til then had profited from government-sponsored privileges, were tackled head-on. When governments changed, the basic reforms remained in place. Why did this revolution succeed?

Speed and the all-encompassing nature of the reforms taken together have sometimes been called the 'Big Bang Approach'. In his book *Unfinished Business*, Douglas said that clear goals and speed were essential to prevent interest groups from dragging you down. Or, phrased differently: 'Opponents' fire is much less accurate if they have to shoot at a rapidly moving target.' Another parallel was that of the blitzkrieg. As one author put it: 'In each case the lightning strike involved a policy goal radically different from the existing configuration, to be attained in a short period, following a surprise announcement.' In any event, Douglas needed to be fast, as it was by no means certain that Labour would win a second term. The reformers rationalised the speed further by pointing out that New Zealand had to catch up fast as it hadn't recovered from Britain's abandonment of Commonwealth Preference more than a decade earlier.

The all-encompassing nature of the reforms was easy to defend: wasn't a comprehensive solution needed for comprehensive economic problems? People lost out from some reforms; and gained from others: they took a wide view, and knew that they were all in it together, rather than some being targeted and others being privileged. Douglas's approach was a radically different one from Muldoon's. Muldoon would only change things if it was Pareto efficient: that is, if at least one person was better off without anyone else being worse off. He therefore changed little and his government was perceived as sclerotic. Some groups disadvantaged by early reforms later supported other reforms. When farmers and manufacturers lost their subsidies, they asked for state spending cuts to bring down interest rates and the exchange rate.

In his book Douglas identified the different aspects of his 'blitzkriegs':

- Abolishing legal privileges favouring special interest groups is essential to reform.
- If there is a solution which works in the medium term, go for it without hesitation: only this will satisfy the people.
- Do not reform step-by-step: determine the goal and reach it in quantum leaps.
- Prior to reform, consensus with interest groups is rarely reached; support will follow when the reforms show success.
- Uncertainty endangers reform; the faster you go, the shorter the uncertainty.
- Don't stop reform until you have completed it; the opponents won't be able to cope as they are too busy.

It is open to question whether the Labour Party would have obtained a parliamentary majority in 1984 if the public had been fully aware of what Douglas intended. The November 1984 Budget was a complete departure from previous Labour Party 'consensus politics'. It owed virtually nothing to Labour's vague election manifesto. In fact, Labour's manifesto had been incredibly vague. Douglas said that the policies were based on views which he had held from as early as 1980, and from fresh papers, including the Treasury's Economic Management Briefing to the incoming government. He also said that there had simply not been time enough to spell it all out to the electorate. The more astute politics watchers probably knew what was coming, as Douglas's views were widely known and published. But whether the public at large was aware when they cast their votes in the privacy of the polling booth is an open question.

Douglas defended some form of secrecy. In a speech to the Mont Pelerin Society in 1989, he stated that obtaining political support before the reforms are implemented compromises their quality, allows opposition to grow, and therefore adds to their cost. He preferred consensus to develop progressively after the implementation, when the benefits to the public are being delivered. This is precisely what happened: there was little public support to reverse the reforms. While I was writing this book I was surprised to find that the New Zealand farmers appreciate their subsidy-free status. They also campaign for the abolition of subsidies elsewhere.

The main reason why the reforms were not reversed was the undoubted economic success they had. Or, as the then Governor of the Reserve Bank of New Zealand Donald T. Brash put it in 1996:

The best security against the reversal of recent reforms is to continue with reforms in order to encourage growth and employment, and to provide increasing opportunities for the unskilled and those on low incomes to raise both their skills and their incomes ... it is actual growth and prosperity, not ideas about the market, that maintain popular support for a free society.

EIGHT

SINGAPORE

I. SINGAPORE'S DEMISE ANNOUNCED

For Singapore, creating wealth was a choice between life and death. The 640 sq. km island swamp gained independence from Britain in 1959. In 1963 it merged with Malaya, Sabah and Sarawak to form Malaysia. Race riots ensued, and Singapore was pushed out of the union in 1965. After Stamford Raffles set up a trading post along the 120 fishermen living there in 1819, Singapore had flourished as an entrepôt for the surrounding area. From its harbour, commodities such as tin, rubber, petroleum, pineapples and palm oil were dispersed to all parts of the globe. This trade was now seriously threatened by its hostile neighbours.

Singapore was based on laissez-faire: its economy was steered by the millions of decisions taken by individuals, rather than government diktat. The commodities trade stopped when Malaysia decided that it would use its own ports. Inspired by racial enmity and fear that its outer provinces would want to join Malaysia, Indonesia imposed an economic boycott on Malaysia and Singapore in 1962. Singapore's demise was foretold worldwide. As if the foreign troubles weren't sufficient, the city state also fought pitched battles with Communist agitators on its streets. Singapore's leaders feared that they would lose power to the Communists if prosperity wasn't produced soon. Both the economic and security situation deteriorated further when Britain announced that it would withdraw from East of Suez by 1971 (it needed the money to pay for welfare and other vote-winning policies). The British bases were responsible for an estimated 20 per cent of Singapore's GDP, and 70,000 jobs. With no natural resources, no productive companies, a largely illiterate population, poor infrastructure and the loss of its entrepôt trade, Singapore now needed to pay for an army, create jobs for the 14 per cent of unemployed workers and the streams of new immigrants, and create prosperity to keep its 2 million population out of the clutches of Communist, racial and religious fanatics. In 1973 Singapore suffered more losses as a result of the oil crisis which quadrupled the oil price.

Britain offered aid to offset the loss from closing their military bases, but the British-educated leaders of Singapore were determined that their country would not be lamed by a British-style welfare state. In his memoir *From Third World to First*, Lee Kuan Yew, who was Singapore's Prime Minister for more than thirty years, recounts how he had visited Malta around that time. He had been shocked to find that its dockworkers, on full pay but unemployed because of the closure of the Suez Canal as a result of the Six-Day War, were playing water polo in the dry dock which they had filled with water. He expressed amazement that they seemed to be quite happy to vegetate on continued British charity. He told the Singaporeans that they shouldn't expect the world to bail them out financially like common beggars.

Urgent action was required if Singapore was to survive, and instead of waiting for its budding businessmen to jump into action, the government ditched non-interference. Growth became the top priority of all government action. Singapore, often dubbed Singapore Inc., became a highly effective engine to create wealth. Lee Kuan Yew decided on a two-pronged strategy. If the Asian neighbours refused to do business with it, then he would focus on trade with America, Europe and Japan instead. Secondly, he would create a First World oasis in a Third World region. In order to inspire confidence to attract investment, Singapore would not only have to unlearn its 'Third World Ways' as reflected in manners, outwards appearance and corruption, but also introduce First World governance and institutions.

They must have done something right. When Lee Kuan Yew took power in 1959, Singapore's GDP per capita was US$400. By 2010 it was US$56,522 (Indonesia US$4,394, Malaysia US$14,670, United States US$47,284). Here is how they did it.

2. A FIRST WORLD OASIS

Rule of law – security – certainty of property – democracy
When it was pushed out of Malaysia, Singapore and its leaders could have perished for four reasons: its racial and religious differences, the Communists, foreign invasion or economic decline. Singapore's leaders realised early on that only the rule of law and the creation of wealth could protect against all four calamities.

Singapore was multi-ethnic with a majority of ethnically Chinese, as well as Malayans and Indians; and multi-religious with Buddhists, Christians, Muslims, Taoists, Baha I, Jains, Jews and Zoroastrians. There were race riots between Malayans and Chinese. There was constant Indonesian and Malaysian agitation: while Indonesia occasionally threatened invasion, Malaysia merely announced it would cut off the water supply. Both attempted to exploit Singapore's racial differences for their own purposes. Singapore's leaders decided to build a Singaporean identity to transcend its differences. They knew that the new state could not be dominated by any one of the communities. They were determined to build a multiracial society that would give equality to all citizens, regardless of race, language or religion. Whether they were 100 per cent successful is debatable, but the leaders tried to be impartial as they were constantly at risk of being thrown out.

One way of creating a Singaporean identity, while also protecting against foreign threats, was to build up an army after the British left. At the time, Singapore had 1,000 soldiers. With 2 million citizens, Singapore required more than a small army. An entirely professional army was unaffordable, so military service for all men was introduced. It became a rite of passage: men learned to live together, and their different religious requirements were respected. This is not the place to discuss the pros and cons of drafts – when a US general disparaged a professional army as 'mercenaries', Milton Friedman famously likened the draft to slavery. The key thing to remember is that nobody would have invested in Singapore if it had been under constant threat of internal or international upheaval.

As a former British colony, Singapore's legal system was based on British common law. Unlike other newly independent states, Singapore didn't set about changing place names or pulling down statues of imperialists: it did not want to upset potential investors. Early on, its leaders decided to curtail a number of freedoms. They said it was necessary to provide security and prosperity; detractors claimed it was done to stay in power. For example, when the Malayan National Liberation Front waged a violent terror campaign in the 1970s, quite a few were detained without protection of traditional human rights. Lee Kuan Yew argued that the terrorists could not have been defeated if they had been allowed habeas corpus, as few people dared to provide evidence against them in open court. Singapore eliminated trial by jury, as it feared it would lead to religious or racial strife. Singapore never accepted the view that criminals are the victims of society. Punishments are harsh and crimes few. At 0.48 per 100,000 people, Singapore has one of the lowest homicide rates in the world.

Singapore's leaders call their political system a democracy; those on the left call it a capitalist dictatorship. It is difficult to form a clear picture, as many commentators base their views on their ideological or emotive certainties. Many political laws for which the Singapore government is criticised exist in Western countries – such as, for example, the prohibition of foreign donations for political parties, or the obligation to publish donations above a certain amount. There are multi-party elections, but opposition to and criticism of the government is made difficult in a number of ways. Again, Singapore's leaders would say this is necessary to provide harmony and prosperity and to reduce ethnic and racial strife.

Political adversaries used to be detained indefinitely under the Internal Security Act. The last time that was applied was twenty-five years ago. Now, similar aims are achieved through legal impediments and co-option of critics. The use of law to stifle dissent has been dubbed 'rule through law rather than rule of law'. Political activity is only allowed under the umbrella of a legal political party. That way, political battles are waged out in the open and can be controlled. It also removes (usually left-wing) 'grass roots support' from political parties. One man, one vote was effectively abolished to protect minorities. Group Representation Constituencies have several Members of Parliament, but at least one must be from a minority race such as Malay, Indian or other. Dissenters are 'let in at sufferance' by the ruling party. Supreme Court judges' appointments are short-term, and may be renewed – or not – at the discretion of the government. Lower Court judges can be transferred from the judiciary to the administration. The government portrays the judiciary as fair, but if one wants to debate the issue, one risks being prosecuted for contempt of court. There is extensive use of defamation, libel and contempt of court action by government figures against adversaries. Lee Kuan Yew has been called 'the most successful individual litigant in history'. As this book focuses on economics this is not the right forum to discuss the rights or wrongs of these departures from basic rules of a free and democratic society. When confronted with the choice between individual liberty and security, Singapore's leaders chose the latter, with a firm dose of self-preservation thrown in for good measure. About one fact most commentators do agree: if Singapore was a truly free democracy as in Europe or North America, its citizens would most probably vote the current leaders back in.

Foreign newspapers and magazines are subject to circulation restrictions if they discuss Singapore politics. When American *Time* Magazine published an article critical of the government of Singapore, its circulation was reduced to one-ninth of its former level. Foreign publications need to apply for an annual permit and need to deposit a substantial bond toward possible legal liabilities – so they are careful. Private satellite receivers are banned in Singapore, except for private businesses (to receive up-to-date information). The government promotes cable television, which it can control. The companies participating in cable are eager to stay in Singapore and exercise self-censorship. Internet service providers whose pages promote political or religious causes need to be licensed. They have to route traffic through proxy servers which filter out pornographic, political and religious sites. The editors of websites are accountable for every posting online, even if it is anonymous. Many Asian countries are trying to adapt the 'Singapore Model'.

It isn't just politics and media which are curtailed. Social

mores are imposed, too. The leadership believes this makes
societal and economic sense. If the population 'unlearns its
third world ways', it will be easier to attract foreign investment. Population growth is strictly controlled. 'Educated
mothers' receive incentives to have three or more children.
The fine for littering is S$300 for a first offence. A second
offender may have to clean dirty estates or beaches and
the media is invited to cover the event (I suspect this measure would be quite popular in many countries). Spitting,
jaywalking, smoking in government offices or on the MRT
trains are subject to fines, too. Gambling, except through the
state lottery, is illegal. Drug trafficking may incur the death
penalty – tourists are warned on their flight embarkation
cards. The rules which are imposed often seem draconian
to those of us with a more easy-going attitude. Most developed countries used to have similar rules imposed by social
control at some point in their history. Many countries have
introduced similar strict rules – New York's popular Mayor
Giuliani's zero-tolerance policing springs to mind.

Investors were unafraid of Singapore, as they knew their
property rights were secure. Unlike many other ex-colonies,
Singapore did not go on a confiscation spree after independence. This, and Singapore's military strength which protected
them from war loss, encouraged multinationals, particularly
American ones, to establish large and expensive operations. Within days of the October 1973 oil crisis, Singapore
declared that it would not block the export of the oil stocks
which foreign oil companies had stored in Singapore; even
though this would have guaranteed their oil supply for six
months. It chose to forgo that potential advantage in order
to keep international confidence in its government. The
strategy paid off. By the 1990s, Singapore was the world's
third largest oil refining centre in the world; the third largest
oil trading centre and a major petrochemical producer.

Population

The high population growth made labour cheaper in the 1950s and 1960s. This created a comparative advantage with other countries. In addition, it meant a greater pool of ingenuity, with the possibility of specialisation and increased productivity (as in Adam Smith's pin factory). Multinationals brought highly schooled and specialised foreign employees with them, who trained local people. When full employment was reached, the scarcity of labour was remedied by organising workers in Johor and the Indonesian island of Batam as part of a triangle of growth in 1994 (similar to Hong Kong factories expanding into Chinese Guangdong).

Low tax and responsible government

In all but two years between 1960 and 1999, Singapore enjoyed annual budget surpluses. On average, government spending was 20 per cent of GDP, as compared to 33 per cent in the G7. Income tax and corporation tax were gradually reduced, and the emphasis was shifted towards a consumption tax on goods and services of just 3 per cent. The top rate of income tax was gradually reduced from 55 per cent in 1965 to 20 per cent today, and most citizens pay no income tax whatsoever. Corporation tax went down from 40 per cent to 17 per cent in the same period. But even that is over-stating it. Many companies can negotiate an even lower rate with the tax authorities, depending upon how much business they bring in – sometimes as low as 5 per cent. There is no capital gains tax and no tax on interest. Import tariffs are 0.4 per cent.

Recent Evolution of the Corporation Tax Rate in Singapore						
1997/00	2001	2002	2003/04	2005/06	2007/09	2010–12
26 per cent	25.5 per cent	24.5 per cent	22 per cent	20 per cent	18 per cent	17 per cent

Singapore had a British-style death tax, aimed at making the rich pay. Evasion was massive, and little was raised. When the death tax was cut from 60 per cent to between 5 and 10 per cent in 1984, far more revenue came in: the rich no longer bothered to pay crafty tax experts to reduce their liability.

While many developed countries increasingly try to fleece the rich to pay for their sky-rocketing government spending and welfare bills, Singapore made a concerted effort to become a sanctuary for the world's wealthy. There is no capital gains tax and no tax on interest. There is no tax on income earned outside Singapore. Almost forty private banks now have operations in Singapore. Citigroup's headquarters for all private banking outside the United States is now in Singapore, as well as the global banking headquarters of Standard Chartered Bank of Britain. In 2001, Singapore increased its banking secrecy laws (except for anyone suspected of being involved in terrorism or smuggling). While many banks moved the handling of their private transactions to data centres in India, Singapore moved its handling back to Singapore.

Labour relations

To attract investment, Singapore had to confront the unions. In the 1950s and 1960s most of Singapore's unions had been taken over by Communists. They engaged in a never-ending series of strikes. The union practices were similar to those used in Britain: in order to stop the Communists, the colonial government came up with the bright idea of bringing in special advisers such as Jack Brazier from the British Trade Union Congress to teach the non-Communist trade unions to become more effective. They taught the Singaporeans how to squeeze employers regardless of the effect on profitability. In July 1966, then Prime Minister Lee Kuan Yew urged the workers of the Army Civil Service Union to discontinue the practices which had had such a ruinous effect on the British economy.' A few months later he told delegates of the International Labour Organisation that they should not kill the goose whose golden eggs they needed. Foreign companies were reluctant to invest, and those who did used machines rather than employing strike-happy employees. A small, privileged group of overprotected and high-salaried unionised workers effectively ruined the economic prospects of other Singaporeans.

Words alone were not enough and the government decided to make an example out of one particular case. Thirteen years before Margaret Thatcher famously won a stand-off with the mining unions, Lee Kuan Yew won a similar stand-off. In 1966 the Public Daily Rated Employees' Union (PDRE) demanded a wage increase for its 15,000 workers. Kuan Yew met them and agreed an increase for 1968, but not 1967. They called a strike, but the Industrial Arbitration Court declared it illegal. The PDRE went on strike anyway, claiming that it was in solidarity with other strikers. The police charged the strikers' leaders for calling an illegal strike; the Ministry of Health declared that the strikers had sacked themselves and that they would have to re-apply for a job (90 per cent did), and the PDRE and other unions were deregistered. Strikes in essential services were banned. From then onwards, trade unions became more reasonable. In 1969, for the first time since the war, there were no strikes at all – eight years before, there had been 153.

After the government won re-election in 1968, several labour laws were passed which laid the foundation for industrial peace. Minimum employment conditions were introduced, as well as limits on benefits and overtime bonuses. Holidays, annual leave, maternity and sick leave were regulated. Companies regained the right to hire and fire and to promote and transfer. Strikes needed to be sanctioned by secret ballot, and contravening officers were prosecuted. Within a year, fifty-two new factories were built. In 1972 the National Wages Council was set up to negotiate annual recommendations for wage increases and other employment conditions; they always made sure that rises never exceeded productivity increases.

Unions reinvented themselves from militants demanding privileges whatever the economic cost into mutual societies through which workers could give direct help to each other, and cooperatives which gave the worker–consumers a share of the profits. They expanded into broadcasting, resorts and condominiums for their workers, child and healthcare, and even a country club with golf course. One added advantage was that it taught many of their members the basic rules of how to run a successful business.

Rooting out corruption

On the day they were sworn in after the election of 1959, the PAP members turned up in white shirts and white slacks to symbolise purity and honesty in their personal behaviour and their public life. They were determined to rid Singapore of corruption. Corrupt leaders had brought many Asian countries to their knees. Corruption is harmful to the wealth-creating forces of the free market economy and reduces economic growth. It creates price distortions as the end product or service costs more than it would in an incorrupt market. The corrupted will try to pass the cost on to the consumer. The higher cost may cause some projects not to go ahead; investment falls. In addition, a covert, upward redistribution of wealth takes place, as the small downtrodden citizen will never be able to offset the bribes he has to pay against the ones he might receive.

In Asia, corruption was rife. The leaders and warlords of Nationalist China, for example, had been guilty of wholesale looting (including creating hyperinflation) – similar to what is called 'kleptocracy' today. A substantial part of the Communists' appeal was that they did not seem interested in personal enrichment. Singapore's leaders' determination was all the more remarkable because those who can end corruption – the political leaders – often stand to gain the most from it. In Singapore it helped that the leaders belonged to the upper strata of society and were already well off.

Small corruption was countered by removing discretionary decision-making powers from low level officials and setting out clear rules instead. Some permits and approvals were abolished. The bribery laws were toughened: anything of value became subject to them; investigators obtained wide-reaching powers, the evidence of accomplices was declared admissible and the fines were increased tenfold. No mercy was shown towards big corruption: to set examples, corrupt high officials were remorselessly prosecuted and fined.

Some other more general measures were introduced to reduce the enticement to accept bribes. In many Asian countries, waging an election campaign is very expensive. Singapore introduced compulsory voting, and the parties usually spend less than the legal maximum on campaigning. In addition, politicians are paid substantial salaries: not just to make them 'well off', so they wouldn't really need to earn more, but also to attract the best people. Running the country is seen as equivalent to running a large corporation of professional office. Salaries of ministers and senior civil servants are high and are linked to salary increases in the private sector, a sort of 'profit-related pay'. As Singapore's issuance of currency is not at the whim of the government, politicians cannot create short-lived booms by printing money (and thereby increase their salary), as in many other countries. Unlike most other developed countries, Singapore finds it quite easy to attract applicants from the private sector to fill public sector jobs. In many countries politicians are too afraid of the electorate to grant themselves salary increases, and therefore resort to substantial and opaque perks which multiply their official salary. Singapore offers few perks to its officials and politicians. When the social democratic Workers' Party attacked ministers for being paid much more than their colleagues in neighbouring countries, Lee Kuan Yew replied laconically that he was both one of the best-paid and one of the poorest politicians in the Commonwealth. According to the World Economic Forum's 2011/2012 Economic Competitiveness Report, Singapore is the least corrupt country in the world.

Welfare

The Singaporean government realised that the best insurance against mishaps and old age is people's own savings. But it refused to rely merely on voluntary saving, as some individuals have less ability to care for themselves, or have catastrophic bad luck. So it decided to do some redistribution. It rejected the Western-style welfare state with its encouragement of laziness, dilution of individual and family responsibility, and immorality of making working people pay for the inactive. Singapore developed a system which ensures that people enjoy welfare throughout their lives without a Western-style welfare state. On the one hand, Singapore introduced measures which would increase the earning power of its citizens, such as free market economics and good education. But for housing, medical care and retirement benefits, they developed a novel interlinked system.

The system was first imposed by the British colonial authorities. Even though Singapore had obtained partial internal self-government, it did as it was told. The Central Provident Fund was set up as a government statutory body under the Ministry of Manpower in July 1955. The British tried to introduce similar systems in many other colonies, but in laissez-faire Hong Kong the authorities royally ignored it. The system forced all citizens except the self-employed and senior civil servants to save for their retirement in a fund regulated and managed by the state. Initially, both individual and employer contributed 5 per cent; the savings could be withdrawn at age fifty-five. It proved inadequate, and the compulsory contributions were increased. This was not opposed, as productivity and wage increases more than offset the increase. By 1984 the contributions were as high as 50 per cent. They currently stand at 40 per cent: 20 per cent paid by the employer and 20 per cent paid by the employee.

The government was determined that working people should save for their own pensions, rather than making future generations pay for it under the pay-as-you-go system which is most commonly used in the developed world. Key to this is that the savings held by the Central Provident Fund remain the contributor's own. The money is inherited by his nominated legatee or according to the intestacy laws. This ensures that the payee does not see his contributions disappear into a pay-for-everybody's-welfare black hole. It also encourages him to be careful in his use of the money, e.g. when he pays his healthcare bills from it. The system encourages across-the-board thrift.

Later, the same forced savings scheme was expanded to pay for other necessities such as insurance, education, investment, health insurance and house purchase. It does mean that the Central Provident Fund is much more than a pension fund: it is an alternative to the welfare state, and one of the main reasons why income tax can be kept so low in Singapore.

The savings in the Fund can be used to pay for a deposit on a 'social' house from the Housing and Development Board, or to buy a private house. In 1961 the government granted itself the compulsory power to purchase land for public purposes such as house building. It was believed that developers should not unduly profit from increases in land values resulting from economic development and infrastructure paid for by the government. House building advanced at breakneck speed. Today, 88.6 per cent of households are home owners – the third highest percentage in the world (after Bulgaria and Hungary).

From 1978 onwards, the government allowed people to use the CPF to accumulate their own savings. The government guaranteed a minimum return for the CPF, and if the money invested in the CPF outperformed that percentage, that surplus could be taken out of the account for personal use. CPF money could now be invested in private, commercial and industrial property, in unit trusts and mutual funds and in gold.

In the mid-1970s the government wanted to provide high quality healthcare for everyone. There was no question of copying the British national health system, which they believed to be a failure. They didn't like the American system, as it left many uninsured and unprotected. Medisave can now be used by people to pay for their and their immediate family's hospitalisation and other medical expenses. As they will be entitled to the remainder, people are responsible with their own healthcare consumption. The Fund can be used for private hospital fees; the competition puts pressure on state hospitals to provide higher service quality. MediShield savings can cover catastrophic illness (prolonged and serious illness). Medifund (1993) is the state subsidy for those whose Medisave and MediShield account has run out of money and who have no family to recoup it.

The health savings account system has important consequences for the cost of healthcare. Throughout the world, there are broadly four systems of health insurance and provision of healthcare. The United Kingdom 'enjoys' an entirely nationalised system whereby all citizens are given the healthcare the state NHS provides them with. Consortia of NHS doctors commission the health services for their members. In countries such as the Netherlands, people choose among competing insurers which in turn choose competing providers. The United States and Switzerland have health maintenance organisations whereby the insurer is also the provider (in-house). In Singapore, there is no intermediary: individuals choose their healthcare providers on a case-by-case basis, and pay for it from the savings in their health savings account. These differences have substantial consequences. Whereas in the United Kingdom system there is no effective customer control and the health services are commissioned by a limited number of doctors, in Singapore several millions of customers control what they purchase from a number of providers. About 68 per cent of healthcare is purchased from the private sector – at around half the cost per capita as in Britain's NHS.

Libertarians will point out that the Central Provident Fund is very authoritarian. The state forces you to save. However, those savings can then, subject to limits, be used for a large number of purposes such as paying for medical care or buying a house. The state uses the Fund to encourage family values and self-reliance. The forced saving means that people have less disposable income. Citizens are forced to deposit their contributions with the government, with only trust as guarantee that those savings will not sooner or later be confiscated, or that the promised benefits will be paid out. In the case of Singapore, with its well-established reliance on the rule of law and good governance, this is unlikely to happen. Still, eventual confiscation cannot be excluded completely: nobody knows what financial position Singapore will be in in the future, or who will be in government. When the British colonial authorities imposed similar systems in India and Nigeria, it ended in tears: the funds were mismanaged and provided low rates of return and poor service. The risk attached to depositing savings with the state is only marginally different from depositing savings with private health insurance in many Western countries: few in Britain will forget, for example, how the Labour government raided the private pension funds by imposing a tax which creamed off £5 billion a year.

In fact, in Singapore this is already being done in a craftier manner. The return on the Central Provident Fund has been meagre. This is no surprise: the state holds the investment monopoly for the Fund and is not annoyed by competitors offering higher returns. The largest of the three Central Provident Fund parts, which provides for retirement benefits, has 99 per cent of its assets invested in non-marketable government bonds. The average rate of return between 1988 and 2008 was 1.3 per cent after inflation (provided the official inflation figures are correct – several authors claim the return is actually negative). Savers are aware of this, and withdraw a lot of money to, for example, buy a house. It is not unusual for more than 70 per cent of the annual contributions to be withdrawn in any one year. The money raised by the state is invested by the Singapore Government Investment Corporation. Its portfolio and investment performance are not made public and CPF members do not know the ultimate deployment of their funds.

It is interesting to compare briefly the Singaporean system with the one existing in Hong Kong. In Hong Kong the colonial authorities also set up a Central Provident Fund to force people to save for their pensions; but because they were too busy dealing with millions of immigrants and because they were not very enthusiastic about interfering in people's lives in the first place, the Fund was never enforced. Unlike the authorities in Singapore, the colonial authorities did not need to be elected, and keeping the Chinese happy and unimpeded had been public policy since they arrived on the peninsula. What followed was an organic growth of private pension funds without compulsion or regulation. The Hong Kong government did provide some welfare:

housing support for the elderly, state education and fully state-funded health services. Old-age security was mostly provided by the family. Later, large corporations introduced occupational pension schemes for their workers. There were no specific regulations until 1993. At that time, 30 per cent of Hong Kongers participated voluntarily in pension schemes. In 2000, the Hong Kong government introduced the Mandatory Provident Fund system. Superficially, it is similar to Singapore's – but one only has to save 10 per cent of one's salary, and those who earn less than HK$5,000 only pay 5 per cent. But the most important difference is that this 10 per cent can be invested in any one of a number of competing private pension funds. The result is that the return is much higher than under the Singaporean system – usually at least 5 per cent. Over a lifetime of saving this makes a huge difference. The 10 per cent over a period of thirty or forty years would pay for 30 to 40 per cent of the final salary. In Singapore, with a compulsory contribution of 40 per cent over thirty-five years, one only ends up with 20 to 40 per cent of the final salary.

The Singaporean system has a strong Confucian line running through it: that of the centralised, efficient and beneficent state. The family unit remains key. Apart from your compulsory savings, you are to rely upon your own family: retired parents can sue their children who fail to support them. In many cases, the compulsory savings system is mere icing on the cake: 90 per cent of individuals over sixty years of age live with at least one of their children. Many do not have formal pensions, especially older women.

Under the umbrella of the Central Provident Fund, Singapore ended up with a health system, a pension system and the promotion of home ownership. The state only helps in the most extreme circumstances. There are a handful of schemes for the needy, from low-income students to elderly persons without kin or savings. All these are means-tested.

There is public assistance for the most destitute of people: out of a population of 4.5 million people, 3,000 qualify. Singapore has not created a Western-style welfare system where incentives to take care of oneself and one's family are replaced by anonymous taxpayers who are coerced into paying – not just for the genuinely needy, but also for the lazy and the opportunist.

3. ATTRACTING ENTERPRISE

Helping the economy
Singapore and Hong Kong have a lot in common: both are small city states, and both were suddenly cut off from their traditional hinterland. But in one respect their development differed quite fundamentally. Unlike Hong Kong, the government of Singapore was a major force in pushing economic development. It made economic growth its key policy, and all other policies supplementary to it. It built up a reputation of reliability, rule of law, and sound macroeconomic policies; it built first class infrastructure and industrial estates; it took equity participations in industries, and it promoted export. This interventionism was a departure from the laissez-faire economy which had flourished before independence. At that time the powers of the free market reigned supreme. As Ronald Coase observed, before independence, Singapore ran as an organism, not an organisation. The extreme responsiveness to changing conditions resulted from the millions of individual decisions taken by its population. When Singapore risked perishing, the government thought it could go faster and better.

After substantial lobbying by the government the British army decided to transfer its possessions to the new government instead of destroying them as was the usual practice. Singapore could have opted to transform the sites into state

enterprises. Instead, most were privatised; if not immediately, then after a few years. Five years after the British
withdrawal, the naval dockyard of Sembawang was transferred to Sembawang Shipyard Limited, a company which
was set up especially. It later became SembCorp Industries, a
conglomerate listed on the Singapore Stock Exchange with
slightly less than half of its shares held by Singapore's sovereign wealth fund, and a majority of its shares held in public
hands. An island which had housed British Gurkhas became
a tourist resort; Fort Canning became a clubhouse for leisure
and recreation; the military airfield was expanded by land
reclamation and became Changi International Airport; and
the Pasir Panjang military complex became the National
University of Singapore.

Immediately after independence, many mistakes were
made. The government put protectionist measures in place
for the local production of refrigerators, air conditioners,
radios, televisions and tape recorders, and for the assembly
of cars. This resulted in the misallocation of scarce resources.
The companies relied on protection instead of trying to
become more competitive. After 1975 Singapore began
to dismantle its protectionism. At one point an EDB officer
asked a Mercedes-Benz director how long Singapore would
have to maintain its protective tariffs for a local car assembly
plant. 'Forever,' the director replied, 'because Singaporean
workers are not as efficient as Germans.' The government
promptly removed all protectionism.

Local businessmen were encouraged to establish factories
of vegetable oils, mosquito repellents, hair cream, cosmetics,
religious offerings and mothballs. Hong Kong and Taiwan
investors set up factories for textiles, toys and clothes.
Unsurprisingly, joint ventures between the state and private
businessmen failed: state companies are driven by subsidies and status, whereas the private sector is driven by the
profit motive. For many years the Jurong Industrial Estate,

the infrastructure of which had been built at vast expense but which remained empty, was nicknamed 'Goh's Folly', after the minister who set it up. It quickly filled when the government granted five years' tax exemption for any business moving in. By the end of 1970, 390 new enterprises had been created.

The Economic Development Board was set up to become a one-stop agency for investors, so they would not have to deal with multiple departments. It financed industry and established new industries and industrial estates. Its main efforts included ship breaking and repair, metal engineering, chemicals, and electrical equipment and appliances. Successful components were split off to run on their own. The development finance section became the Development Bank of Singapore: it financed Singapore businessmen who needed venture capital but who could not obtain it from the established banks who were excessively prudent and who had only experience in trade financing.

The government founded new industries such as the National Iron and Steel Mills; Neptune Orient Lines (shipping), Singapore Airlines, the Insurance Corporation of Singapore, Singapore Petroleum Company, Chartered Industries of Singapore (a mint and ammunition factory), and Keppel Corporation (initially a local ship repair yard). There was always great fear that these state companies would become a drain on state funds, as was the case in most Western countries. In Singapore, they were run as proper companies, with the firm understanding that they had to be profitable or be shut down. They were always led by managers under contract, and never by state employees. Many of these companies became efficient, profitable, and competitive – Singapore Airlines, for example, is the most profitable airline in Asia and passengers routinely vote it the best in the world. Some government monopolies such as the Port of Singapore Authority, Singapore Telecom and

Public Utilities Board were turned into separate companies. Some of the state companies were subsequently sold (e.g. National Iron and Steel Mills is now part of Tata Steel); others were listed on the stock exchange, with Singapore's sovereign wealth fund keeping a shareholding. All insist that they are proper independent companies who receive no state subsidies or preferential treatment from the government, despite being government-linked.

From the above, it appears as if the government of Singapore was merely interested in the big players. Nothing could be further from the truth. It persistently tried to make it easier for private individuals to set up businesses. Singapore tops the World Bank's Doing Business 2012 list of 183 countries for the ease and speed it offers would-be businessmen. Bottom of the list is Chad. As Jim Powell of the Cato Institute points out:

> The process to set up a legal business takes three days in Singapore; sixty-six days in Chad. It takes twenty-six days to obtain a construction permit in Singapore, 154 days in Chad. Filing fees, taxes and other costs of starting a business are 0.7 per cent of per capita average income in Singapore, whereas they amount to 208.5 per cent of per capita average income in Chad. In Singapore, an estimated eighty-four hours are required each year to maintain tax-related records and prepare tax returns, versus 732 hours in Chad. Total taxes consume 27.1 per cent of corporate profits in Singapore, 65.4 per cent of corporate profits in Chad.

Financial centre

In 1968 Singapore set out to become the financial centre of Asia within ten years. There was a time gap in the international banking world between the closure of the banks in San Francisco and the opening of the Swiss banks. Singapore could nicely fill the void to create 24-hour around the world banking. Singapore was still a third-world country, and it took some convincing to attract foreign banks. A number of hindrances to a flourishing financial sector were quickly lifted. All foreign exchange restrictions on all currency transactions were lifted. All Asian dollar deposits were exempted from statutory liquidity and reserve requirements. Withholding tax on interest earned by non-resident depositors was abolished.

One great competitive advantage was its stable currency: early on, it had decided not to have a central bank which could print and create currency at will. Instead, the Monetary Authority of Singapore (MAS), a currency board, keeps the value of the Singapore dollar within a certain fluctuation band of a basket of currencies of its main trading partners.

Singapore's removal of financial regulations does not mean that its supervision of the finance industry was weak. There were frequent complaints of overregulation. It was claimed that in Hong Kong all is allowed that is not expressly forbidden, and that in Singapore all is forbidden that is not expressly allowed. Singapore's leaders often stressed that the difference was that Hong Kong, as a colony, enjoyed the backing of the British government if all else failed; whereas Singapore had no such guarantee. Singapore's supervision was strict in order to inspire trust in investors. If the MAS had doubts about a financial institution's credibility, it refused to issue a licence. For example, the Bank of Credit and Commerce International (BCCI) repeatedly applied for a licence – even engaging the services of the former British Prime Minister Harold Wilson. The MAS stood firm and kept refusing; and found itself vindicated when later in the BCCI's bankruptcy it transpired that it had been swindling its customers all along.

Singapore's existing financial sector was conservative and stale. Its policies were so cautious that they prevented expansion into other financial activities. The big banks didn't need to be entrepreneurial as they enjoyed government protection. The banks wanted a continuation of the restrictions on foreign banks opening more branches or even ATM machines. More qualifying foreign banks were allowed to open branches and the limits on foreign ownership of local bank shares were lifted. The commission rates and access to the stock and futures exchange were freed. The setting up of asset management companies was encouraged. For many years the state's Central Provident Fund invested people's individual savings' accounts in a very conservative manner. Surpluses were placed in bank deposits and government-linked companies. No use was made of fund managers to increase the returns and none of the money was invested in new industries. The rules were changed to allow for market investment techniques.

By the 1990s the foreign exchange market was the fourth largest in the world. When the market became jittery, banks were told to provide full information on their hidden reserves, their non-performing loans, and their regional loan exposure, to allow investors to take a considered view without any suspicion of secrecy. The banks' openness and liability for their own actions inspired trust and stability, while elsewhere in the Western world failing banks were bailed out by the taxpayers. There was no stock market bubble, and not a single Singapore bank faltered during the Asian Financial Crisis of 1997–8. In the 2007 world economic crisis Singapore's exposure to sub-prime mortgages was limited, but it suffered from falling exports to the US and Europe.

The special case of multinationals
To bypass their hostile neighbours and to focus on trade with the world, Singapore attracted American multinationals. Multinationals offered the spectrum of high-tech large-scale operations creating many jobs. American businessmen

liked Singapore's 'no begging bowl' approach. They liked
the political and economic stability Singapore offered. They
liked the sound labour relations which meant that no strikes
would endanger their supply chains. They knew that unlike
in other third-world countries, their investments would
be safe from confiscation and war loss in Singapore. They
enjoyed direct access to the government, and could speak
freely about overregulation, the rise of the Singapore dollar
or restrictive hiring policies for foreign workers. Some foreign
investments failed, usually because of competitive changes
in technology and markets. There were always enough new
companies to fill the void – a classic example of creative
destruction: the necessity to allow uncompetitive companies
to go belly up to allow better ones to be founded or grow.

In his autobiography, Lee Kuan Yew observes that
attracting multinationals was not fashionable at the time.
In the eyes of development economists, multinationals were
exploiters of workers, land and raw materials. The 'dependency school' claimed that multinationals perpetuated colo-
nialism by extracting raw materials from poor countries for
little money and selling them expensive consumer goods
produced in wealthy countries in return. Prime Minister Lee
Kuan Yew and Deputy Prime Minister Goh Ken Swee didn't
buy the development economists' narrative.

Raul Prebisch's Dependency Theory urged third-world
countries to close off their markets and to start manufacturing
substitutes for the foreign imports to thwart the exploitation by developed countries. This ran counter to Ricardo's
Law of Comparative Advantage, which proved that countries must produce what they are most competitive at, and
import the rest. Singapore briefly flirted with protectionism
and import substitution while it was part of Malaysia, but
rejected it afterwards. It suffices to compare the evolution of
Singapore's economy with those economies which stuck to
Prebisch's teachings to form a balanced view.

Singapore was not above presentational trickery in order to attract investors. Everybody travelling to Singapore will see the wide glamorous palm-tree-lined avenue from the airport into the city. It was built for precisely that reason: to impress upon every visitor that Singapore is competent, disciplined and reliable – without any word being spoken. The whole city-state has been sanitised for decades.

4. SINGAPORE'S PRINCIPLES

Prime Minister Lee Kuan Yew was always dismissive about ideology and said that they applied what worked instead. Perhaps he didn't want to admit that he had been ideologically wrong. When he started out in politics he believed in the fairness of socialism, with equal shares for all. But pretty soon he became aware that an economy could only develop if individual were incentivised to work hard. Why then did he not copy Hong-Kong's laissez-faire model? Hong Kong was not subject to regular elections, as Singapore was. Unlike Hong Kong, Singapore's leaders therefore redistributed income to soften the harshness of free market competition. In order to get elected, the People's Action Party was positioned firmly as a centre party. It has been in power since 1963. Time and time again, Lee Kuan Yew stressed the difference from Hong Kong: 'Because people are unequal in their abilities, if performance and rewards are determined by the marketplace, there will be a few big winners, many medium winners, and a considerable number of losers. That would make for social tensions because a society's sense of fairness is offended.' Or: 'A competitive, winner-takes-all society, like colonial Hong Kong in the 1960s, would not be acceptable in Singapore.'

In fact, the PAP party is an eclectic mixture of Western

and Asian concepts, with paternalism, technocracy and communitarianism at its heart. The Confucian ideal of a 'strong centralised state governed by wise bureaucrats' is omnipresent. Government guides daily social life through an arsenal of interventionist measures. Singapore's sovereign wealth fund, which manages US$142 billion in assets, allows for a great deal of government control over business and industry. A lot of effort is put into training top civil servants. Intelligent pupils are identified early on; they obtain scholarships at the most prestigious foreign universities. In return, they have to work eight years for the civil service, where they often earn higher salaries than in the private sector.

But while Singapore is intervention-happy, rejects laissez-faire, and wants to help the poor, it is also hostile to a Western-style welfare state. As Kuan Lee puts it:

Watching the ever-increasing costs of the welfare state in Britain and Sweden, we decided to avoid this debilitating system. We noted by the 1970s that when governments undertook primary responsibility for the basic duties of the head of a family, the drive in people weakened. Welfare undermined self-reliance ... For nearly four decades since the war, successive British governments seemed to assume that the creation of wealth came about naturally, and that what needed government attention and ingenuity was the redistribution of wealth ... We have used to advantage what Britain left behind: the English language, the legal system, parliamentary government and impartial administration. However, we have studiously avoided the practices of the welfare state. We saw how a great people reduced themselves to mediocrity by levelling down.

It doesn't do socialism, it doesn't do laissez-faire and it doesn't do welfare statism. So which policies does Singapore apply to help the less well-off?

The lifeline of development aid which was thrown at newly independent countries (in most cases never to go away), was firmly rejected. Singapore increased its prosperity through its own labours. The social problems are solved by focusing on traditional family help, and by forcing people to save for their own future through the Central Provident Fund. It obliterates the necessity of a welfare state to keep social peace; it provides capital to make the economy grow, and the saving on welfare spending allows Singapore to keep taxes extremely low. However much Lee Kuan Yew claimed that he was 'of the centre', it is difficult not to see traditional centre-right values in this. Singapore does not see it as a moral duty to take from the rich to give to the poor. It has a different understanding of morality: that of encouraging and rewarding people who save for themselves and their families, to encourage responsibility, and to see state welfare as a safety net for extreme circumstances only.

Singapore interfered, intervened and dictated the road towards economic prosperity. Lee Kuan Yew argued that they couldn't wait: 'Had we waited for our traders to learn to be industrialists we would have starved.' As state support for the economy has been part and parcel of Singapore's development for the last forty years, it is difficult to guess what would have happened without it. In Hong Kong, such state assistance was absent – and Hong Kong performed as well as Singapore. Hong Kong's 'purity' vis-à-vis government meddling is the reason why it, and not Singapore, is the world's greatest success story for economic freedom.

Singapore's steering of the economy was a process of trial and error. Contrary to Western countries, it closed down its state companies which made losses. Much interventionism was only short-term, and was eventually reversed. Initial protectionism disappeared, taxes went down dramatically, and many companies founded by the state were at least partly privatised. There is virtually totally free trade, with foreign companies enjoying free access to Singapore's markets.

Singapore's economic success created many jealous rivals and enemies – rivals such as other Asian countries which stayed behind in a third-world quagmire, and enemies such as those hostile to market forces, and development economists who couldn't stomach Singapore's success after it abandoned Raul Prebisch's mantras. Critics point out that the claim that Singapore was a third-world swamp when the PAP took power in 1959 is merely a myth concocted by the PAP to portray themselves as the saviours of the nation. Singapore had experienced significant inter-war industrialisation. The per capita income was over one-third of that of the UK. However, by the late 1950s it was declining. Per capita exports fell by almost half between 1937 and 1957. It deteriorated further when Malaysia and Indonesia refused to trade with it. Some rapid thinking was required to replace this source of prosperity. The small city state of Singapore focused on trade with the world, and thrived.

It is said that Singapore's development was 'predestined', 'inevitable', and the result of happy coincidences. Wasn't Singapore located at a crossroads of sea trading routes? Many countries are located at important sea routes, and could have established free ports – for example right next to Singapore. *Yet they didn't.* When Indonesia was busy enforcing its ruinous trade boycott of Singapore, it talked about establishing its own free ports. No such thing happened. Perhaps there was some truth in the Singapore government's belief that Sukarno's government was incapable of creating anything which would be free from official incompetence, endless procrastination and corruption. Neighbours Indonesia and Malaysia came nowhere near Singapore's growth in the years after separation and confrontation: between 1966 and 1972 the average growth rate was 13.9 per cent in Singapore, 5.5 per cent in Malaysia and 6.4 per cent in Indonesia. The 'location' argument is a strange one at the best of times – wasn't the Republic of Venice, which was one of the most successful merchant nations for close to 1,000 years, built on a swamp at a lost corner of the Adriatic Sea nowhere near international sea routes?

It has been said that Singapore was 'lucky' with its timing – that multinationals were just then searching for low-cost locations to manufacture their products. The United States, for example, operated a special advantageous tariff for offshore assembly. This may be so, but why was Singapore chosen, and not the Philippines, or Indonesia, or Brazil? Surely time is equal for all?

Some say Singapore merely continued its long tradition of free trade. They may have had a tradition of openness, but the continuation of a tradition does not take place if a government decides otherwise. Singapore did have a tradition of free trade – Stanford Raffles himself established a free port when he founded Singapore in 1819. Why was it that this remained so even when in the 1930s directing and curbing trade became so popular elsewhere? The answer is that there was always a strong lobby among Europe's merchants which resisted any attempts by special-interest groups to have trade restricted for their own benefit. In addition, when trade with Indonesia and Malaysia was cut off the traditional interest groups who traded in commodities lost power as and when they were outperformed by the new industrial classes. The old interest groups could not pressurise the government into adopting protectionism – a process not dissimilar from the loss of power of powerful pre-war special interest groups in Europe after the war; or from the loss of power of the landed gentry and the guilds during the industrial revolution in England in the eighteenth and nineteenth centuries.

Singapore consciously continued free trade after independence, and removed the few remaining barriers which existed. It continues to do so today: the US–Singapore Free

Trade Agreement of 2002 eliminated all the remaining trade barriers between the two countries. US telecommunications suppliers, insurance companies, delivery firms, banks and law firms were thought to enjoy huge economies of scale but were allowed free access to Singapore. Singapore seemingly gave a lot, but knew that even unilateral free trade usually benefits the freeing country. In 1992, Singapore was one of the original signatories of AFTA, the Asian Free Trade Area. Its members aim to abolish all tariffs and non-tariff barriers between them. Unlike the EU, it does not impose an external tariff, leaving its members free to decide and compete between them. The other members are Brunei, Indonesia, Malaysia, Philippines, Thailand, Vietnam, Laos, Myanmar and Cambodia.

5. CONCLUSION

Singapore doesn't smell anymore. In his book *La Nouvelle Richesse des Nations*, the French philosopher Guy Sorman recalled how in the early 1960s Singapore was a city of the senses: on the Chinese market, visitors were struck by the curious mix of fermented fish and carbide lamps which illuminated the streets. The miserable lived on immobile houseboats and there were ambulant traders and bicycle rickshaws ridden by skeleton-like opium addicts all over the place. The whole was framed by a motley lot of Victorian facades eaten away by equatorial mould.

Today, Singapore doesn't even look like Houston or New York. It looks just as Western, but far more prosperous. According to the 2012 Index of Economic Freedom, the most densely populated country in the world after Monaco is the second most economically free, out of a total of 184 countries. According to the World Economic Forum's 2011/2012 Economic Competitiveness Report, Singapore is the second most competitive country in the world. Singapore's institutions continue to be ranked highest in the world for their lack of corruption and for their efficiency. The efficiency of its goods and labour market is ranked highest as well, and it comes second in the world for its financial market development.

Milton Friedman said that Singapore was a company which organises its 3 million employees along market principles. Its leaders liken it to a company with almost 5.2 million shareholders who can change the board at elections. Whatever it's called, mass prosperity is the outcome. It is not all bliss, of course, but then it has to be judged by earthly standards. The high-handed social authoritarianism makes many a libertarian queasy.

Singapore advanced from the third world to the first in a time frame of about thirty years. This was not achieved automatically, or by coincidence. Singapore forced people to save, thereby obliterating the need for the welfare state which has dragged down so many other developed countries. It reduced its taxes to staggeringly low rates. By the 1990s its GDP per capita was twenty times higher than its neighbours. Singapore runs like a Swiss watch. Singapore is a good example of how fast a Heaven on Earth can be created.

NINE

HOW TO CREATE MASS PROSPERITY

If Julius Caesar had met George Washington in 1760, he would have found the world barely changed. He would have been served food prepared by slaves in a stately home. The average age would have been twenty-eight to thirty-five. Just 250 years later he would have heard talk of missions to Mars and of people travelling to the other side of the world in just twelve hours to go on holiday. What had happened?

The subtitle of this book, How to *Create* Mass Prosperity, would make any principled free marketeer cringe. Governments don't create prosperity; individuals do. As Adam Smith taught us 237 years ago, productivity increases make wealth grow. If people are left free, their desire to improve their lives will make the pie grow. Economic freedom is what steers all progress. If allowed to proceed unchecked, individuals beavering away will deliver standards of civilisation, and overcome adversity, at levels as yet unknown.

Free markets create wealth and lift the less well-off out of poverty. When there are no regulations to stop them, people can use their talents to improve their situation, and social mobility increases. Talent is much more evenly divided than capital: allow those who work the hardest and have the most talents to thrive on their freedom, and the market will redistribute its bounty more evenly than regulated societies do. The endless variety of the free market is more likely to offer opportunities to even those with few talents. The disadvantaged are the least likely to profit from regulation, as they have the smallest leverage with government. Do away with big government and those at the bottom of the ladder will climb it. The free market is therefore intrinsically social.

Rulers always think that they can do better than the ruled. Their attempts to improve on the self-correcting free market damage the vehicle through which individuals create a better life for themselves. The reason is Hayek's Knowledge Problem: a small group of leaders will never have the detailed knowledge that millions of individuals have of their own circumstances, and of the alternatives to reach the best results. This is why the public sector always undershoots the private sector. This is why the public sector needs to be kept as small as possible: it is financed by taking resources away from the private sector which can achieve so much more with it.

When the state takes over responsibility for our lives, we become like animals living in herds who are led by shepherds. Most of us have become 'subject' to others: to special interest groups, to democratic majorities or to the state. The degree to which we have lost our liberty can be measured by the degree to which we have to part with the fruits of our labours. When tax is 50 per cent, you work one day out of two for the state and you are only half free. In the United Kingdom, the Adam Smith Institute annually calculates 'Tax Freedom Day'; the calendar day on which people become free of tax. Tax freedom days are rarely brought forward.

Government cannot improve our lives, because it doesn't even know what a better life is: it means something different for every one of us. Most have a vague idea what sort of life we want and how to achieve it. We try, and we make mistakes. The more people try, and the more errors are made, the better, as more good methods will manifest themselves. Increasing prosperity therefore implies risk, uncertainty and failure. When the government tries to take risk out of our lives, it destroys the mechanism by which we can find out what is best for us and how to achieve it. When governments take decisions instead of allowing individuals to take them, failure is national instead of individual. This does not mean that those who are risk-averse need to live in terror: they can take out private insurance, or join a mutual society, or choose for themselves that they want a quiet and easy and less prosperous life. But even when they do nothing, the advance by others under a free market economy will advance them.

Because people are risk-averse, many leaders try to insure people against the vicissitudes of life through state welfare. When the state is grown to pay and administer welfare, it brings growth to a halt. In excess, it may even *reduce* growth and prosperity: not only is welfare paid for through taxes on the productive sector; but it also incentivises people not to be productive. People end up safe, but poor. This is what Eastern Europe found when it tried Communism. Welfare is also used to care for those of us who have been unlucky: the poor, the sick and the disabled. Most of us agree to a state safety net. Not just out of compassion, but also out of self-interest: after all, everyone can have a bout of bad luck. But few agree to a safety hammock, and that is what welfare states have mostly become. Many countries which successfully transformed their economies found alternatives to the traditional Western welfare state which did *not* impede growth and prosperity. But ultimately, the best way to make people better off is to create wealth. Who will the redistributor take from once the wealthy have been stripped bare? Redistribution is finite; wealth creation is infinite.

Some leaders have conscientiously created mass prosperity. They went against the flow. Instead of protecting people against life, they let them get on with it. They tore down the prison walls which served to keep people safe. Instead of stifling human ingenuity and productivity by clipboard-wielding bureaucrats, they abolished rules and controls and limited themselves to setting up stable frameworks such as the rule of law and property rights. Their politicians were the rarest of species: those who are so unselfish that they reduce their own power to empower others. Those countries boom. Their people prosper. They create wealth beyond their wildest imagination. As the French businessmen told the interventionist Finance Minister Colbert in the eighteenth century: '*laissez-faire*', or leaving them be, is what lifts people out of poverty and misery. It isn't rocket science: everybody can do it, by following the routes they show us.

We have just read about eight countries which managed to dramatically increase mass prosperity. You will have noticed that they share similar traits. There are two dimensions to the creation of mass prosperity: *how to do it*, and *what to do*.

HOW TO CREATE MASS PROSPERITY

Catastrophes spark extraordinary reforms. They paint the options in black and white and trigger calls for dramatic change. The civil war against absolutism in England, Mao's famine, the civil war in Chile, Nazism in Germany, mass immigration to Hong Kong and Singapore's risk of being wiped out, all sparked exceptional politicians to take exceptional measures. In all cases, loss of prosperity stood at the heart of the conflicts. Countries which decline slowly, such as Western Europe, do not react: in the medium term, people are still quite happy to continue as before, and don't want the risk of change. They tend to see growth levels of 0–1 per cent as quite an achievement – while elsewhere countries grow by 8–10 per cent. It is their children or grandchildren who will pay. It was the dramatic decline of Britain and America which sparked its population to vote for the great

reformers Ronald Reagan and Margaret Thatcher. This does
not mean that slowly declining or slowly growing countries
can't change their course. New Zealand was the least likely
reformer of the eight countries we discussed; yet its reforms
were phenomenally successful.

Speed is of the essence. The faster the reforms are begun,
the faster they will yield results. This is extremely important,
as all reforms hurt initially. Leaders in democratic countries
will especially want to take action from day one, as they will
face re-election soon. When the reformer takes office, all
the plans must be ready. FDR understood this – hence his
introduction of fifteen pieces of major legislation in his first
100 days in office. Freshly elected, governments benefit from
a short-lived honeymoon during which the population will
give them the benefit of the doubt and during which the media
can't really attack them in the light of the popular mandate
the politicians just obtained. Fast reforms have the added
advantage that special interest groups don't have the time
to organise protest. This tactic was successfully applied in
New Zealand. In occupied Germany, Erhard announced reforms before the Allies had a chance to block them. Some
reforms may fail, and it is best to have as much time as
possible left to fix them. Undemocratic regimes often live in
the mistaken belief that they have plenty of time left. It was
this mistake which caused the Tiananmen demonstrations:
reform went too slowly and this allowed plenty of time to
notice its inevitable mistakes and for opponents to organise
themselves (including the Communist hardliners).

Reform must be total and all-encompassing. This is not
just because most political actions have side-effects, but also
because it evens out the winners and the losers. People who
lose out because of one reform may gain from another. When
everybody is in it together, they will perceive the reforms as
being fairer.

Half-hearted reforms produce half-baked results. This is

the folly of the 'third way': instead of going for what works best (the free market economy), leaders compromise for political reasons into something that is but a shadow of what could be. Margaret Thatcher used to say that those who stand in the middle of the road get hit by traffic from both directions. A typical example is the part-privatisation of state companies in China. Those companies would perform so much better if they were privatised completely.

Reform is more difficult in democratic societies, as special interest groups are better organised. The colonial government of Hong Kong was able to ignore pressures from special interest groups to grant privileges, as it was appointed by London. The only truly democratic country I have discussed is New Zealand; Thatcher's Britain, Reagan's America and Václav Klaus's Czech Republic would have been equally fine examples. In Chile, the economic reforms under the right-wing dictatorship were so successful that they were not reversed when democracy returned and the left gained power. In New Zealand, the left started the reforms and the right continued them. Erhard introduced his reforms during the occupation, but once democracy was reintroduced his party stayed in power for fifteen years. Chinese leaders should feel more confident about introducing democracy: if China is really becoming as prosperous as they claim, its leaders' democratic re-election should be a piece of cake.

Special interest groups are the single greatest danger to reform. Unlike the population at large, which has dispersed interests, special interest groups have direct usually pecuniary interests and are well-organised. They must be dealt with early in the reforms, though not all at the same time, as they might unite their forces. These special interest groups typically include industries which are 'too big to fail': monopolies and quasi-monopolies, the public sector and trade unions. 'Tackling' them does not mean confrontation. It may be possible to convince them that taking away some privileges is to their advantage. When New Zealand farmers realised that the subsidies they received increased inflation, they started to advocate abolishing them. Trade unions in Singapore transformed themselves into successful organisations more akin to mutual societies. To fight the privileges of special interest groups, it might be possible to engage the help of those who suffer under them: e.g. the consumers, or the taxpayers, or, as the case of the monopolistic trading companies in eighteenth-century England, the 'free traders': aspirational new entrants into the markets who want to compete with the monopolies. In the case of post-war America, the special interests proved too strong. With only a two-year majority, the Republicans were unable to block the special interest groups from gaining the upper hand again.

The message must be clear and must be repeated. The most likely help for reformers will come from the small and the downtrodden. The person who wants to set up a business but is stopped by excessive red tape, or companies blocking competition; the small taxpayers; the consumers: they have the most to gain from the abolition of privileges granted by the state. They will be less organised than special interest groups; and it will be hard to mobilise them. Reform would be extremely difficult if the media were to be dominated by a special interest group or by reform-hostile opinion (e.g. by institutional bias). One way of ensuring that the population at large rather than special interest groups effectively dictate public policy is by organising regular referendums. Public consultations of 'stakeholders' or public meetings are no good as they tend to be dominated by special interest groups or a few vocal individuals. Hard-working families with children are rarely represented in public consultations or at public meetings as they simply don't have the time to do it. Widespread participation, including by those who are too busy with work or family chores, can be ensured by online voting or postal voting.

Concern for the less well-off must be at the top of the reform agenda at all times. Not just because it is morally right; but also because the support for the reforms by society as a whole will wane if misery is allowed to exist. As Adam Smith said, the less well-off have the most to gain from the abolition of privileges granted by the state to special interest groups: the poor have the smallest bargaining position and are unlikely to have obtained benefits from state regulation. State hand-outs and state services are usually captured by the vocal middle and upper classes. The poor also have the most to gain from free markets as it will increase prosperity the most. Even when there are only crumbs, there will be more when the pie is bigger.

MEASURES TO CREATE MASS PROSPERITY

Reduce the size of the state. The easiest way to create prosperity is to reduce the body that reduces it: the state sector. The state sector consumes wealth through its spending, and destroys it through its regulations. Most activities the state engages in are non-productive in nature. They are paid for by taxes on the productive sector, which can therefore re-invest less. The larger the state sector, the more potential investment capital that is consumed. Secondly, the bigger the state, the more it will regulate. Because of the Knowledge Problem, state regulation usually fails. This invariably leads to regulatory failure spiral, which makes matters worse. Beware of politicians who say they will regulate better, rather than less! The one thing the state must set up is a framework within which the private sector can thrive. Especially the rule of law must be guaranteed.

The state needs to be reduced to its smallest possible size. That is typically achieved by reducing the number of state employees, privatising state companies, outsourcing state functions to the private sector (full privatisation achieves better results, but that may not always be politically possible), and reducing the welfare state.

Privatisations. As many state companies and state services as possible need to be privatised. All eight countries in this book implemented drastic privatisations. If possible, competition needs to be introduced, e.g. by splitting the state company up into separate entities before privatisation. If there is no competition there is a danger that the rules to prevent monopolistic pricing will be so stifling that they make it less likely that a new competitor will turn up. When companies are privatised they are usually brought under a heavy regulatory regime, to assuage the fears of the public. The problem is that this excessive regulation tends to stay in place forever, even when the fears have faded into a distant memory. It is therefore better to incentivise businessmen to start competing, than to micromanage the existing monopolist. The more excessive the monopolist's prices are, the more people will switch to alternatives, and the more new entrants will be tempted to compete. The only monopolies which last are those imposed and protected by law.

Opposition to privatisation can be reduced by giving or selling shares to the state employees. After privatisation, people are usually made redundant, as state companies typically maximise employment at the expense of productivity. In Chile, privatised state companies ended up employing more people after a short transition.

Anything less than total privatisation – that is, sale of 100 per cent of the company, including voting rights – will perform less well. When the state keeps an interest in the company, there will always be a risk of political interference. Politicians will typically make companies focus on political priorities instead of increasing wealth-creating productivity. They will try to give legal advantages to the company, which again reduces productivity and market competition.

Increasing productivity is the reason companies are being privatised. The underperformance of Chinese state companies, or part-state companies, exemplifies the detrimental nature of political interference. State shareholdings in private companies are at their least harmful when they are small and/or 'blind', that is, if the state (typically through a sovereign wealth fund) buys the shares, but does not otherwise interfere in the running of the business.

State spending needs to be cut, as it takes place at the expense of the productive sector. Remember: when state spending is cut, the private sector will invest more than the shortfall, as it is more efficient. The best method to cut state spending is to cut state revenue first. Revenue comes from money printing, debt and taxation. Some countries have introduced constitutional limits on these. In most Western countries the state prints money to pay for its profligacy and prudent savers pay by having their savings reduce in value through inflation (it is sometimes called the inflation tax). When money loses its value quickly, wealth creation becomes impossible. At the very least, the government needs to be prevented from printing money at will. This can be done by making the central bank independent. Sadly, as the central bankers are usually still dependent upon government for their appointments, perks and future career prospects, the independence is more often an ideal than a reality. Introducing a gold standard makes it difficult to devalue the currency as it will be highly visible (it can be done if the government decides that the paper money will henceforward entitle the bearer to less gold). A gold coin standard might be the solution, though not practical. In Hong Kong, the currency is issued by private banks. This works well – the Hong Kong dollar is the eighth most traded currency in the world.

Debt makes our children responsible for today's irresponsibility. It reduces growth for future generations. A prosperity-creating government will need to repay the existing debt. This can be done by achieving systematic budget surpluses, which in turn can be achieved if most other measures in this package are carried out. The national debt should be visible for all and include all liabilities, including future pension liabilities. Both debt and taxation ceilings could be limited in the Constitution. John Cowperthwaite's principle of a balanced budget was written into the Basic Law of Hong Kong.

Low tax. There is an inverse correlation between taxation and growth. At 100 per cent taxes, nobody would work. Reduce taxes, and people are incentivised to go the extra mile. Reducing taxes will often lead to total higher revenues, as the economy will grow and capital and income flight will be reversed. Some taxes are less harmful than others: a consumption tax is the least harmful. This should be flat, so as not to favour specific sectors and not to encourage tax evasion and tax avoidance. Countries such as Hong Kong, or Britain during the industrial revolution, which slashed 'sin taxes' saw their revenue rise. A business tax is always harmful, as companies can move their wealth-creation elsewhere. Among business taxes, taxes on financial institutions are the most harmful, as they don't have factories and machines to take with them when they move countries. High-income taxes encourage people to work in the black economy, or not to work at all, or to emigrate. Cutting the highest marginal tax rates is the most beneficial, as the higher the tax rate, the greater the incentive will be to avoid it. When Prime Minister Gordon Brown introduced a 50 per cent income tax rate for the highest earners (up from 40 per cent), it led to a reduction in tax revenue of £7 billion. Sixty-two per cent of those high-earning taxpayers either left the country or re-arranged their tax affairs. When high marginal tax rates are cut there has always been a pronounced Laffer Effect (total tax take growing notwithstanding lower tax rates). It is not a good idea to lift people out of tax altogether, as you build a constituency of people who have a vested interest in keeping taxes as high as possible for others (thereby reducing growth and prosperity).

The simpler, lower, and flatter the taxes are, the less bureaucracy and evasion, and the more generally accepted the taxes will be. Taxes should stay stable over the long term: changing taxes annually is a mistake, as business investment decisions usually cover several years. Compare Hong Kong, where the tax system has basically remained unchanged since 1940, with Britain where it changes every year. When there is tax uncertainty, certain wealth-creating investments will simply not take place. Tax reformers should use the 'big bang' approach so people who lose out through one reform, gain by another.

Deregulate. Excessive regulation always favours the strong and harms the weak, as the weak have less bargaining power to encourage the government to rule in their favour. Unequal regulation distorts the allocation of goods towards the greatest productivity in the free market. Regulation harms competitiveness of companies which try to sell their goods on the international market. International regulation – that is, monopolistic regulation – is extremely dangerous, as it is precisely the competition between different regulatory systems which keeps regulation to some extent in check (e.g. tax competition makes it impossible for a country to tax excessively, as the citizens can flee). One of the great examples of successful deregulation was the industrial revolution in Britain: when mercantilist rules which stifled the economy were swept away, the economy produced unparalleled wealth.

There are many ways to cut red tape, such as sunset clauses (laws expiring automatically after a set time), a one-in, one-out rule, or employing a private agency to propose scrapping and simplifying existing regulations. Some countries exempt small businesses from certain regulations. This is better than submitting them to inappropriate regulation, but it gives an unfair advantage to the small instead of the best (as in a free market). Rules which need abolishing most are those which restrict free market competition: e.g. rules limiting the numbers of entrants into professions or industries. One sector which can profit a lot from deregulation is the financial sector, as it is this business which can most easily move abroad. Banks behave irresponsibly if they know that the state will bail them out, therefore no such guarantee must be given. The financial sector developed successfully during the industrial revolution and in Hong Kong without financial regulation. The extensive regulation of the financial sector over the past decades has not reduced financial volatility and risk. As human ingenuity is endless, the rules are circumvented, and crashes and frauds still occur. The volatility can only be taken away when financial activity is outlawed altogether. Such action would seriously impede wealth creation and prosperity.

The rule of law. The rule of law is the minimum legal framework which helps the free market function. If you want investment and growth, you have to provide a rule of law. China had to reintroduce courts, law and protection of private property, because foreigners would not have invested otherwise. When property rights were eroded in Chile, it led to civil war and a collapse of the economy. The rule of law typically includes certainty of law, no retrospective laws, restriction of political power, politicians being subject to the law, an independent judiciary, 'negative' human rights, the protection of persons and private property, and fair, accessible and independent courts. It does not include 'positive' entitlement rights which necessitate taking private property from others.

Safety. If there is no safety of property or person, creating wealth will be extremely difficult. This includes international safety (threat of invasion and terrorism) and domestic safety (crime and public order). Safety can be obtained in the minimal state: one could, for example, outsource parts of the army.

Police can be outsourced as well. The wealthy of the world already enjoy first-rate private security firms; there is no reason why this could not be expanded. It is the poor who suffer most from an absence of law and order, as they cannot buy their way out. Less well-off residents could be given vouchers, so they can purchase the policing they want. In addition, the more public space is privatised, the less the 'public' police will be needed; as private security firms can do the task. Providing security may be a means by which politicians obtain excessive power – the rule of law ought to prevent this.

Abandon privilege. Politicians grant legal preferment to their pet groups; markets grant favour to whoever is the best. The Knowledge Problem means that markets are more likely to identify success (politicians usually pick losers). Treating everybody equally (equality before the law) has the additional advantage that it does not cause jealousy or distrust. So out go all differentiations between race, sex, religion, sexual orientation: the state must treat every individual in the same way.

Take care of the poor. All measures to increase growth and prosperity must be assessed on their social impact. The best welfare is economic growth. If radical reform fails to improve the lives of the poorest among us, human compassion will turn support away from the reforms. However, helping the feeble is not synonymous with introducing comprehensive state welfare. Most welfare can be replaced by insurance and savings (voluntary or compulsory), mutual societies and private charity. Chile successfully privatised its pensions system. Singapore and Hong Kong introduced compulsory savings plans. The Hong Kong system produces higher yields as there is competition between the private investment companies, whereas the Singapore system is a state monopoly. In Chile, the replacement of the repartition system by accumulated savings had the added benefit of providing huge amounts of capital to invest in the productive sector. There will always be people who are left behind and who cannot lift themselves out of poverty without help. I believe they are relatively small in numbers, and charity should be able to take care of them. But if this is not possible, then the state could provide systems which are, as far as possible, limited both in time and in scope (a safety net instead of a safety hammock). It is better to give the less fortunate money or vouchers than to provide state services for them, as they will know best where their priorities lie and how the money is best used.

Free trade. Free trade, even introduced unilaterally, benefits all parties. Chile, post-war Germany, Hong Kong, Singapore and New Zealand all had or have free trade. Free trade increases competition, competitiveness and growth. There is really no excuse not to introduce it. Freeing trade is likely to incur the opprobrium of special interest groups which dream of state protection. But let us not forget that many producers benefit from free trade: they may be able to import cheaper components to manufacture their products. Consumers' power is not to be trifled with.

If countries work together, free trade areas are preferable to customs unions. In free trade areas, countries liberate trade between them, and they decide individually what they do vis-à-vis third countries. In customs unions they also need to agree the external tariffs between them, making it more likely that there will not be total free trade as some are always likely to object. As such, free trade areas such as the North American Free Trade Association or the European Free Trade Association are more likely to create prosperity than customs unions such as the European Union.

CONCLUSION

The choice is yours. Will your children live in poverty, under the status quo, or be prosperous beyond your wildest imagination? Do you choose regulation, a 'third way' or freedom? Recently a friend said to me: 'France has been declining for decades. But it has declined so gracefully!' This book is no guidance to graceful decline; this book is about creating a much better world.

In every example in this book, comprehensive economic reform was triggered by a dramatic event: war, hunger, civil war and serious economic decline. It is too early to decide whether the 2007/2008 world economic crisis (which has now been running for five years) will be of such magnitude as to force certain countries into dramatic economic change. I believe it might, and I believe that will be a good thing for everybody else in the world.

Nobody can predict what sort of countries long-term high growth will create. During my brief lifetime I have seen the coming into being of the mobile phone, the CD, the video and then the DVD, the PC, email and the internet. When the past looks primitive, the present is on the right track. But it can be even better. Dramatic growth in prosperity can lift civilisation up to levels as yet unimaginable. It will allow us to conquer poverty, resolve energy needs and cure diseases.

Mass prosperity will only come about in countries which copy the method the eight countries in this book applied so successfully. Leaving people free to pursue their dreams and their aspirations as they see fit will create Heavens on Earth.

J. P. Floru
Hope Bay, 10 December 2012

ACKNOWLEDGEMENTS

I am especially grateful to Dr Madsen Pirie of the Adam Smith Institute, who, apart from being a great example and an inspiration, encouraged me to write this book and made it possible for me to do so.

A warm thanks to everybody who advised, made suggestions and put me on the right track: James Bartholomew, Professor David Beito, Dr Eamonn Butler, Dr Stephen Davies, Dr Tim Evans, Shane Frith, Robert D. Garber, Professor Pierre Garello, Dr Oliver M. Hartwich, Tim Hewish, Stephen Hoffman, Dr Christoffer Koch, Dr Dominique Lazanski, Professor Mark Littlewood, Jamie Myatt, Dr Tom G. Palmer, Tony Penman, Daniel Pycock, Ruth Richardson, Gonzalo Schwarz, Deborah Thomas and Dr Richard Wellings.

I thank the unsurpassed Allister Heath, Editor of *City A.M.*, for writing the foreword. I have never disagreed with anything he's written.

I thank the team at my publisher, Biteback: the Managing Director, Iain Dale, who enthusiastically supported this project; Katy Scholes, who markets this book; Olivia Beattie, Publishing Assistant; Namkwan Cho for the beautiful design; and Sam Carter, Editorial Director, who followed this project day-to-day.

Endless admiration and special thanks to those who read entire chapters of this book long before they were anywhere near comprehensible: David Beito, Christoffer Koch, Grégory Van den Bergh, Dominique Lazanski, Shane Frith, Stephen Davies and François Feuillat.

I thank my family and friends who, for almost one year, put up with my silences, annoyance, rants, nervousness, despair, frustrations and absences; whose food went cold; who were waiting at the station; who did not receive my calls and whom I didn't visit. I promise I'll make up for it (until I start writing again).

And to François, who bore it all.

BIBLIOGRAPHY

I used numerous essays, articles, news reports and books – too many to list here. These are the main books and publications I have relied upon:

Acton, Lord, *Essays in the History of Liberty: Selected Writings of Lord Acton* (Liberty Classics, 1985)

Avineri, Schlomo, (ed.) and others, *Communitarianism and Individualism* (Oxford University Press, 1992)

Baerg, William R., *Judicial Institutionalization of the Revolution: The Legal Systems of the People's Republic of China and the Republic of Cuba* (Loyola of Los Angeles International and Comparative Law Review, 1992)

Bastiat, Frédéric, *Selected Essays on Political Economy* (The Foundation for Economic Education, 1975)

Berg, Maxine, *The Age of Manufacturers* (Routledge, 1994)

Booth, Philip (ed.) and others, *Towards a Liberal Utopia?* (Institute of Economic Affairs, 2005)

Brash, Donald T., *New Zealand's Remarkable Reforms* (Institute of Economic Affairs Occasional Paper, 1996)

Briggs, Asa, *The Age of Improvement 1783–1867* (Longmans, Green and Co. Ltd, 1959)

Butler, Eamonn, *Adam Smith: A Primer* (Institute of Economic Affairs, 2007)

Butler, Eamonn, *The Condensed Wealth of Nations* (Institute of Economic Affairs, 2011)

Cheung, Martha P. Y. (ed.) and others, *Hong Kong Collage* (Oxford University Press, 1997)

Coase, Ronald and others, *How China Became Capitalist* (Palgrave Macmillan, 2012)

Coates, Austin, *Myself a Mandarin: Memoirs of a Special Magistrate* (Heinemann Educational Books, 1975)

De Soto, Hernando, *The Other Path: the Economic Answer to Terrorism* (Basic Books, 2002)

Dyble, Colleen (ed.) and others, *Freedom Champions: Stories from the Front Lines in the War of Ideas* (Atlas Economic Research Foundation, 2011)

Easton, Brian, *The Commercialisation of New Zealand* (Auckland University Press, 1997)

Eiras, Ana, *Chile: Ten Steps for Abandoning Aid Dependency for Prosperity* (Heritage.org, 2003)

Ekelund, Robert B., *Mercantilism as a Rent Seeking Society* (Texas A&M University Press, 1982)

Fleming, Thomas, *The New Dealers' War* (Basic Books, 2002)

Floud, Roderick and others, *The Economic History of Britain since 1700* (Cambridge University Press, 1981)

Folsom, Burton and others, *FDR Goes to War* (Threshold Editions, 2011)

Folsom, Burton, *New Deal or Raw Deal* (Threshold Editions, 2009)

Friedman, Milton and Rose, *Free to Choose* (Harcourt, 1990)

Friedman, Milton and Rose, *Two Lucky People* (University of Chicago Press, 1998)

Friedman, Norman, *The Fifty Year War* (Naval Institute Press, 2000)

Fulbrook, Mary, *A Concise History of Germany* (Cambridge University Press, 1991)

Gillies, Peter and others, *Ludwig Erhard* (Ernst Freiberger-Stiftung, 2010)

Gillespie, Nick (ed.), *Choice: The Best of Reason* (BenBella, 2004)

Grantham, Alexander, *Via Ports: From Hong Kong to Hong Kong* (Hong Kong University Press, 2012)

Gregg, Pauline, *A Social and Economic History of Britain 1760–1955* (George G. Harrap & Co. Ltd, 1950)

Halper, Stefan, *The Beijing Consensus* (Basic Books, 2010)

Hayek, F. A., *The Counter Revolution of Science: Studies on the Abuse of Reason* (Liberty Press, 1979)

Hayek, F. A., *The Fatal Conceit: The Errors of Socialism* (University of Chicago Press, 1991)

Hayek, F. A., *The Road to Serfdom* (University of Chicago Press, 1994)

Heckscher, Eli F., *Mercantilism* (George Allen and Unwin Ltd, 1935)

Higgs, Robert, *Crisis and Leviathan* (Oxford University Press 1987)

Huff, W. G., *The Economic Growth of Singapore* (Cambridge University Press, 1994)

Ishihara, Kyoichi, *Inflation and Economic Reform in China* (The Developing Economies, 1990)

Juurikkala, Oskari, *Two Tigers: One Fit, One Fat Cat, in Pension Provision: Government Failure around the World* (Institute of Economic Affairs, 2008)

Kearns Goodwin, Doris, *No Ordinary Time: Franklin Roosevelt* (Simon & Schuster, 1994)

Larroulet, Cristian, *The Battle of Ideas in Chile* (Atlas Economic Research Foundation, 2011)

Lee, Kuan Yew, *From Third World to First: Singapore and the Asian Economic Boom* (HarperCollins, 2011)

Lindert, Peter H. and others, *English Workers' Living Standards During the Industrial Revolution* (Economic History Review, 1983)

Lipson, E., *The Economic History of England* (A & C Black Ltd, 1931)

McCloskey, Deirdre, *Bourgeois Dignity: Why Economics Can't Explain the Modern World* (University of Chicago Press, 2011)

Mierzejeweski, Alfred C., *Ludwig Erhard* (University of South Carolina Press, 2004)

Miller, Terry and others, *2012 Index of Economic Freedom* (The Heritage Foundation, 2012)

Mokyr, Joel, *The Enlightened Economy* (Penguin, 2011)

Morris, Jan, *Hong Kong* (Penguin Books, 1997)

Palmer, Tom G. (ed.) and others, *The Morality of Capitalism* (Jameson Books, 2011)

Palmer, Tom G. and others, *After the Welfare State* (Students For Liberty & Atlas Network/Jameson Books, Inc., 2012)

Pennington, Mark, *Robust Political Economy: Classical Liberalism and the Future of Public Policy* (Edward Elgar, 2011)

Pirie, Madsen, *Economics made simple: How money, trade and markets really work* (Harriman Economics Essentials, 2012)

Pirie, Madsen, *Freedom 101* (Adam Smith Institute, 2008)

Popper, Karl, *The Open Society and Its Enemies* (Routledge Classics, 2003)

Rand, Ayn, *Capitalism: the Unknown Ideal* (Penguin Group, 1967)

Richardson, Ruth, *Making a Difference* (Shoal Bay Press, 1995)

Rothbard, Murray, *An Austrian Perspective on the History of Economic Thought* (Ludwig von Mises Institute, 2006)

Rowley, Charles K. and other, *Economic Contractions in the United States: A Failure of Government* (Locke Institute and Institute of Economic Affairs, 2009)

Sally, Razeen, *New Frontiers in Free Trade: Globalization's Future and Asia's Rising Role* (Cato Institute, 2008)

Sally, Razeen, *Trade Policy, New Century* (Institute of Economic Affairs, 2008)

Schlichter, Detlev, *Paper Money Collapse* (John Wiley & Sons, Inc., 2011)

Schumpeter, Joseph A., *Capitalism, Socialism & Democracy* (Routledge, 1976)

Senior, Ian, *Corruption – The World's Big C* (Institute of Economic Affairs, 2006)

Serra, Pablo, and others, *The Effects of Privatizations on Chilean Firms* (Universidad de Chile, 2001)

Shell, Orville, *Mandate of Heaven* (Warner Books, 1995)

Sorman, Guy, *La Nouvelle Richesse des Nations* (Fayard, 1987)

Spadaro, Louis M., *New Directions in Austrian Economics* (Sheed Andrews McMeel, 1978)

Speer, Albert, *Inside the Third Reich* (Weidenfeld & Nicolson, 1970)

Taylor, Frederick, *Exorcising Hitler* (Bloomsbury, 2012)

Thatcher, Margaret, *The Path to Power* (Harper/Collins Publishers, 1995)

Tooze, Adam, *The Wages of Destruction: The Making and Breaking of the Nazi Economy* (Penguin, 2007)

Valdés, Juan Gabriel, *Pinochet's Economists: The Chicago School in Chile* (Cambridge University Press, 1995)

Van Der Kiste, John, *William and Mary* (Sutton Publishing, 2003)

Wang, Yanlai, *China's Economic Development and Democratisation* (Ashgate Publishing Limited, 2003)

Wellings, Richard, *A Beginner's Guide to Liberty* (Adam Smith Institute, 2009)

Ziyang, Zhao, *Prisoner of the State: The Secret Journal of Chinese Premier Zhao Ziyang* (Simon & Schuster, 2009)

INDEX